(above) "The Tuskegee Experiment" statue on the grounds of the U.S. Air Force Academy, Colorado Springs, Co. The inscription at the base of the statue reads: "The Tuskegee Airmen of World War II. They rose from adversity through competence, courage, commitment, and capacity to serve America on silver wings, and to set a standard few will transcend."

(r.) Inscription on the back side.

"THE TUSKEGEE EXPERIMENT"

THE ORIGINAL TUSKEGEE AIRMAN EVOLVED DURING WORLD WAR II AT A SMALL ARMY AIR-FIELD NEAR TUSKEGEE, ALABAMA IN WHAT WAS CALLED THE "TUSKEGEE EXPERIMENT". THE EXPERIMENT INVOLVED THE TRAINING OF BLACK PILOTS AND GROUND SUPPORT PERSONNEL TO FORM THE 99TH PURSUIT SQUADRON. THIS SQUADRON WAS LATER JOINED BY THE 100th, 301ST, AND 302ND SQUADRONS FORMING THE 332ND FIGHTER GROUP. THEY COURAGEOUSLY FLEW COMBAT IN THE P-40, P-39, P-47 AND P-51 AIRCRAFT, DISTINGUISHING THEMSELVES WHILE FLYING OVER 1500 MISSIONS, AND NEVER LOSING AN ESCORTED BOMBER TO ENEMY FIGHTERS IN THE EUROPEAN THEATER OF OPERATIONS. OTHER BLACK PILOTS, NAVIGATORS, BOMBARDIERS AND ENLISTED CREW PERSONNEL FORMED THE 477TH BOMBARDMENT GROUP (MEDIUM) FLYING THE NORTH AMERICAN B-25. AT THE END OF THE WAR IN EUROPE, ELEMENTS OF THE TWO GROUPS WERE JOINED TO FORM THE 477TH COMPOSITE GROUP FLYING P-47's AND B-25's. THE COMPOSITE GROUP WAS DEACTIVATED IN MAY 1946 AND THE 332nd FIGHTER GROUP WAS REACTIVATED. THE GROUP CONTINUED UNTIL JUNE 1, 1949, AFTER PRESIDENT HARRY S. TRUMAN INTEGRATED THE ARMED FORCES.

RED TAILS
BLACK WINGS

*The Men of America's
Black Air Force*

by

JOHN B. HOLWAY

Yucca Tree Press

First Printing - February 1997

Library of Congress Cataloging in Publication Data

Holway, John B.

    Red Tails, Black Wings: The Men of America's Black Air Force.

        1. World War II - 1939-1945, Air war. 2. World War II - 1939-1945, Black airmen. 3. World War II - 1939-1945, Fighter pilots. 4. World War II - 1939-1945, Integration of services. 5. Tuskegee Airmen
        I. John B. Holway. II. Title.

Library of Congress Card Catalog Number: 96-061290
ISBN: 1-881325-21-0

Cover design by Fine Line Graphic Design
Jacket photos: Smithsonian National Air & Space Museum; Clarence Lester.

To the Tuskegee Airmen and

to Jim, John, Diane, and Mona

The way you paved as Black Eagles has led us to today where black GIs are again serving their nation in combat, this time side by side with their buddies of every hue and color, race and creed, from every town and city in America. This time, all are equal. From the top GI to the bottom, we are all measured only by our competence and the content of our character. And that's *the way it should be."*

— General Colin L. Powell,
Chairman, Joint Chiefs of Staff
Address to the 20th Annual
National Convention,
Tuskegee Airmen,
10 August 1991 —

We were daring, we were stylish, the way we took off, the way we banked, the way we joined forces, the way we buzzed, the way we crushed our caps, the way we always had our dress uniforms totally pressed, the way we always had our trench coats draped across our arms. When you're on top, you stand a little taller. That's the kind of thing that gave us our reputation.

— Roscoe Brown,
Commanding Officer
100th Fighter Squadron —

A pilot or man of whatever color is just as good as he proves himself to be. Our pilots had pretty good alibis for being failures if they wanted to use them. When the test came, they had to fight just as men, Americans against a common enemy.

— Colonel Noel Parrish
Commanding Officer
Tuskegee Army Air Base —

Table of Contents

List of Illustrations

Maps

Photographs

ACKNOWLEDGMENTS

The author is grateful to the many former 'Red Tails' and their families for the loan of individual photographs. Acknowledgment is also given to the following for permission to use the photographs indicated.

The Tuskegee Airmen, Brandon Publishing Company — Toppins (C-9), Weathers (C-10)

Gen. Benjamin O. Davis, Jr. — (16); Hall (C-4)

Denver Public Library, Western History Department — Love (6)

James H. Fischer — (C-18)

Arthur Freeman — Coleman (26)

Alan Gruening — P-51 (C-16 bottom)

Harold Hurd — Bragg (30)

Elmer D. Jones — Hall & Coke (91); Brooks (C-2); Rayford (C-8); Rogers (C-8), Smith, Thomas (C-9); (C-14 top)

National Archives — James, Jr. (C-4)

Noel F. Parrish — (49)

Frederic Remington — *Buffalo Soldier* (6)

Schomburg Center for Research in Black Culture (photographs and Prints Division), The New York Public Library, Astor, Lenox and Tilden Foundations — Brown (34); Watson (C-9)

Smithsonian Institution Air & Space Museum Archives — Powell & First Transcontinental Flight (30); Coffey (34); (85); Davis (C-1); Hannibal Cox (C-2); Deiz & Elsberry (C-3); Jefferson (C-5); Lawrence (C-6); Ross (C-8); (C-15); (C-17); (329 top)

Squadron/Signal Publications (C-16 top)

William R. Thompson — Driver (C-3); Fuller (C-4); Roberts (C-8); Thomas (C-9)

Tuskegee University Archives — Robinson (34)

United States Air Force — Bullard (26); (44); Anderson (49); (75); Cannon and Hall (91 top); Archer (C-1); DeBow (C-3); Marshall, McDaniel (C-6); (C-10 bottom); (C-11-13); (176); (183); (329 bottom)

United States Air Force Academy — fontispiece

United States Army — (290)

Alekandr Zivkovic — (214)

Foreword

How did a ground pounder come to write about flyers? My only military acquaintance with airplanes was jumping out of them during the Korean war.

In 1982, I attended the opening of the Smithsonian's exhibit on the Tuskegee Airmen, where I met Colonel George 'Spanky' Roberts, a former commander of the Red Tails, and Lou Purnell, another former Red Tail and curator of the exhibit. The subject was entirely new to me, and during an extended lunch Roberts gave me a long account of the outfit and his own experiences before, during, and after his great adventure in World War II.

My experience was in writing oral history, primarily baseball, so I was particularly attracted to stories that other writers had neglected. The Red Tails' story cried out to be written. Charles Francis has also written a fine history of the unit, but I couldn't resist learning more. I began attending Tuskegee Airmen conventions and button-holing veterans. It was like eating popcorn, I couldn't stop.

I want to salute Charles E. Francis, whose living and painstaking pioneering work, *The Tuskegee Airmen* (Branden Publishers, Boston, 1988), inspired countless readers, including myself. It will be read a century or more from now, whenever future generations want to learn the exciting story of this chapter in history.

Fourteen years later I was still collecting stories and watching the men of that colorful era take shape and come to life on the computer screen. I hope the reader will enjoy getting to know them as much as I have.

John B. Holway
February 1997

Mediterranean Area of Operations for the 99th

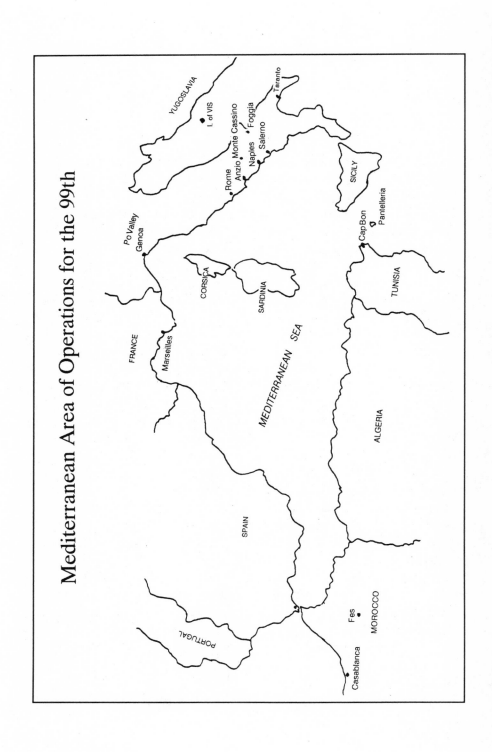

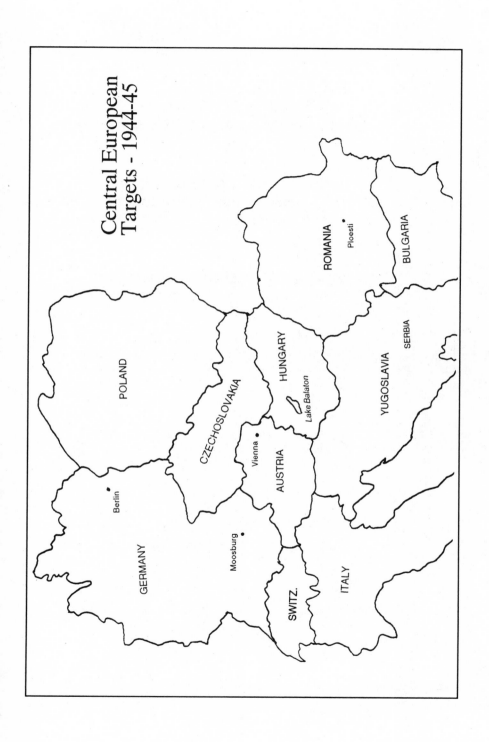

Central European
Targets - 1944-45

POLAND

GERMANY

• Berlin

• Moosburg

CZECHOSLOVAKIA

SWITZ.

AUSTRIA

Vienna •

HUNGARY

Lake Balaton

ITALY

YUGOSLAVIA

SERBIA

ROMANIA

Ploesti •

BULGARIA

Source: General Benjamin O. Davis, Jr.

1

Black Rifles

From Bunker Hill to Desert Storm, African Americans have played a part in every American war, with the possible exception of the Mexican War, although our school books and movies don't always show them there. The marriage of blacks and the armed forces has been a stormy one, with many ups and downs.

The best days were the thirty-five-year period, 1863-98, that is, from the Civil War through the Spanish-American War. Then things went down hill for the next forty-three years, 1898-1941. By the time of Pearl Harbor, anti-black virulence in the Armed Forces was probably the strongest it had ever been since Appomattox.

The story begins with Columbus and his African crewman, Pedro Alonzo Nino. Blacks sailed with Balboa to Panama and fought with Cortez in Mexico, with Pizarro in Peru, and with Ponce de Leon in Florida.

One of the most amazing stories is that of the black slave Estevan who accompanied Fray Marcos de Niza into what is now Arizona and New Mexico to search for Cibola, the fabled 'seven cities of gold.' Estevan, a huge, colorful man, was sent ahead by Fray Marcos and was killed by the Zunis at Hawikuh.

Black men helped settle the colony of Jamestown. Some one hundred fifty years later Abijah Prince and others shouldered muskets with the colonists in the French and Indian Wars, the prelude to the American Revolution.

The American Revolution

Some five thousand blacks served in the Revolution — ten thousand counting irregulars, says historian Alan Gropman. Most of them lived and died unknown, but a few found their way into military records.

Crispus Attucks, the big Indian-African, was the first American to fall in the Revolution in the Boston Massacre of 1770. Peter Salem, a Massachusetts slave, stood with "the embattled farmers" of Concord and fired one of the shots "heard 'round the world." A few days later he and a black free man, Salem Poor, waited on Bunker Hill until they could "see the whites of their eyes," when Salem shot and killed the British commander. Lemuel Haynes joined the attack on Fort Ticonderoga to bring cannons to Washington to drive the British out of Boston.

George Washington, a slave owner, had used Negroes on the Virginia frontier, but when he took command of the Continental Army, he tried to get all blacks out of the ranks, although his slave, William Lee, was at his side in every battle. As the Americans' fortunes became desperate, Washington let other blacks into the ranks. Agrippa Hill fought at Saratoga, Edward Hector at Brandywine, and Austen Dabney at Cowpens. Fifteen year-old James Forten was thrown into a British prison ship, where he gave up his chance to escape so a younger white prisoner could go free.

The governor of Rhode Island bought freedom for slaves for a black battalion to stop Benedict Arnold's invasion.

The English also wooed black slaves. In Virginia the royal governor promised freedom to those who joined his 'Ethiopian regiment.'

Prince Whipple, the son of an African king, crossed the Delaware with Washington (see Emanuel Leutze's famous painting). Oliver Cromwell also crossed the Delaware, fought at Brandywine, shivered at Valley Forge, and watched the British surrender at Yorktown. An African-American spy, James Armistead, waited on Lord Cornwallis' table at Yorktown and reported every plan Cornwallis made.

Negroes sailed with John Paul Jones — according to Gropman, one-fourth of all American seamen were black. One, Deborah Gannett, was a woman; another, Henri Christophe, was a future emperor of Haiti.

Most of these "black founding fathers" had no historian, wrote poet John Greenleaf Whittier, but they "bore their full proportion of the sacrifices and trials."

Once victory had been won, however, they were all mustered out. Many received pensions of land or money, even from states in the South. Others died penniless.

In 1803, when two Virginians, William Clark and Meriweather Lewis, set out on their epic journey to the Pacific, they received critical help from an Indian woman, Sacajawea, and a strapping black man, known only as 'York.'

The War of 1812

Again both sides competed for Negro troops in 'America's second revolution.' The British recruited ex-slaves in Maryland and Virginia. Blacks were called into federal uniform over the objections of President James Madison of Virginia. Again, white enlistments weren't filling the ships, so blacks sailed with Commodore Perry and "met the enemy" on Lake Erie. "They seemed absolutely insensible to danger," Perry said. Louisiana had black militia companies, and six hundred Negroes fought with General Jackson at New Orleans. After the victory, Jackson told them, "I expected much of you ... but you surpassed my hopes."

However, once more after victory the black troops were dismissed, and most who had expected freedom were returned to their masters instead. In 1819, Jackson led the Army into Spanish Florida to recapture slaves who had fled to the Seminole Indian nation.

Later, Negroes also died at the Alamo and helped win Texas independence at San Jacinto.

The Civil War

When John Brown raided Harpers Ferry, one of his men who fell was a Negro, Shields Green. Many Northerners, including leaders in Lincoln's own Republican party, opposed both slave labor and free black labor in western states; both were considered threats to white working men.

After the Union's Fort Sumter fell in 1861, over one hundred students from Wilberforce College tried to volunteer to fight but were told, "This is a white man's war." Lincoln didn't want to lose the four pro-slavery border states that had remained loyal.

Then once more, when the war news grew desperate, the country turned to African Americans. "Men of Color, to Arms!" posters proclaimed. Frederick Douglass declared: "Let the black man ... get an eagle on his buttons, a musket on his shoulder, and bullets in his pocket, and there is no power on earth that can deny that he has a right to citizenship."

The 1991 movie, *Glory* dramatized the story of one all-black regiment, the 54th Massachusetts. There were one hundred seventy others. One out of every eight Yankee soldiers and one of every four seamen was black, though they served for less pay than their white comrades. More than one hundred eighty thousand African Americans served, and more than thirty thousand died. The black casualty rate was higher and the desertion rate lower than those of the rest of the Army. Martin Delaney, a graduate of Harvard Medical School, rose to the rank of major.

Ex-slave Harriet Tubman volunteered at the head of a contingent of men to raid behind Southern lines. Mixed Indian and Negro forces under the Creek chief, Opothayohola, and the

Cherokee, Six Killer, fought as irregulars in Kansas and Missouri.

Nineteen blacks won the Congressional Medal of Honor. The first, Sergeant Robert Carney, had run away from Virginia to go to sea. Fighting with the 54th in an assault on Fort Wagner, South Carolina, he seized the flag and carried it alone to the gates of the fort, where he was shot in the scalp. But, he boasted, "The flag never touched the ground, boys."

On the sea, Robert Smalls commandeered a Confederate ship and sailed it through a Southern blockade at Charleston.

The Southerners, who fought savagely against ex-slaves on the battlefield, finally recruited them themselves as the war grew desperate. They offered freedom to up to three hundred thousand blacks and, in fact, did form a few companies, though it was much too late to save the Confederate cause.

Lincoln declared that "Negroes have demonstrated with their blood their right to citizenship." After Appomattox, William Tecumseh Sherman, the nation's top general, recommended integrating the Army, but the idea was rejected. The Navy did likewise.

The West

Jim Beckwourth helped blaze the trail to California that the Forty-niners followed in the great Gold Rush. It's estimated that one-fifth of all cowboys were black, though none are to be seen in modern movies and television shows. The very word 'cowboy' derives from the pejorative term for Negroes, 'boy.' Nat Love ('Deadwood Dick') was a gunslinger and cattle puncher. Bill Pickett[1] invented the rodeo sport of bulldogging. His buddies, Will Rogers and Tom Mix, went on to Hollywood stardom, but Pickett was nixed.

The Indian Wars

To fight its Indian wars, the Army formed four black regiments, two cavalry and two infantry. One of every three cavalry

James Beckwourth
Frontiersman, scout, explorer

Nat Love
Cowboy

Buffalo Soldier
by Frederic Remington

troopers in the West was African American. The Indians called them 'buffalo soldiers,' perhaps from their woolly hair, perhaps because they fought with the tenacity of a wounded buffalo. The blacks were strictly segregated and fought almost entirely under white officers. They guarded stage coaches (bumping along on top, not inside), fought Geronimo, and helped capture Billy the Kid. One died with Custer. (Oddly, Custer had turned down command of a black regiment.)

Hollywood, which loves to depict the cavalry galloping to the rescue, carefully depicts only white cavalry. However, artist Frederick Remington captured the truth in canvases such as "Ninth Cavalry to the Rescue." He gave the black troopers high marks for doing the toughest jobs without complaining. They were given the worst posts and the worst nags in the Army, but the blacks' alcoholism rate was lower than whites' and their desertion rate was one-tenth as high. Young John Pershing commanded a black company, winning the nickname, 'Black Jack,' which he called "an honor."

Buffalo Soldiers won thirteen more Medals of Honor on the plains, although this was only three percent of the total in the period. The first one went to Emanuel Stance, who stood only five feet tall. George Johnson won one for leading twenty-five troopers against one hundred Indians. Moses Williams stood by his white lieutenant under fire and saved the lives of at least three comrades. One soldier cited for bravery, William Cathy, turned out to be Cathy Williams, a woman.

The black-Indian Seminole Scouts were possibly the most decorated unit in the Army. Small, red-faced Lieutenant John Bullis lost his horse in an attack by thirty Comanches. "We can't leave the lieutenant, boys," cried Sergeant John Ward, who, with bugler Isaac Ward and Private Pompey Factor, galloped back, guns blazing. Bullis leaped up behind Ward "and just saved my hair." All four won Medals of Honor.

One Medal of Honor winner was later shot-gunned in the back by a sheriff at a New Year's Dance. It was one of many racial incidents that flared on the frontier.

At Fort Concho, Texas, rioters attacked a black sergeant, so the troopers strode into a saloon, ordered a quick drink, turned, and fired into the crowd of cowboys and gamblers, killing two. Police arrested two soldiers, and when their comrades staged a shoot-out at the jail, each side lost one man killed.

The Academies

Prejudice was rife at West Point and Annapolis as well. In the 1870s two black plebes were forced out of the Naval Academy. From 1870-89 twenty-two black cadets were appointed to West Point, but only twelve actually entered, and of those, just three graduated.

In 1877 Cadet Johnson Whitaker was found tied to his bunk and beaten unconscious, with his ear slit. An official inquiry concluded that he had done it to himself! He left soon after.

Henry Ossian Flipper was the first to graduate, in 1881. He was later court-martialled for embezzling funds, a case that remains a mystery.[2] Flipper claimed he was railroaded because he had gone riding with a white lieutenant's fiancee. However, one apparently objective study suggests that his Mexican mistress had stolen the funds. We will probably never know the truth.

John H. Alexander graduated from West Point in 1887 but died seven years later, leaving little record.

The third graduate was Charles Young. Born in a Kentucky log cabin in 1864, he was the son of a free black soldier in the Union Army. He entered West Point in 1884, enduring what the Washington *Post* would call "a lonely cadet life" in "a silent environment." One classmate, later Major General Charles Rhodes, wrote that "we esteem him highly for his patient perseverance."

Another cadet, from South Carolina, came to Young's defense after a Yankee classmate made a remark "that reflected on the chastity of the Negro's female forebears." The Carolina paladin met the other in a bare knuckles duel behind the barracks at four o'clock one morning.

Young wrote poems and composed songs, played the piano, harp, and cornet, and spoke French, German, and Spanish. But he was apparently no student, graduating last in his class. He would be the last black in West Point for forty years.

Cadet Charles Young,
West Point, 1884-1888.

Young served with the cavalry in Nebraska and Utah and, after Alexander's death in 1894, was the only black officer in the Army.

When the Spanish-American War broke out in 1898, Young hoped for a combat command. But that would have meant a promotion to colonel, a move the Army forestalled by giving him command of a volunteer regiment in the States.

The Spanish-American War

Twenty-two black sailors died in the sinking of the battleship *Maine* in Havana harbor, the incident which ignited the war. One of them earned the Medal of Honor.

The Army accepted two hundred thousand black volunteers, and some one hundred African-Americans received reserve commissions. Eight states, including Alabama, formed Negro regiments. Some nine thousand African Americans saw service in Cuba under a former Confederate officer, General Joe Wheeler.

When the 10th Cavalry left for Cuba from its base at Missoula, Montana, townsfolk postponed church to turn out to wish them farewell. But in Florida, the reception was different. They were herded into the holds of segregated troop ships, where they were kept for a week in burning heat with only candles for light while white troops occupied the upper decks.

All four of the Army's regular black regiments and several militia outfits saw action in Cuba. The 25th seized the Spanish flag at El Caney, although an officer from the white 12th regiment, which arrived after them, demanded that they give it to him. They complied, but only after tearing off a corner to prove they'd been there first.

The black horse soldiers were brigaded to Teddy Roosevelt's Rough Riders. With Pershing at their head, the 10th Cavalry charged up San Juan Hill. When Roosevelt arrived, the 10th was already on top, and its band broke out with "A Hot Time in the Old Town Tonight." Pershing said he could have "taken our black heroes in our arms."

Initially, TR also praised his black comrades, declaring that "I could wish for none better" and "they can drink out of our canteens."

Frank Knox, Roosevelt's deputy, declared, "I never saw braver men."

Blacks won another six Medals of Honor.

In the Philippines, which were acquired from Spain, black infantry regiments helped put down an insurrection. It was "the white man's burden," as poet Langston Hughes wrote, but blacks helped bear it.

Philippine governor (and later President) William Howard Taft wrote that prejudice was "almost universal throughout the country. It is a fact, however, as shown by our records, that the colored troops are quite as well disciplined and behaved as the average other troops" and showed less "intemperance." Communities which were at first hostile later "entirely changed their view and commended their good behavior to the War Department."

But trouble lay ahead.

The Brownsville Incident

In Brownsville, Texas across the river from Mexico, violence followed the pistol-whipping of a Negro National Guardsman by a local policeman. One civilian was killed and a policeman wounded, and cartridges found the next morning implicated the soldiers.

All denied guilt, and no court martial was ever held. Nevertheless, President Roosevelt ordered three companies of the 25th discharged *en masse* without honor. Among the group were seven Medal of Honor winners. However, a Senate investigation concluded that the cartridges could not have come from Army weapons and suggested that townspeople planted the evidence themselves.

Seventy years later President Richard Nixon exonerated the men, including the last living survivor, who was allowed to enter a Veterans' Administration hospital. But Brownsville left a strong impact among African-American troops for years to come.

Meantime blacks were again eased out of the post-war military. By 1917, only three percent of the army was black.

One of the African-Americans commissioned in the Cuba crisis was the son of a middle-class Washington family, Benjamin Davis. When he applied to West Point, he was turned down, so he enlisted with a view to winning a regular commission through the ranks.

Riding with the cavalry in the Utah desert, Davis met Young, who coached him on the coming exam, which Davis passed in 1901, finishing third among twenty three candidates. Of the twelve who won their bars that day was another Negro, John Green.

There were only a few career paths open to a black. He could serve as a lieutenant in a black regiment until he was promoted above white officers in the same unit. Then he had to be assigned either as a military attache to a black nation or as an ROTC instructor in a black college. At that time there were only two independent black nations, Haiti and Liberia, and only two black colleges that offered ROTC, Wilberforce in Cleveland, and Tuskegee in Alabama. For the next two decades, Davis and Green followed each other from one of these assignments to the next.

In Liberia, Young was wounded rescuing an embassy officer from a tribe of "man-eating folk." In 1916, by then a lieutenant colonel, he rode with Pershing in Mexico, pursuing the bandit, Pancho Villa.

World War I

Both Young and Davis hoped for battlefield commands as colonels at the head of black regiments, something unprecedented in United States history.

When Pershing was given command of all U.S. troops in France, he nominated Young to the rank of full colonel. However, a lieutenant from Mississippi protested to his senator that this would put Young in command of white junior officers, and President Woodrow Wilson, a Virginian, agreed that this could produce "trouble of a serious nature." Doctors flunked Young on his promotion physical, though he rode a horse from Ohio to Washington, D.C., to dramatize his good health. He was forced to retire and died in 1922 in Lagos, Nigeria.

As for Davis, the Army sent him on a tour of China and Japan.

If America's two top black soldiers were not allowed to go to France, over three hundred thousand colored soldiers did, thirty thousand of them in combat. A black Officers' Candidate School was established and turned out seven hundred second lieutenants.

Meanwhile, another race riot erupted. In Houston the black 24th Infantry regiment went on a rampage after a soldier was clubbed and jailed for trying to stop a policeman from beating a black woman. Sixteen civilians and four soldiers were left dead.

A quick and secret court martial was held, the largest mass murder trial in U.S. history. The all-white tribunal sentenced nineteen soldiers to death, and they were summarily and secretly hanged before a judicial review could be held.

President Wilson rallied the country to a war "to make the world safe for democracy." "Why not make *America* safe for democracy?" asked the NAACP. However, W.E.B. DuBois, founder of the NAACP, urged African Americans to "close ranks"; the country first, then rights, he declared. A. Phillip Randolph, head of the Pullman Porters' Union, asked dryly what rights blacks had ever won by their wartime sacrifices?

The Army's four regular black regiments were all kept home. Most African-American soldiers were assigned to service or labor battalions. When men of an Illinois regiment refused to sit in the back of a streetcar in Virginia, the Army tried to disband the unit.

Two black divisions, one reserve and one National Guard, did serve in France. Pershing welcomed them: "They are American citizens, and I cannot discriminate against them."

The reserve 92nd left a controversial record. It had been parceled out to seven sites for training to allay public fears of twenty thousand black men with guns in one place. As a result, it never developed an *esprit.* Most of its recruits were illiterate and its general, a white man, was a racist. At the battle of Meuse-Argonne, it was severely criticized for its performance, although Pershing didn't join the criticism. "The only regret expressed by colored troops," he said, "is that they are not given more dangerous work to do."

No men of the 92nd, serving under the U.S. flag, received Medals of Honor, although their white officers did. One black doughboy, Henry Johnson, repulsed an attack by twenty Germans, fighting with grenades, rifle, rifle butt, and a bolo knife (machete). Another, William Butler, rescued five com-rades, killing eight enemy in the fight. The Germans reported they had been attacked by "an enemy group of overwhelming numbers."

Seventy-three years later, in 1991, President George Bush presented a Medal of Honor retroactively to Corporal Freddie Stowers, who was killed attacking a fortified hill. He was arbi-trarily selected from among four men nominated.

Meanwhile, the 93rd Division bandmaster was beaten for not doffing his cap in town, whereupon members of the unit marched on the town and shot it up. The division was hastily shipped overseas to the French.

The black troops fought in the Meuse-Argonne campaign, losing twenty-five hundred men in hand-to-hand fighting. The 371st regiment lost half its men. The 369th New York Infantry — 'the Men of Bronze' — spent more than six straight months on the line, a record among all American regiments, and boast-ed that it never lost a trench or a prisoner. French General Goybet declared that they showed "complete contempt for danger," and Pershing called them "second to none." They were awarded 171 *Croix de Guerre*. The 93rd returned to a ticker-tape parade down Fifth Avenue.

Between the Wars

White sailors refused to eat or bunk with black shipmates whose roles were restricted to mess stewards, and in 1919 the Navy cut off all new black enlistments.

That year bloody race riots erupted in several cities. In Chicago alone thirty-eight persons were left dead and five hundred injured. Lynchings spread across both North and South — seventy-seven were reported in all; some blacks died merely for wearing their old uniforms. The hooded Ku Klux Klan paraded openly down Washington's Pennsylvania Avenue.

In this atmosphere, Pershing, then the Army chief of staff, in 1922 commissioned a study of how to utilize blacks in the future. The panel concluded that they should continue to be employed in combat so that whites would not make all the sacrifices, but it recommended continuing traditional segregation.

The low point came in 1925. The Army War College released a study which concluded that "the cranial cavity of the Negro" is smaller than a white man's and therefore he is inferior in intelligence, unless he happens to have "a heavy strain of white blood." It added that a black is superstitious, subservient, and "a rank coward in the dark." In addition, he is prone to "petty thievery, lying, promiscuity, and ... atrocities connected with white women." Socially, the War College said, the Negro could not associate with "any except the lowest class of whites," although it conceded that "Negro concubines" did sometimes attract white men who were otherwise considered "high class."

As for the Negro officer, the War College said, he shared "all the faults and weaknesses of character inherent in the Negro race, exaggerated by the fact that he wore an officer's uniform." Even Negroes didn't want to serve under Negro officers, it said.

This provided the foundation for Army policy for the next fifteen years and was still quoted approvingly well after Pearl

Harbor. Army recruitment policies reflected this attitude. In the 1930s African-Americans made up less than two percent of the men in the Army as scarce Depression openings went to whites.

Davis was then a colonel and, aside from three chaplains, the only black line officer on active duty. In 1929, it appeared that he might be joined by another African-American officer when Alonzo Parham was admitted to West Point. However, Parham flunked out in his first year.

West Point was about to get another cadet and the Army another black officer in the person of Benjamin Davis, Jr.

B.O., as he was called, was born in 1912 while his father was serving on the Mexican border. When the boy was twelve he sat with his father, mother, and younger sister on the porch of their Tuskegee home one summer night with the porch light defiantly lit and grimly watched torch-waving Ku Klux Klansmen march past. The next year:

> My father paid five dollars to a barnstormer to give me my first ride in an airplane. Two years later I was living in Cleveland, twirling the dials of the family Atwater-Kent radio, listening avidly to the daily reports of Lindberg's solo flight.
>
> Newspaper accounts of air battles of World War I reached a crescendo with Lindberg's flight. Lindberg has remained one of my heroes throughout these sixty years. But I couldn't think of any course of action that would let me get into aviation.

The youth attended Western Reserve University and the University of Chicago before a West Point appointment appeared. Did he know of how Charles Young had been treated a half-century earlier, and did he know what was in store for him?

> No, as a matter of fact, I was naive, as I look back. I had excelled in high school, I was confident of my ability, and I thought there was nothing unusual about being a black cadet. The roof kind of caved in on the third night when I went to attend a meeting and was told I was not supposed to be there.

Davis soon discovered the reason: His fellow cadets were meeting to debate 'the nigger problem.' "I learned later the

General B.O. Davis, Sr.   Cadet Benjamin O. Davis, Jr.

The Davis family.

purpose of the meeting was to instruct my classmates to make me withdraw from the Academy. For four years I was 'silenced.' I became an invisible man. My classmates treated Filipino, Nicaraguan, and Thai cadets better than they treated me."

Not another cadet spoke to him. Davis roomed alone, sat alone on the bus going to football games, and when he attended mandatory dance classes, he also danced alone. Although he was assigned a table at the mess hall, Sunday breakfast was "open seating," and he was forced to go from table to table, mess tray in hands: "Request permission to join your table."

"Permission denied."

This 'silencing' was usually reserved for violations of the honor code, and Davis asked himself how it was reconciled with West Point's motto of "Duty, honor, country."

> West Point is supposed to train leaders, but there was no damn leadership at all. The superintendent, Lieutenant Colonel Richardson, an old cavalry officer, was a fine gentleman, but he wasn't about to interfere with what went on. The first captain of cadets was William Westmoreland [later commander of U.S. forces in Vietnam]. If he'd been a true leader, he would have stopped that crap.
>
> It was designed to make me buckle, but I refused to buckle. They didn't understand that I was going to stay there, and I was going to graduate.
>
> I was not missing anything by not associating with them. They were missing a great deal by not knowing me.

In 1935 another black cadet, seventeen-year old Felix Kirk-Patrick, entered but was released in a year for too many disciplinary 'gigs.'

Davis survived and graduated in 1936, 35th in a class of 276. Ordinarily his marks would have given him his choice of arms, and he chose the Air Corps. It was denied on the ground that there were no black air units for Davis to join. In fact, he had only two choices, infantry or cavalry. One general urged him to drop out of the Army and study law. "The general did me a favor," Davis wrote. "He brought out my stubborn streak."

Assigned to the Infantry School in Fort Benning, Georgia, Davis and his bride, Agatha, drove south. When they had to stop along the road to "answer calls of nature," they were careful to choose "a treed area so we wouldn't be any more embarrassed than we were."

At Benning, they discovered that the 'silencing' had not ended. The Officer's Club refunded Davis' check for dues with the note that he wouldn't be using the club. According to Army etiquette, Lieutenant and Mrs. Davis made an appointment through the adjutant to call on the post commandant. They arrived to find the front door open and lights on inside, but no one answered their knock. Davis slipped his card under the screen door and left. The next night the commandant's card mysteriously appeared under his own door.

Davis was assigned to the black 24th Infantry regiment. "I was the training officer for young black recruits. What happened to them after they were trained? They were given duties as servants in officers' quarters. The 24th had no combat mission."

2

Black Wings

In 1911, Tom Steptoe of Chicago became one of the first airmail pilots in history when he flew a four-mile leg of an experimental route in Long Island. He later urged Congress to appropriate money for a permanent air mail service, though his idea was rejected as impractical. Nothing in his record suggests that he was not white; however, some Chicago veterans claim that he was actually a very light-skinned Negro.

Eugene Jacques Bullard

The first American black pilot we can identify for sure was Eugene Jacques Bullard, who flew with the French in World War I and may have downed two German fighters, though neither was confirmed.

The son of a Martiniquan father and Creek Indian mother, Gene was born in 1894 in Georgia, where he listened to his father spin stories of a paradise named France, where *egalite* and *fraternite* reigned. When masked Ku Klux Klansmen made a midnight ride around the family cabin, young Gene decided to run away to find that fabled land.

For the next two years he lived with gypsies, broke and rode racehorses, hoboed on freight cars, and stowed away on a ship to Scotland. He supported himself as a 'target' in carnivals and later by hefting heavy loads as a Liverpool longshoreman. At sixteen he became a boxer, fighting all over Europe as far away as Russia, until he finally reached his promised land, France.

When World War I broke out, Gene enlisted to defend his adopted country in the famous Foreign Legion, reputedly the toughest soldiers in the world, in their distinctive *kepi* headgear with white cloth hanging down behind. He carried a machine gun in the Moroccan Division in the great battle of Artois Ridge, where 175,000 men were killed or wounded. At Champagne, he attacked along with five hundred men, of whom only thirty survived. He himself fought his way out of an encirclement, receiving "a little head wound."

Eventually Corporal Bullard donned the steel helmet of the French *poilu* or doughboy, and joined the 170th Regiment — 'the swallows of death,' as the Germans called them. He trudged 'the Sacred Way' under the greatest artillery barrage the world had yet seen and into the trenches of Verdun. "It was clear we were heading for hell," Gene later wrote. Some 650,000 men on both sides would be killed, gassed, or wounded — "men and beasts were hanging from the branches of trees."

A shell knocked out most of Gene's teeth, and almost every man "got one more hole in him than he was born with.... We were damn near wiped out dodging from shell hole to shell hole under fire." When his machine gun grew too hot to fire, he threw it away and, diving into a crater, looked up to see a German dive in on top of him. "I pulled the trigger. Thanks be to God, I pulled it in time." Bullard leaped back out, his face whiter than the German's.

That night Bullard led a patrol to pick up weapons and food and was knocked unconscious by an exploding shell. When he came to, the village was "like a Chicago slaughterhouse.... Those who could walk, jump, or hop were doing just that. I had a hole in my left thigh" and expected at any moment to receive "a surplus hole somewhere else." He doused his wound with the only first aid he had, iodine, which made him "leap into space."

Sergeant Bullard volunteered for the French Air Service, though U.S. officials tried to prevent it until Gene felt that "I was fighting two wars." Nevertheless, he was accepted. Another volunteer American flier, James Norman Hall, co-author of *Mutiny on the Bounty* described the new cadet: "Suddenly the door opened to admit a vision of military splendor.... (Bullard's) jolly black face shone with a grin of greeting and justifiable vanity." He wore tan aviator's boots, "which gleamed with mirror-like luster," above vivid scarlet breeches and a black tunic. He also wore a *Crois de Guerre*, the *fourragere* [shoulder cord] of the Foreign Legion, and an enormous pair of wings." While the other pilots gasped, Hall "repressed a strong instinct to stand at attention."

With his mascot, Jimmy the monkey — dressed in a tiny uniform, tucked inside Bullard's own jacket — Gene flew his bi-winged Spad fighter on patrol over Verdun at speeds up to 125 miles an hour. He called it a *cage au poule* — a chicken coop — held together with wire and glue. On the side he painted his motto, "All blood runs red." He described his first mission.

> In the distance we spotted four big German bomber planes with sixteen German fighter planes to protect them.... As the *Boches* kept coming, we got the signal from the Commandant to divide into sevens and maneuver into fighting position. Then the attack was on.
>
> An air battle generally lasts from one to three minutes — very rarely as long as three. In this one everything happened so fast that I didn't have time to get frightened. All I could see were burning planes earthbound and a long trail of smoke coming from one of the German bombers which ... exploded in the air....
>
> I started shooting at every damn enemy plane that I even thought might be heading in my direction. It was all very confusing with planes roaring by and the smoke-filled air resounding with the tat-tat-tat of machine guns.

When he landed, Bullard found seven bullet holes in his tail.

On patrol November 7, 1917, "I was sure I had my first *Boche* victim in the air." He had his adversary in his sights and pursued him until "I was being machine-gunned from the ground by the Germany infantry," and he made a forced landing just inside friendly lines. When his mechanic arrived by truck with a doctor, they found Gene and Jimmy walking around the plane counting the bullet holes. There were ninety six in all.

When the United States entered the war, Bullard applied for the U.S. Army Air Corps, but the American doctors told him he had flat feet. He replied that he had walked all over France in the infantry. Next he was informed he had large tonsils. "To this I replied that luckily I was not an opera singer." All the other American fliers were transferred to their country's Air Corps. But not Bullard.

After the war, he returned to the prize ring, played drums with a Montmartre jazz band, married and divorced a French countess, and opened his own nightclub, where he played host to Charlie Chaplin, Rudolph Valentino, F. Scott Fitzgerald, Gloria Swanson, Ernest Hemingway, and others.

As World War II approached, Gene joined the *deuxieme bureau*, the French intelligence agency, and eavesdropped on German officers in his club.

With the 1940 German invasion, Bullard, then forty six, hiked to the front to join his old regiment but was warned to get away before the Germans discovered his spy activities. So Gene joined the thousands of refugees fleeing Paris. An exploding bomb damaged a vertebrae, but he limped and bicycled two hundred miles to the Spanish border, where he boarded a ship bound for America.

In New York, Gene once again supported himself by lifting heavy loads on the docks until a bus driver punched him, blinding him in one eye. For formal occasions at the French embassy, he donned his old Legionnaire's uniform, and General Charles de Gaulle himself embraced him and presented him with the Legion of Honor, France's highest decoration.

In 1951, Dave Garroway, host of the new NBC-TV 'Today' show, heard Bullard's story and broadcast a nationwide plea to find the old warrior. Bullard was indeed discovered – operating the elevator in the NBC Building in New York.

Ten years later Gene succumbed to cancer in his small rented room in Harlem, surrounded by model planes and photos of his famous Parisian friends. He was buried in his Legionnaire's uniform, and he left behind a fascinating manuscript of his adventures. It was published in 1969 by P. J. Carisella and James W. Ryan under the title *The Black Swallow of Death*. His bust was unveiled at the Smithsonian Air & Space Museum in January 1993.

Bessie Coleman

Meanwhile, another intrepid pilot had become the first acknowledged African American to fly in the United States. She was Bessie Coleman, 'the black Amelia Earhart.' Both women were photogenic and colorful and began their flying careers at about the same time, in the early 1920s.

Like Bullard, Coleman had to go to France to win her wings. Also like Bullard, she was half-Indian, a pretty Texan, who was born in 1893, five years before Earhart. Her father, who concluded that the only thing worse than being a Negro in Texas was being an Indian, left his family and escaped the state. Little (five-foot, two-inch) Bessie picked cotton in Texarkana, attended a one-room school, and helped her mother raise twelve children. Moving to Chicago, she manicured nails near the White Sox park on the fringe of the then roaring Chicago underworld. She may have danced in Negro stage reviews, opened a chili parlor, and saved her tips for flying lessons.

At that time there were only a handful of women fliers in America, black or white. (The first female aviator, Baroness de la Roche of France, earned her wings in 1910. The first U.S. woman, Harriet Quimby, made her first flight in 1911 and died in a crash the following year.) Facing the double handicap of being a woman and a black, Coleman found U.S. airports closed to her.

So she took French lessons and, in 1920, sailed to France. Strangely, there is no evidence that she met Bullard; in fact, she never mentioned him in her writings and probably had never heard of him. She enrolled under a French ace, and, according to Bessie, one of her fellow students crashed and died in the first week, "a terrible shock to my nerves." For nine months she walked every day to the airport and back — Bessie claimed it was nine miles each way, possibly an exaggeration. At any rate, she finally came home with an international pilot's license.

But Coleman was still unable to break into the white male world of flying, so she sailed back to Paris to learn stunt flying. Bessie had a great sense of style, according to her biographer, Doris Rich, and designed dashing flying togs for herself. She looked equally stunning in a fringed and beaded evening dress on the dance floor.

To raise money for her dream of opening a flying school for blacks, 'Brave Bessie' came home again to barnstorm in air shows across the country, doing loops and figure-eights and parachuting to the oohs of the crowds. However, Rich writes that Coleman faced prejudice, not only from the white world, but also from blacks, both men and women. The Negro press scolded her for scandalously breaking with tradition.

While Coleman couldn't enforce integrated seating at her shows, in her home town in Texas she did succeed in eliminating separate entrances.

A crash and a broken leg grounded her for a year, but by 1926 Coleman had raised almost enough money for her dream of a flying school and planned one more show, in Jacksonville, Florida, to put her over the top. The day before the show Bessie declared, "I'm on my way now" and went up with a white mechanic at the controls of a flying crate that, according to Rich, shouldn't have been allowed off the ground. Coleman wasn't wearing a 'chute and may have unbuckled her belt in order to stand and peer over the side of the cockpit. The plane suddenly flipped over and Bessie was thrown out, falling a thousand feet to her death.

A monkey wrench was later found lodged in the engine. Ever since, the suspicion of sabotage has hovered over Coleman's death. Rich, however, suggests a less sinister explanation:

There was no firewall between the cockpit and the engine, and a loose wrench may have slid into the engine.

Today, the anniversary of her death, April 30, is still marked with a fly-by of planes dropping roses on her grave in Chicago.[1]

Hubert Fauntleroy Julian

By far the most flamboyant of all early black fliers was Hubert Fauntleroy Julian, 'the black eagle of Harlem.'

Born in Trinidad in 1897, Julian moved to Canada and took his first airplane ride with the great World War I ace, Billy Bishop, in a Sopwith Camel. Moving to the United States, in 1924, Julian decided he would be the first man to fly the Atlantic, from New York to Africa, in his plane, 'Ethiopia I.'

A boy named Harry Sheppard, a future Red Tail, remembered him: "He was flamboyant, ebullient − a little foppish, I'd say − full of grand ideas, undaunted by anything."

"He was my inspiration when I was a kid," laughed Louis Purnell, who would also go on to fly with the Red Tails. "He was the most elegant rogue in black aviation."

Purnell recalled:

Julian didn't want to be classed as a Negro, because he was from Trinidad. His attire was a derby, monocle, finely trimmed mustache, formal collar with the tips bent, a morning coat with tails, striped trousers, and spats. It befitted his character. He had that haughty air about him. When he was flying, he'd wear riding breeches and leather boots. I thought he was glamorous.

When I was about six years old, he came through Wilmington, where I lived, going to churches and speaking to collect funds for the flight [to Africa]. After he passed the plate at church, he pulled off this trick at a big air show:

He was supposed to jump out and descend in a 'chute while playing a saxophone. He had a big open LaSalle touring car with the top pulled back, and he rode in front of the grandstand with his flying suit and disappeared over a hill at the far end of the airport.

The plane took off and circled us, and out he jumped, but as far as I could see there was no evidence of a saxophone.

(above); Bessie Coleman popularized flying among black youth. *(below)*: Eugene Jacques Bullard, America's first black aviator who flew for the French. *(right)*: Hubert Fauntleroy Julian, the clown prince of black aviators.

The plane landed at the far end of the airport, over the same hill, and our attention was turned to the displays of different planes in the hangar. But I happened to see a truck go by — what attracted my attention was the billowing 'chute in the back. It was another guy, altogether different, in the truck, with a scuffed-up suit. Anyhow, a switch was made, and a moment later Hubert Julian once more rode in front of the grandstand with an open 'chute in the back.

Finally Julian got his plane to the Harlem River, took off, and managed to get as far as Flushing Bay, about five miles away. He landed smack in the middle of the bay. That was the end of his flight.

> He'd pull all kinds of stunts. He was the only guy who ever made a parachute jump over New York City without a license — and landed on the skylight of a police precinct station!
> He was a pilot in Haile Selassie's air force in Ethiopia and wrecked the whole air force — it had about two planes. They fired him.

Another black aviation pioneer, Cornelius Coffey, recalled Julian: "He was a parachute jumper, but I question whether he was a pilot. Julian had the world in a jug and the stopper in his hand. But they told him not to fly the emperor's personal plane, and when he crashed it, they were going to expel him."
According to Purnell:

> Julian would sell or smuggle arms to both factions in any uprising.
> But he was the only Negro who could go into the White House unannounced and be received. This was during Franklin Roosevelt's time.
> Although he may have been a bit of a deceiver, he was quite a showman, quite a showman. He was the clown prince of aviation. You'll find his whole personality in the book, *The Black Eagle of Harlem* by P. Nugent. You're going to die laughing.

Purnell once asked the famous African-American aviator and instructor, Albert 'Chief' Anderson: "Where did you get your inspiration from, Chief?"

Anderson broke out in a grin. "Don't tell me you were inspired by the same fool I was — Hubert Julian?"

"We both fell out of our chairs laughing," Purnell said.

After commanding Ethiopia's new air force, in the 1950s, the 'Black Eagle' smuggled weapons to Cuba's Fidel Castro. In 1964, he was arrested in the Congo for carrying concealed weapons on a plane to the rebel province of Katanga. He was thrown in prison, boasting to his guards that "I have a fourteen-room mansion overlooking the Harlem River." Scheduled for execution, Julian was rescued by the African-American U.N. official, Dr. Ralph Bunche. Finally, Julian was picked up in London for shop-lifting. In 1982, Purnell phoned to invite him to a program at the Smithsonian. "I understand he had died," Lou said. "He would have run the whole show!"

In 1927, Charles A. Lindberg captured the nation's imagination with his one-man flight across the Atlantic, and African-Americans dreamed of one day being 'the brown Lindy.' Lindberg himself reflected the prevailing stereotype of blacks. In his autobiography, *We*, he told of an elderly African-American woman who asked if he could fly her "up to Heaben." He also recounted giving a ride to a boastful black passenger, who promised to wave a red flag throughout the flight to signify to friends below that he was not afraid. Lindy said he put the plane into a loop, and the passenger immediately cringed on the floor of the cockpit, hanging on for dear life.

Meanwhile, in 1927, the year of Lindberg's trans-Atlantic flight, two African Americans. Joel 'Ace' Foreman and Artis Ward, climbed into a small JN-4 'Jenny' to attempt a cross-country flight. They made it from Los Angeles to Chicago before they were reportedly arrested for flying an unlicensed plane.

About that time, a mysterious figure known as 'Samuel Sauzereseteo' reportedly flew from Moscow to Berlin and followed that with a flight from Belgium to the Congo. He was reported to have been black, but little else is known about him.

*   *   *

Bill Powell

An Army veteran, Bill Powell returned to Paris in 1927 for the Armistice Day parade. He visited Le Bourget airport, scene of Lindberg's arrival, took his first airplane ride, and was hooked. (He too didn't look up Gene Bullard, suggesting that Americans still had not heard of the 'Black Swallow.')

Bill returned to the States and tried to take flying lessons. However, although he held an engineering degree from the University of Illinois, he was turned down by the Air Corps and several civilian schools. Finally, Powell was accepted at a flying school in Los Angeles and recruited seven more students to form a Bessie Coleman Club. One woman mortgaged her house, and Powell put down six thousand dollars of his own savings to purchase two biplanes.

The Flying Hoboes

In 1932, James Herman Banning was one of eighteen thousand licensed American pilots. Twelve, including himself, were black.

His ambition was to be the first African American to cross the country by air. But he had two big problems. One, in those Depression days, he didn't have enough money to buy gas. Two, he didn't have a plane to put it in.

Banning had been born twenty-seven years earlier in the little town of El Reno, Oklahoma. After studying engineering for two years at Iowa State College, he applied at flying schools in the Chicago area but was turned down by them all.

In 1926, he finally found an army lieutenant in Iowa to give him lessons. After three hours and forty-five minutes of air time, Herman watched his mentor crash into a cornfield in a ball of flame and smoke. The pilot was killed.

Herman poked through the wreckage, found the motor more or less intact, and bought it. From other spare parts, he nailed and glued together a fuselage of wood and canvas around the engine, then patiently built and attached two pairs

FIRST TRANS-CONTINENTAL FLIGHT

J. Herman Banning and Thomas C. Allen, the Flying Hobos, and
the bi-wing they flew on their trans-continental flight.

Pioneer black pilot, Bill Powell

Pilot Janet Bragg, an active member
of the Challenger organization.

of wings to the body. When he climbed into the cockpit, the ignition coughed and sputtered, the propeller turned, and Banning at last had a plane he could solo in.

In 1928, Banning joined Powell's group in Los Angeles, and he and Powell climbed into one of the planes to attend an air show. Navigating by road map, they took a wrong turn in the desert, ran out of gas, and crash landed on a strange beach, where the sun rose over the ocean and set over the land. For five days, with almost no food or water, they trekked across the sand until they reached a fishing village, where they learned they were on the east coast of Baja California. They bought gas and hauled it back coolie-style on poles.

On Labor Day 1931, the Bessie Coleman Club achieved its greatest triumph − the first all-Negro air show, before fifteen thousand people in Los Angeles. It starred parachute jumper Lottie Theodore. Other daredevils, such as Marie Dickerson Coker, Willie 'Suicide' Jones, and Dorothy Darby, also barnstormed around the country.

Meanwhile, a cocky kid named Tom Allen was hanging around the airfield in Oklahoma City, working in trade for flying lessons. The only instrument on planes in those days, Tom recalled, was an oil gauge. By his fifth hour in the air, he said, he was doing loops and spins. When the other fellows at the field told him he was "too yellow" to solo, he jumped into a plane and took off and landed before anyone could stop him. He helped Powell set up air shows in Oklahoma, then Tom thumbed his way to Los Angeles, arriving with empty pockets, to join Bill's club.

Meanwhile, a prize of a thousand dollars had been offered to the first black who could fly across the country, coast to coast. (The feat had actually been accomplished in 1911 by Cal Rogers in his biplane, 'The Gin Fizz.' He took forty-nine days.)

Powell and another club member, Irvin Wells, decided to try. They headed east over the desert, putting down frequently for gas and to catch a few hours sleep. They were doing all right until they came to the mountains east of El Paso. Flying at night without an altimeter, Powell crashed into a peak, flipping the plane. The two airmen climbed out and scrambled over rocks and skirted cacti and howling coyotes, until they spotted the lights of a ranch house and arrived in time for breakfast.

Meanwhile, Banning and Allen decided to try to reach New York. Arthur Dennis, a character known as 'Small Black,' a leader of the 'sporting class' [gamblers] in Los Angeles, bought them a plane, the 'Eagle Rock.' It was a surplus World War I plane, with a 100-horsepower engine, though Allen said it looked like "some of the horses were dead." They still didn't have enough for gas, but decided to stay with friends on the ground and pass the hat to buy enough gas to get to the next stop. They laughingly called themselves 'The Flying Hoboes' and climbed into their seats. They wore no 'chutes but gamely buckled the chin straps of their leather flying helmets, pulled their goggles down, waved to four well-wishers at the field, gunned the engine, and bumped down the runway.

As Allen later put it, "We angled down into Arizona and New Mexico, listening to the motor very close." Lodging, Allen would reminisce, was hard to find, and they often went to bed hungry. At Yuma they sold a suit of clothes and a wristwatch for ten dollars worth of gas. In New Mexico, they were grateful they carried no parachutes — "the extra weight would have made us crash at the end of the runway," Allen noted.

Approaching the mountains where Powell had come to grief, they flew in fog so thick they couldn't see their wingtips. "We just lucked through," Tom said. That night they slept in a one-room shack as hogs rooted in pens next to them.

In Carthage, Missouri, the 'Lindberghs of their race' were forced down with engine trouble, then sputtered into St. Louis. There they picked up contributions ranging from nickels to a two-dollar bill — eight dollars in all. The gas pump thirstily drank it all up. At Pittsburgh the presidential election was in full swing, Franklin D. Roosevelt against Herbert Hoover, and the local Democratic Party agreed to finance the rest of their flight if they would drop campaign leaflets from the plane. They eagerly agreed.

And so they finally arrived over the tall buildings of Manhattan, landing, not in a shower of ticker tape, but in a shower of political leaflets. It had been two weeks since they had left. The

'Flying Hoboes' were hailed and treated to dinner, but they never did find the sponsor who had promised the thousand dollars.

Back in Los Angeles, Banning and Powell agreed to fly together in an upcoming air show, but Powell had to cancel. Banning went up with a Navy pilot who stalled and crashed back to earth, killing Banning immediately.[2]

Chief Anderson

In 1933, C. Alfred 'Chief' Anderson and Dr. Albert Forsythe became the first African Americans to fly round trip coast-to-coast.

Anderson, one of the most beloved of the early black pioneers, was the first to qualify for a transport pilot's license, the highest rating. Raised in the Blue Ridge Mountains of Virginia, he once told an interviewer how he started flying: "It was impossible for blacks to fly then. They would just point-blank tell you, 'We don't take colored people up.' So I bought a second-hand plane. Naturally, I had to learn, but nobody would teach me, so I taught myself. I became familiar with the feel of it and watched what other people were doing, and when it came time to solo, I just did what they did."

Forsythe was born in the Bahamas and raised in Jamaica. He had earned a medical degree from McGill University in Canada and set up practice in Atlantic City, when he came to Anderson and asked Chief to teach him to fly.

After their cross-country flight, Forsythe proposed an ambitious twenty-nation goodwill tour to the Caribbean and South America. They borrowed some money and bought a Lambert Monocoupe, "The Spirit of Booker T. Washington."

They made the over-water hop to Nassau safely, landing on a dirt road at dusk by the light of automobile lights. They continued to Havana, Jamaica, and Haiti, but engine failure forced them down in the mountains before they reached Santo Domingo, where they had to wait three weeks for new parts. Then they continued down to Puerto Rico and the Virgin

34

Pioneer Black Aviators
(above l.): Willa Brown; *(above r.)*: James Peck;
(below l.): Cornelius Coffey; *(below r.)*: John C. Robinson.

Islands and island-hopped the Lesser Antilles to Grenada and Trinidad, almost to the coast of British Guiana on the South American mainland. Heavy with fuel, they took off from a primitive field, clipped a bamboo tree and crashed, ending their trip.

Cornelius Coffey and Johnny Robinson

Two auto mechanics, Coffey and Robinson, met in 1925 in Detroit, where Robinson was hiding out from Chicago gangsters. When Bessie Coleman was killed the following year, they decided to carry on her dream, "realizing," as Coffey put it, "that it was rough for African Americans to get into aviation."

As told by Coffey, an eighty-eight-year-old in 1993, they traded a second-hand Hudson car plus two hundred dollars for a Hummingbird biplane, including four hours of free lessons, and took off. Next they mailed applications to the Curtis-Wright master mechanics course, but when they reported for class, they were stopped at the door. They threatened to sue and were grudgingly admitted with the warning that "we won't be responsible for what happens to you."

"We accepted the challenge," Coffey said. "It was plenty rough." At first the other students were hostile, but at graduation in 1931, the director declared, "These two young men have proven themselves beyond a doubt. This school will now be open to every African-American student. If they know any others, we'll enroll that class and make these two the assistant instructors. The doors will always be open."

Cornelius and Johnny recruited thirty more students, and the Challenger Pilots Association was born.

"Coffey was a brilliant man, but very quiet," one of his students, Chauncey Spencer, remembered. "He wouldn't say twenty words all day."

Among the first students were Janet Harmon Bragg and Willa Brown.

A registered pediatric nurse, Bragg came from Georgia, the granddaughter of a Cherokee Indian. She saved her money and bought a plane, which she allowed the club to use.

Brown, a preacher's daughter from Kentucky, was the glamour girl of black aviation. Enoch Waters, editor of the Chicago *Defender*, recalled his first meeting with her — "a shapely young brownskin woman, wearing white jodhpurs, a form-fitting white jacket and white boots." When she "strode into our newsroom ... all the typewriters suddenly went silent."

She soon became Mrs. Coffey. "Many people wondered how those two got together," a later student, Felix Kirkpatrick, said with a smile and a shake of his head.

On the anniversary of Bessie Coleman's death in 1931, Coffey, Brown, and Bragg made a memorial flight over the grave, inaugurating a custom that continues to the present.

In 1934, Coffey and Robinson went on a barnstorming tour of the South in Bragg's plane. In Georgia, Robinson tried to take off overloaded with fuel and clipped a chimney. "I felt a thud," Coffey said, "and turned to look. The stabilizer on the tail was practically gone; the only thing holding it was the top wire. There was a tree right in the line of our approach, and the left wheel caught the top limb and swung us around ninety degrees. We cartwheeled to the left and completely washed the plane out." Luckily, they walked away.

After Julian muffed his chance in Ethiopia, Robinson rushed to the embassy and applied for the job. While Coffey stayed home to recruit others and ship parts and equipment, Robinson bought himself a uniform, named himself a colonel, and flew to Addis Ababa, the embattled capital bracing for an invasion by Mussolini's Italian army. The African-American press dubbed him 'the brown condor,' who would lick Mussolini as 'the brown bomber,' Joe Louis, had licked the Italian ex-world champ, Primo Carnero.

The first enemy Robinson licked was Julian in a knock-down fight in an Addis Ababa hotel room, and Julian finally left town. Johnny found that Ethiopia had only a handful of obsolete planes and a few European aviators. In 1936, the capital fell and Robinson escaped one jump ahead of the invaders.

The self-effacing Coffey sold his own plane to buy Johnny a ticket home, where five thousand people gave him an ovation and eight thousand more tried to squeeze into the hero's banquet.

The two friends started a new ground school and borrowed a thousand dollars for a plane. Coffey invented a new carburetor that wouldn't freeze, permitting year-round operations. The system is still in use today, though Coffey never got a dime for it. But because they could fly twelve months of the year, they paid the loan off in six months. Coffey said:

> The rates we could charge the students were unbelievable — six dollars an hour dual and four dollars solo. If you sold empty bottles, you could get enough money to buy a fifteen-minute flight. And after the student soloed, we could rent the airplane to him for four dollars an hour! It allowed many of our people to fly who wouldn't be able to otherwise.
>
> And *we* made money too! Our actual expense was $1.98 an hour — gas, oil, and hangar. So it helped all the way around."

Coffey continued teaching — and learning. He took a course in the 707 jet engine, taught in the public schools and remained actively working until his ninetieth year, when he died in 1995.

Robinson returned to Ethiopia in 1944. Ten years later he was flying blood plasma to a hospital when he collided on takeoff with a student, caught pneumonia, and died. He is buried in Addis Ababa.

Janet Bragg died in 1993 and Brown in 1994 at the age of eighty-six.

James Peck

In 1936, the Spanish civil war broke out, and hundreds of Americans volunteered to fight against General Francisco Franco and his patrons, Hitler and Mussolini. Among those was a handsome, soft-spoken Pittsburgher, James 'Jimmy' Peck, reputedly the world's first African-American ace.

Peck caught the flying bug watching World War I fliers in a field near his Pittsburgh home, and after two years at the University of Pittsburgh, he won his pilot's license and applied for appointments to the Air Corps and the Navy. Neither service bothered to answer.

Jimmy worked as an elevator operator and as a trap drummer with the Victor Recording Orchestra. After the war erupted in Spain, Peck and another black, Paul Williams, sailed to France, made a fourteen-hour march across the Pyrenees mountains, and arrived in Valencia during the worst air bombardment of the war. He wrote that the civilian suffering he saw gave him a personal motive to fight.

Flying with Spaniards, Dominicans, Brazilians, and Russians, Peck was credited with five victories over Italian and German planes. He wrote about his experiences in two books in a poetic style reminiscent of France's Antoine de Saint-Exupery. Jim described his first sight of enemy planes while on an aerial patrol.

> At our approaching speeds, the dots — I make out nine of them — become larger and round.
>
> We open with a solid wall of fire. Grayish threads of smoke stream from the pointed noses of the enemy craft as they reply — tracers [bullets]. One of the planes veers crazily, turning cartwheels like a kid's kite gone mad, and their formation scatters. I line up on one of the enemy, who is pulling up slightly below and to my right.
>
> A tiny streamer flies from the pilot's helmet. I had to choose the best pilot for an enemy. Only the squadron commander wears that ribbon! I'm not so frightened as I'm going to be in just a moment.
>
> Suddenly it happens — my ship is hit. A long burst of slugs chews its way into my lower wing with a succession of thudding impacts.
>
> I'm hitting him, too — I can tell by the path of my tracer bullets. As his biplane flashes by close beneath, I pull up into the tightest wingover turn that I can execute.
>
> But the commander has outwitted me by making a left turn. He executes an Immelmann — half a loop, the ship rolling right side up at the top — then, before I realize it, his guns are spewing more of those slugs into my tail. This guy is clever.
>
> I whip into a tight vertical turn. He sticks behind me as if I were towing him on an invisible rope. Our ships wind up chasing each other around in a circle, nearly opposite each other. Perhaps if I take the initiative I may gain a momentary

advantage. That is all that one gets in modern combat. But whoever breaks the circle leaves himself wide open for an interval. This decision is the most momentous I have ever been called upon to make in my young life.

I roll over on my back − upside down. The pull-up slows down one's forward speed and the other plane gains during this interval.

I stop the biplane's roll, and the commander's plane is directly opposite, and he is just waking up. But he is too late. From my inverted position I clearly see the glass and metal frames of his goggles, the gray, set face, that streaming ribbon. I fire all four guns.

Tracers and a crazy line of bullet holes stitch along the bottom of his cockpit and creep back along the fuselage. That ugly, black cross on the plane's rudder seems to disappear in a shower of flying tracer, metal and fabric. Then the ship is gone.

A cloud swallows him up, like some eerie thing devouring a victim. Victory in my first combat.

Reviewers hailed the books − *Armies With Wings* and *So You Want to Fly* − and excerpts appeared in the New York *Times*, London *Chronicle*, *Harpers Magazine*, and *Reader's Digest*. Peck devoted only two chapters to his own exploits and in them did not claim to have bagged five planes. Still, the story grew, and there is probably no way either to confirm or disprove it.

In 1972, Peck was working on the B-1 bomber project at North American. His last known address was San Diego in the mid-1980s. After that his trail petered out.

Chauncey Spencer

By 1939, war clouds were gathering across Europe. The government was gearing up a Civilian Pilot Training Program (CPT) to prepare college men for the Air Corps if war broke out. The black press − the Pittsburgh *Courier* and Chicago *Defender* − and many other Negro voices were clamoring to include black colleges in the program. Chauncey Spencer found himself a catalyst in the campaign.

Spry and hearty in 1996 at the age of eighty-nine, he called himself "a sixth-generation American" with roots going back to 1705. As a fifteen-year-old in 1921, he took a train to Chicago to see Coleman put on an air show and met the famous aviatrix. He remembered her as tiny, enthusiastic, and determined.

Eleven years later, Oscar DePriest, the only African American in Congress, visited Spencer's hometown of Lynchburg, Virginia, on a speaking tour and dined at the Spencer home. He suggested that the youth to go back to Chicago to Coffey's new school. Soon Spencer was flying, stunting, and parachuting. "A friend dared me to go up and race another parachutist down. I crawled out on the wing and jumped," free-falling for two thousand feet. Soon he was performing at shows with Janet and the Coffeys, doing barrel rolls, wingovers, and spirals. Bill Powell came all the way from Los Angeles to see them.

Chauncey and his friend, Dale White, were working on a black history project for the government's Works Progress Administration (WPA), when, he recalled:

> Enoch Waters of the *Defender* tried to interest other people outside of Chicago in aviation. Dale and I planned to fly to all the Negro colleges, but Waters said, "Why do that? Why not try to get into Congress and get support there?"
>
> My mother and father came out to one of the air shows, and they put up the first five hundred dollars to rent a Lincoln-Paige biplane with a radial engine and only two instruments, the flight instruments and the oil gauge. We called it 'Old Faithful.'
>
> George and Ed Jones ran the numbers racket in Chicago [similar to today's lottery but then illegal]. Enoch, Dale, Coffey, and I went to see them at their business 'front,' a Ben Franklin five-and-ten-cent store on 47th Street for money for fuel and supplies. George turned to his secretary and said, "Give Coffey a check for a thousand dollars."
>
> So on the 9th of May 1939, Dale White and I jumped off from Harlem Airport, Chicago, at six o'clock.
>
> Then Fate stepped in. Flying over Ohio, the engine threw a crank shaft, and we made a forced landing in a field. We sent word back to Chicago, where Coffey got the parts and said, "Don't worry, I'll be there this afternoon." And he was. We rebuilt that plane in two days and one night.

After Coffey tested it in flight, we took off and stopped overnight at West Virginia State College and met the student body. In Pittsburgh we met Jim Peck and spent six to eight hours with him — a very quiet man. Then we flew directly into Washington.

Edgar Brown, a friend of my family, was a top tennis player and head of the Federal Workers Union, which broke down segregation in restaurants in Washington. We took a little train under the Capitol building, and when we came into the corridor of the Senate Office Building, someone said, "Good morning, Ed."

Edgar said, "Good morning, Senator, how are you?"

It was Harry Truman. He asked a few questions: "Are you citizens? Do you pay taxes? You mean to tell me, because of your color you can't get into the U.S. Air Corps?"

"Yes, sir."

"Well, I'll see that that doesn't happen again." He said he'd like to meet us at the airport.

When we got there, I said, "Would you like for us to take you for a flight?"

He said, "No, but I see you've got guts to fly that plane all the way from Chicago."

We visited the Committee on Military Appropriations. Next we went to New York for a parade on the birthday of Joe Louis. On the way back I got a telegram from Enoch Waters: The Committee had appropriated money for the CPT, including Negroes.

But it was all purely by accident. If we had flown straight into Washington, we would have missed Harry Truman. Fate designed that delay. There were two ways we got into aviation—Faith and Fate. I say I was "the right man at the wrong time."

How do you like *that* story?

3

The Tuskegee Experiment

Civilian Pilot Training (CPT) was a landmark in black aviation history. Coffey: "It was the first time the government became involved in paying for flight training for African Americans. Until then, we were on our own. We got the training started early enough so when the Air Force finally decided to train black pilots, most of my students ended up in the 99th Fighter Squadron." His proteges included Jack Rogers, Clarence 'Lucky' Lester, Felix Kirkpatrick, and Hannibal Cox.

The NAACP pushed for integrated training, but one youth, Spann Watson, wondered, if a big white university had twenty thousand students and only twenty CPT spaces, what chance would he have had of getting one of them? Segregation, he thought, was the best hope he had of flying.

The Air Corps commander, General H.H. 'Hap' Arnold, called the question of Negro air units academic. It was unthinkable for black pilots to order white mechanics to service their planes, and it would take nine years to train black ground personnel; the approaching war would be over by then.[1]

The Marine commandant, General Thomas Holcomb, declared that the Marines "are a club that doesn't want them."

The Navy restricted blacks to cooks, mess stewards,[2] and work crews. President Roosevelt's idea to integrate the Navy was to put a Negro band on each ship — "the colored race is very musical," one official pointed out. Navy Secretary Frank Knox, the old Rough Rider, nixed it; he thought blacks should join the Army instead.

Secretary of War Henry L. Stimson upheld the other Services. "Leadership," he insisted, "is not embedded in the Negro race." Meanwhile, the Pittsburgh *Courier* dubbed the coming war, a war to "make the world safe for hypocrisy."

By mid-1940, when Hitler's army goose-stepped down the Champs Elyses, completing its conquest of most of Western Europe, the Army still didn't know what to do with Ben Davis, Sr. None of the major commanders wanted him. The NAACP asked Douglas MacArthur to give him a job befitting his rank of colonel; the general did not reply. When it urged a general's star, the Army answered that he was too old. Wearily, Davis went back to Wilberforce College for his fourth tour teaching ROTC, a captain's position.

His son, B.0. Davis, was also assigned to ROTC at Tuskegee Institute, "a useless existence" that consisted of giving one forty-five-minute lecture a day.

But the presidential election was coming up, and Republican Wendell Wilkie was making inroads into the Negro vote. Just before election day, orders arrived promoting Davis to brigadier general. He was assigned to the Inspector General's office to investigate race problems. However, despite the star on his collar, he was still not allowed to go to the post movie or eat with white officers. Rather than dine alone, he decided to skip lunch.

After the election, Roosevelt favored opening the Air Force to blacks, though without "intermingling" the races. When Congress passed a new draft law requiring all Services to enlist Negroes, the Air Force complied by forming all-black "Aviation Squadrons (Separate)." In fact, the men were used as laborers.

Then in March 1941 Eleanor Roosevelt arrived at Tuskegee and watched the CPT pilots go through aerial acrobatics. Chief Anderson recalled:

> The first thing she said was, "I always heard the colored can't fly an airplane."
> I said, "Oh yes, they can, Mrs. Roosevelt."
> She said, "Everybody here is flying. You must be able to fly. As a matter of fact, I'm going to find out for sure. I'm going to take a flight with you."
> It caused a lot of consternation among her escorts. "Oh, Mrs. Roosevelt, you can't do that!" But she was a woman who, when she decided to do something, she was going to do it.

Lou Purnell, a CPT cadet, watched the entire scene. "It sent the Secret Service men into a tizzy. They didn't know what to do."

Someone called the White House, and President Roosevelt reportedly told them, "Well, if Eleanor wants to fly, she's going to fly."

She told Anderson, "Come on, let's go."

"She got in the plane with me," Anderson said, "and we had a delightful flight. She enjoyed it very much. When we came back, she said, 'Well, you can fly all right.' I'm positive that

Chief Anderson and his famous passenger,
Eleanor Roosevelt.

when she went home, she said, 'Franklin, I flew with those boys down there, and you're going to have to do something about it.'"

Meanwhile the NAACP agitated to integrate the Air Force. Spann Watson recalled: "No less than Thurgood Marshall came to Howard University and wanted someone for a test case to sue the U.S. government. The man they selected was Yancey Williams, a senior, a year ahead of me, who was in the CPT class with me. I was Williams' backup.

Before the case could be brought to court, Watson recalled, "I remember as clear as yesterday, I heard the announcer over WOR radio say the Air Corps was going to form a Black Eagle Squadron."

To avoid 'hobbling' the defense effort with integration, the Air Corps decided to train the black pilots on a separate field. (Meanwhile, the infantry was training white and black officers together at Fort Benning, Georgia.) Segregated schools for enlisted specialists would be too expensive, so they would be trained alongside whites at regular Air Corps schools.

Coffey hoped the school would be located in Chicago, but this was turned down because of the weather. The Air Force had a choice of California, Texas, or Alabama and made what many felt was the worst possible choice – the deepest part of the Deep South – Tuskegee, Alabama at the Institute founded by Booker T. Washington. Racial tension plagued the new school; nobody wanted it there. The people of the town appealed to their senators to keep it out of their bailiwick, while the NAACP opposed the whole idea of a segregated school.

In a blistering report in 1943, Judge William Hastie, a black civilian aide to Secretary of War Henry Stimson, blamed both the Institute and the Air Corps for the Jim Crow conditions at Tuskegee. He said the school had bid for the Air Force contract as a source of revenue – "a mess of pottage."

The Institute replied defensively that "when Negroes are not segregated, they are subject to humiliation."

Watson agreed:

> The NAACP, of which I was a great supporter, because everything I got had been spearheaded by it, wanted to integrate the training with white cadets, but we'd have been blown

away! No one would ever have graduated, they'd have found a way to wash us out. If I'd gone to a white school, no way in hell I'd have had a chance. When they handed out the good things, they wouldn't have given me a thing. I only know four or five black people who had a chance to fly at a white university. So sometimes segregation is not so good, and sometimes it is.

The announcement of a Negro flying unit sent black men across the country scurrying to the recruiting offices. What kind of men were they? One of the later replacement pilots, Roscoe Brown, called them the cream of black youth of their generation. "We had a group of high-achieving people who had their own egos and a disproportionate percentage of leaders. That was implicit in the way we were selected: They went out and recruited the brightest and the best.

Bill Campbell, one of the first candidates, disputed that notion. The Tuskegee Airmen were chosen with exactly the same criteria as all Air Force recruits, he said.

However, Brown's close friend, Lee Archer, sided with Brown. "The cadets were uniformly arrogant and conceited, a different type of people from those I had left in New York. It was a group just like me. If there was a modest, shy man there, I didn't meet him."

The first student chosen and the commander-presumptive of the squadron to be formed, was Lieutenant B.O. Davis. However, the doctor conducting his pre-flight physical apparently hadn't been briefed and dutifully reported that Davis had contracted an advanced case of leprosy. The frantic Air Force quickly found another doctor and explained the situation, and this time the leprosy symptoms were found to have magically vanished. Davis and his wife hastened to their new assignment in Tuskegee, "aware of the high stakes game we were about to be involved in."

The second student selected was George 'Spanky' Roberts from West Virginia. I met Roberts, then a rotund man in a goatee, in 1982 at the opening of the Smithsonian exhibit on the Red Tails.

I'm Indian, black, Caucasian, a little Jewish. Our son married an Armenian, so our grandchildren have that to add to their lineage.

My father was a Kentuckian. He had been a jockey and done a little baseball pitching, and when World War I came around, he wrote asking to be in the combat engineers, the glamour service. They wrote back OK, but when they got a look at his face, they said uh-uh, they didn't want any niggers. He was later drafted and became a first sergeant in a port battalion. He had eleven 'slaves' in his organization, people who had never heard that there had been a Civil War or an Emancipation Proclamation. A great many whites didn't know they were violating the law either.

I grew up in Fairmont, West Virginia. I remember seeing Josh Gibson, the great baseball batter, hit in a little coal-mining town, Grant Town, near Fairmont. On up behind the playing field were hills, and the ball went out of the park at least twenty feet above the fence and still climbing. It must have gone seven hundred feet, allowing for exaggeration over the years.

I've loved flying all my life. When I was junior high school age, my parents dug up the money from some place to take a hop in a four-seater aircraft. The pilot asked me if I'd like to fly it. I had to stand up to reach the pedals, but I flew the airplane for probably twenty minutes.

I went to West Virginia State College, which was a segregated institution at that time, taking psychology, sociology, and engineering. I was pretty young, and with hazing what it was, I said, "I'll spank you if you don't let me alone." I was small enough that the upperclassmen thought it was funny, so I became Spanky, and it followed me all the years of my life.

I had been haunting the hell out of the Air Corps to let me enroll. Finally I got a telegram from the War Department that the Air Corps was opened to blacks, and I was the first one accepted as a flying cadet. [Davis, who was already commissioned, was not a cadet.]

Two other cadets were CPT graduates: Mac Ross from Dayton went to West Virginia State, Roberts' alma mater. "A real slick guy," said Spann Watson, "a real glossy officer in his dress and demeanor."

Charles DeBow of Indiana attended Hampton Institute. Lou Purnell recalled him as "very loquacious, verbose, with a sarcastic sense of humor."

Another in that first class was Lemuel Custis, the first black police officer in Connecticut.

> I came out of college right in the middle of the Depression — the Great One, I'm talking about. There weren't any jobs, particularly for young blacks who had some education. I didn't want to hang around the street corners and do nothing — my mother and father had raised me that you have to go out and work for anything you got. So I became a cop, walking a beat. When the Air Corps opened up, I jumped at the chance and never regretted it.
>
> Honestly, I don't know why I was selected in the first group. There were a couple of us who didn't have the benefit of going to schools that had CPT, so I was a real greenie who had to start from scratch. I think Davis and I were the only ones. We had to climb a little higher mountain than the others did."

Roberts' choice as the standout of the first class was John Anderson of Toledo University, a Phi Beta Kappa and sixteen-letter man chosen on the Little All-American football team.

In all, thirteen students were selected. According to Roberts, the base commander, Major James 'Straight Arrow' Ellison, told them: "Take a good look at the man on your left and on your right, because on graduation day they won't be there."

"Of course we didn't believe it," Spanky said. "We promised each other that we'd hang in there no matter what."

Watson was upset at being passed over. "We were the ones who had been pushing the fight to get in, but when they made the call for the first class, most of them were strange names to us, not the people who had been out battling to get in. Where some of them came from, it beats me."

The supervisor of primary instruction was Captain Noel Parrish, an old cavalry sergeant, who had been commissioned in 1939 as a CPT instructor in Chicago, where he had met Coffey and Willa Brown. The school had hoped Johnny Robinson

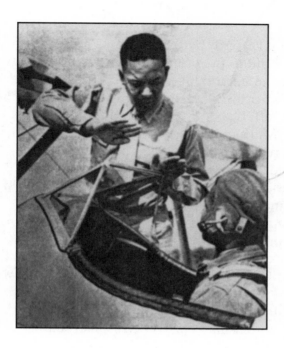

(*above*); C. Alfred 'Chief' Anderson instructs a
cadet during primary training at Tuskegee Institute.

(*below l.*): Lieutenant Colonel Noel F. Parrish,
he gave them the opportunity to succeed.
(*below r.*): Chauncey Spencer.

would also to take part, but negotiations fell through. Jim Peck declined to submit to the prejudice in Alabama.

However, the celebrated and revered Chief Anderson was given charge of primary flight training. "Good old Chief," Purnell recalled, "affable, a good-mixer, an all-round person. He's the 'Ancient Mariner' of black aviation. He was flying when most of us were in diapers, and he's still flying today."

"Chief Anderson was even then a legend to us," Custis declared. "Without him, some of us, including me, would not have been able to make it."

Parrish and Anderson began recruiting a staff of civilian instructors, both black and white.

One who volunteered was lanky, soft-spoken Bill Campbell, a graduate of CPT at Tuskegee Institute, who was working as, of all things, a stenographer at the school (he had graduated in business administration).[3] He defended the white instructors from charges of racism, citing two basic instructors, both white.

> One was a young captain from Indiana. He'd been told I was a licensed pilot, and one of the things he said when he got me was, "You won't have any trouble here." The other was a young first lieutenant from Union Springs, Alabama, sixteen miles from my home. They both treated me just like I'd want anyone to treat me, whether white or black. I didn't know of any racial incidents. All of them had volunteered. I firmly believe those people were there because they said, "I'd like to be."

"There were a bunch of fine white instructors, whom I kept up with after integration," James T. Wiley, another black instructor, agreed. "You have to give them a lot of credit. I don't know if I'd have done it — give up a chance for a career and a chance to make general, as some of them did, in order to train blacks."

Every Tuskegee Airman interviewed enthusiastically agreed. The cadets faced plenty of racial and other problems, but flight instruction was not one of them. All gave the instructors enthusiastic thumbs up.

Wiley was a studious engineering type.

I grew up in Pittsburgh. All the schools I went to, all my friends were mostly white kids. I was competing very well: Some of the guys could beat me up, and some couldn't. I owned my own newspaper route — you bought a route in those days — and I made money. I was one of the few guys around who had something going for him. I graduated from high school with a bunch of money and got a scholarship to the University of Pittsburgh for four years. I worked in the steel mills in the summer time, so I always had money and I had a car available to me. I was a physics major. I was educated, and I thought I would be able to walk out and get a job. But there was no job opportunity for me.

All his white classmates got jobs. It was 1940, and Wiley learned later that the Manhattan Project to build an atomic bomb was just starting that year. Some of his classmates "just disappeared," presumably into secret government jobs. He would have liked to work on that project too. However, instead, "I went to graduate school at Carnegie Tech, where I entered Civilian Pilot Training. I was a good pilot; they couldn't turn me down, because I was as good as, or better than, anyone else. And I knew it."

When Wiley was offered a job as primary flight instructor at Tuskegee, "I saw an opportunity, and I grabbed it. I had never been in an all-colored outfit before, but, as a black person, I'm so happy that I had an opportunity to go to Alabama and meet these fine black guys. Tuskegee was an oasis in the middle of the desert. I made a lot of good friends. My eyes were open to a new way of life."

Big, burly Daniel 'Chappie' James, a football star for Tuskegee Institute and another CPT graduate, also applied. "Chappie was a giant of a man physically," remembered Charlie Bussey, a future cadet. "Must have weighed 260-280 pounds, six-foot-five. Chappie was playful, liked to wrestle — I was always getting slammed against the wall. And hyper-extroverted. He could sing, dance, tell jokes, and fly an airplane. At the club if the floor show wasn't real sharp, he'd get up and take over from them."

"Can I tell any Chappie James stories?" fellow instructor George 'Bill' Terry asked. "None that you can print, except that he was a bad gambler. He'd lose, and we wouldn't lend him any money until he was going home, because he was married."

Terry himself had been an athlete at UCLA.

Jackie Robinson and I were teammates. We were the first two blacks to play basketball in the Pacific Coast Conference − that was before they knew Negroes could play basketball. I had played against Jackie in junior college. Tuition at the university was fifty dollars a semester − that was a lot of money − but only five dollars at the junior college level. He was a forward and the top scorer in the PCC. I played everything, center most of the time; that was back when they were still using a jump ball after every point, not taking it out of bounds like they do now.

I was a political science major, just finishing college, and they started the 'Bruin Squadron' at UCLA. One thousand took the test, about 250-300 guys passed. They had it on the front page of the Los Angeles *Times*:

BRUIN ATHLETES
JOIN THE AIR CORPS.

The colonel called me up at school: "Why didn't you tell us you were colored?"

"Why didn't you ask me?" In 1940, they didn't have race on the form.

I was already sworn in, but I got a letter saying I was too tall and weighed too much. I was six-foot- two-and-a-half, 172 pounds, nineteen years old, a graduate of UCLA, and in perfect condition. They said the restriction was five-feet nine inches, one hundred sixty pounds. They didn't have the same damn restrictions for Chinese or anybody else. But they told me to go home and wait.

A month later Dr. James 0. Plinton, later vice president of Eastern Air Lines, called me on the phone. He said if I paid my way to Tuskegee, they'd teach me to fly and make me an instructor.

Both Terry and James itched to join the Air Corps themselves and fly fighters with their students. But they were too big.

Do fighter pilots have to be small to fit into the planes? "Bull!" Terry exploded. "Chappie flew all kinds of planes. It was difficult to get into a P-39, but all those other planes, you could fly. Ben Davis was six-foot-one."

Black enlisted specialists had also started training. One was Harry Sheppard, the son of a West Indian fisherman. After grammar school in Barbados, he attended New York's DeWitt Clinton high school (which produced two other Tuskegee Airmen, Lee Archer and Wilmer Sidat-Singh), and the City College of New York, CCNY.

> I had very little interest in aviation. Early in 1941 I was studying electrical engineering at CCNY, working in the day and going to college at night — money was hard to come by. My cousin was a student at the Manhattan School of Aviation Trades and said, "Harry, they just opened the Air Corps to Negroes."
>
> I said, "That's fine, Walt, why don't you join?" This was for airplane mechanics and technicians, mind you, not for pilot training. He pestered me to the point where I began to think: The storm clouds in Europe were getting darker and darker, and we couldn't avoid getting embroiled in it. So I finally thought, "Boy, here's a chance to get into a branch of service that wasn't oriented to menial, heavy physical labor."
>
> So bright and early one Monday morning around the 30th of March, my cousin and I went out. The test was history and current events, civics, economics, mechanical skills, and math. Well, Walter failed, and he was out; I passed, and I was in. They inducted me as a private, twenty-one dollars a month. My cousin got a job a week later as a machinist making $175 a week. My father almost died. He said, "I thought you knew something about arithmetic." I thought he was going to kill me.
>
> About 275 of us entered the 99th Pursuit Squadron. We were communications technicians, hydraulic specialists, electrical specialists, fuel systems specialists. There wasn't one guy who wasn't at least a high school graduate. We had college students and college graduates and people who were in the teaching profession. We were young and full of vinegar and the other thing.
>
> Fred Archer and I enlisted together. I called him Stinky, and he called me Alfalfa — remember in the 'Our Gang'

movies, the one with the cowlick back there? I used to have one like that. Fred was an armorer and an ordnance man, took care of the guns and ammunition, and retired as a chief master sergeant. He would have made a very fine officer, but he never seemed to care about it.

The group was ordered to the Air Corps Technical School at Chanute Field, Illinois for seven months of intensive training. Sheppard enrolled as an engine mechanic and achieved a propeller specialist rating.

We went to class eight solid hours a day, from 6:30 to 2:30. After school we had our manual of arms, regular basic training. We were segregated as a group, of course, but we were going to an integrated Air Corps school. The instruction was excellent. We studied together late into the night. We were really a proud outfit. We left Chanute Field in November of 1941 with the highest grade point average of any group that had ever passed through there or would pass through in the future.

A bunch of us were sent to Maxwell Field, because Tuskegee didn't have enough accommodations. We performed guard duty and swept the streets, although we were mechanics and they needed mechanics on the line. They were teaching British, French, and other cadets at Maxwell Field, but they wouldn't relax and allow us to ply our trades.

Finally, as more tents were erected at Tuskegee, Sheppard and the others moved in. He worked on engines at night and instructed cadets by day. "The first time I saw Captain Davis, I almost fell over backwards, I was so proud. He was straight as an arrow and still maintains that erect posture today. The crease on his pants could have sliced bread. He was very quiet in class, but when he asked a question, it was a penetrating question."

Some forty to forty-five primary instructors gave the students their first lessons on the Stearman PT-17, an open cockpit biplane that cruised at eighty miles an hour. It had a narrow landing gear, which made it susceptible to ground loops, that is, a cross-wind could lift one wing, making the other wing hit the ground while the plane spun around. After the cadets mastered the Stearman, they went twelve miles from the Institute to Tuskegee AFB, which was still being built. There they flew the BT-13 Vultee 'Vibrator,' a metal monoplane with enclosed cockpit, radio, flaps, and wider landing gear.

The cadet considered most likely to succeed, Anderson, was the first to wash out. When white cadets flunked, they were reassigned to another field. Black washouts had nowhere else to go. They reverted to buck privates in the ranks at Tuskegee, a humiliating situation.

"Even having CPT didn't guarantee that they'd get their wings," Custis said. "There was more than simply your ability to fly; there was also ground school and overall conduct. I was consumed with making it, not washing out. Next to my wife, flying has been the greatest love of my life."

Advanced training, in the AT-6, introduced the students to formation flying. The trainer cruised at one hundred sixty miles an hour, requiring faster reflexes. It also had retractable landing-gear, which gave the students something else to worry about.

Conditions were primitive as the Air Corps began building a school. The men lived in tents. The mess hall consisted of four walls and a sand floor, a tin stove was used to boil water, and November rain turned everything into 'Mud City.' Chauncey Spencer, an undercover agent for Judge William Hastie, a Negro official in the War Department, reported that two hundred blacks were crammed into a twenty-by-twenty-foot dining room and ate sitting on empty soft drink crates. The white personnel dined at tables with linen cloths and were served by black waitresses in uniform. White officers also slept, washed their hands, and went to the base theater and Officers' Club separately. The PX cafeteria was divided in half; the relatively small number of whites dined in one half, the blacks, who greatly outnumbered them, lined up outside in the other half. Even the blood was segregated. (Ironically, an African American, Doctor Charles Drew, had pioneered the use of blood plasma.) A story that always brought smiles was of the white officer who needed an emergency transfusion to save his life, and the only blood available was from a black. He passed out, still refusing a transfusion, which his wife then authorized.

Spencer, at thirty-five, was too old for pilot training and spent the war as employee relations officer at Patterson Field (now Wright-Patterson Air Force Base), Ohio, trying to enforce integration. In his book, *Who Is Chauncey Spencer?* (Broadside Press, 1975), he described the experience as months of frustration. While white officials told him to "drag his feet" on integration, black employees sought special favors. One side called him a Communist, the other, an Uncle Tom.

The town of Tuskegee was the domain of Sheriff Pat Evans, a 'fat frog,' in Purnell's words. Town police arrested a black enlisted man, and when a black officer asserted jurisdiction and tried to take the prisoner into military custody, the police arrested him too and beat his driver up! Ellison succeeded in getting the MP released and returned to base, but this only enraged the townspeople, who were already in an uproar over armed Negroes. Ellison was promptly transferred.

His replacement, Colonel Frederick von Kimble, strictly enforced segregation. "An aloof type of person," Wiley said, "typical of commanders of colored troops at that time. They were in it for the rank. A colonel has to be a leader, especially with pilots, who are intelligent; you wreck their spirit by being very authoritarian. You're supposed to inspire them and come down and be friendly with them. I never saw Kimble."

Evans demanded that MPs carry no guns; if they did, he disarmed them and locked them up with Kimble's approval. It almost caused a revolt on base when a black nurse was beaten and thrown off a bus for refusing to move to the back. When General Davis came down to observe conditions, he was closely guarded by Kimble. Even being caught with a copy of the Pittsburgh *Courier*, the country's leading black newspaper, in one's footlocker was cause for discipline.

"I was scared as hell of the South," Charles Dryden admitted. "I had read all through my youth of lynchings and the cruelty of whites to blacks if someone didn't say "yes sir" or didn't move off the sidewalk when he was expected to. I had a healthy respect for the cruelty of the crackers down there."

Even fun-loving Bernard Knighten, another future cadet, stayed on base and hit the books rather than go downtown: "If you went downtown, you got thrown in jail. I didn't like jail."

Tuskegee, Davis wrote, was a prison camp, and his wife penned a long poem beginning, "Dear Mom, this is a hell of a hole."

Partly as a result of Spencer's report, von Kimble was transferred.

His replacement was a Southerner, Parrish, who quickly acted to defuse the worst of the tension. Although many things were outside his control, Parrish listened sympathetically to complaints, joined the black Officers' Club and regularly dined there, and, as Davis said, treated the students on an "equal man-to-man" basis.

Parrish gave up his own hopes for a combat command and stayed in Tuskegee to make the experiment work. "Tuskegee wasn't supposed to succeed," said Roberts, "but Colonel Parrish decided that, instead of making it fail, he would make it succeed."

"We can't say enough for that guy," Lou Purnell declared. "He had to be a buffer between the black cadets and the white citizens of the town. He was neither on their side nor our side, but he sure did protect his troops."

Cadet Herbert Carter, a Southerner himself, called Parrish "a very wise-man with vision beyond that day and time. He judged people by their performance and their potential and not by their color. The flight instruction was second to none. Parrish insured that it produced quality pilots."

Lee Archer flew Parrish to Washington a number of times.

> On the flight back you could almost see the depression as he got beaten up by the top brass. He ended up with only one star because he defied the system. But without him, I don't think the Tuskegee experiment would have gone anywhere. That man was an integral part of the Tuskegee Airmen. We look on him as one of us. I loved the guy.

For decades afterward, at reunion dinners, when Parrish' name was called, everyone applauded with a standing ovation.

The first class was taking advanced training when Pearl Harbor hit. "We didn't have radios or any contact with the outside world," said Roberts, who didn't hear the news until December 10.

Of the original thirteen, only five graduated: Davis, Roberts, Custis, De Bow, and Ross. On March 7, 1942, they received their wings before a statue of Booker T. Washington. Recalled Purnell, who was three classes behind them: "There's no way to describe their elation, standing on the platform with their uniforms rippling in the wind. They had done the impossible."

Nobody left after the ceremony as Second Lieutenant Roberts, joined by his fiancee, took his second oath of the afternoon, a marriage vow. "There were major generals, a lieutenant general, and our parents. It was on the Pathe news reel, in the magazines, and all the rest of it."

De Bow was stopped on the street in Montgomery by a white civilian, who asked him: "Why do you boys want to fly anyhow?" He thought about the question for several days and put his answer into an article in *The American Magazine*. First, he decided, he was flying for his parents, who had worked hard at menial jobs to give him an opportunity. Second, he was flying for his race, to prove himself as Booker T. Washington and George Washington Carver had in the field of science. Third, he was flying for his country; however imperfect, it could open doors and was a much better option than Nazism.

4

THE 99TH

More cadets headed toward Tuskegee.

C.C. Robinson, who held a degree in chemistry, boarded a Pullman in South Carolina after the ticket agent dithered for fifteen minutes whether to honor the government voucher. It was 2:30 p.m. when the train pulled out, but "as soon as I got on, the porter came by and wanted to put me to bed. Twenty minutes later the conductor came by with the same thing, to get me out of sight. I said, 'No, no way.' I went to bed with everyone else."

Charles Dryden of New York found that, "even though I had a Pullman ticket, when I went up to the dining car, they'd pull the curtain around my table."

Johnny Briggs from St. Louis recalled: "When I got off the train at Montgomery to change for Tuskegee, having a first-class ticket, I was going to the back of the train. The conductor stopped me: 'Where you going, boy?' He put me right behind the engine, where the blacks sat, with the smoke and fire right in front of us.

"St. Louis was segregated, but it was nothing like the Deep South."

Despite Jim Crow, in August 1941, ten cadets enrolled in the second class.

One, Clarence Jamison, a pre-med student from Cleveland, knew the Davis family from when the senior Davis had taught ROTC at Wilberforce. Jamison was one of six children whose father worked two shifts to send them all to college. Clarence was in his third year at the University of Chicago when he and a buddy, Sherman White, signed up for CPT "just on a whim" for extra credit. When war broke out, Clarence wrote to Eleanor Roosevelt to get into the Air Corps, and "it seemed to work, because I got a letter from the War Department and soon after that I was accepted. I was the oldest in my class. I felt protective of the other guys. I felt more mature and had much more flying experience than they did."

A second cadet was Sidney Brooks. "He was very athletic," his classmate, Charles Dryden, remembered, "loved playing touch football and basketball. And a ladies' man. He was like a big brother to me. I was a kid, didn't know how immature I was. He helped me grow up."

A third was Dryden. As a baby he had thrown pieces of paper in the air, babbling, "Airplane, airplane," and later learned to read on pulp magazines such as *G-8* and the *Battle Aces* about the exploits of World War I airmen. Dryden was studying mechanical engineering at CCNY when he signed up for CPT, one of two blacks in the program.

Thanks to CPT, Dryden found ground school − navigation, meteorology, theory of flight, engines − a "snap."

> But two-thirds of the class washed out. Some were good pilots, but they were victims of the quota. Lang Caldwell had finished all the requirements, but the night before graduation he was told, "You're not going to graduate tomorrow." Obviously, they had counted the numbers and decided someone's got to go. The whole cadet corps was shocked. I understood he went to medical school and he's still quite bitter about it, and I can understand why.
>
> Only three of us graduated − myself, Clarence Jamison, and Brooks.[1] The highlight of my entire life, even up to now,

was receiving my wings. I've never had such euphoria before or since as I did that day.

Those who were of large physical build were assigned as bomber pilots. The little runts like me went to fighters.

A month behind, the third class formed. One of the cadets was Lee Rayford of Washington, D.C. "The most handsome of all the original 99th," Dryden said. "The women were just wild about handsome flying boys with silver wings and glib talk."

"He was the lover-boy," agreed Jamison. "But you never would pick him for a soldier; he was strictly a civilian in uniform. The life of the party, loved to party, a lot of fun to be around. And a damn good pilot. In the evening at the bar, he'd get the stick in his hand and show what he'd do to this man or that man."

Rayford's classmate, Bernard Knighten, recalled him as a "happy-go-lucky poker-playing guy. We called him 'General,' because he was kind of chubby."

Sherman White from Montgomery, Alabama had been Jamison's best friend at the University of Chicago and married a fellow student. When White and Jamison signed up for CPT together, "the instructor wanted to check our coordination, so he had us drive a car. Sherman didn't know how! He bluffed his way through." White learned to fly before he could drive.

"A lot of guys didn't have a car in those days," Knighten said. "I never had a car, and I had no prospects of getting a car."

Knighten, his roommate, agreed, "White was the most uncoordinated man. He couldn't even march. In a review one head would be bobbing up and down at the wrong time − it was always White."

Spann Watson. "He was an easy-going, nonchalant man. I used to get on edge, and Sherman would say, 'Heh, Spann, calm down, calm down, it'll be all right, calm down.'"

Knighten himself was the son of a bricklayer from Tulsa and graduated from high school in St. Louis, the same school that produced two other Tuskegee Airmen, Jim McCullin and the flamboyant Wendell Pruitt. "Pruitt had two gorgeous sisters," Knighten said, "I used to go around with the older one."

Knighten graduated from Dillard University, majoring in "football and social science," but the only job he could find was as a Pullman car waiter on the Chicago-Los Angeles run. He recalls having a drink in a Chicago bar when the radio announced that Negroes were going to be admitted to a new flying cadet program. "I had never been in an airplane," he said, "I had never touched one and had no real desire to fly." But he took the exam anyway. He also put in for law school and divinity school, to cover all bets. When he got home from his next road trip, there were three letters waiting — accepting him into law school, the seminary, and the aviation cadets. He picked the cadets. "Somebody up there really hated me.

"Most of us had never been inside an airplane before we got down to Tuskegee. My first ride was the first time I had been in an airplane.

"We had a little feud going between the northern boys and the southern boys," said Knighten, who considered himself a Chicagoan. "We called them 'Bandanna Heads' because they wore headbands in the cotton fields. I don't know what they called us."

"Knighten was a funny fellow, a funny fellow," C.C. Robinson remembered. "Happy-go-lucky. Liked women."

"Another non-soldier like me," Jamison smiled. "He'd take out the band that made his dress hat stiff, then crumple the hat. We'd have dress parade, and he'd look the sloppiest, even when he was trying to look like a soldier. Davis tried his best to make a soldier out of him, but he was wild, undisciplined. He was a brainy guy, though, and he did have good flying skills."

Knighten:

One day flying the Stearman biplane I got lost, but I didn't panic. I looked for a big level field, set the airplane down before I ran out of gas, and got out to congratulate myself. The schoolhouse nearby declared a recess, and the teacher lined the students up and brought them to the field. Within minutes, the school kids were all over the airplane, standing on the fabric wings, pulling on the struts and kicking the tires. I certainly was not going to tell those white kids in Alabama that they couldn't do this. So when the sheriff arrived, I quietly told him that this was Uncle Sam's property, and he made them all move away.

After I removed my goggles and helmet, he asked me, "Boy, where you from?" I told him I was born in Tulsa, Oklahoma. He beamed, "I knowed it." Then he turned to the crowd: "It's all right, folks, he's Indian. I could tell by his high cheek bones."

Hazing by upperclassmen was an Army tradition. A future cadet, Walter Palmer, described it in his book, *Flying With Eagles*.

> All Pre-Flight cadets were called 'Dodos,' because that extinct breed of bird was incapable of flight.... We had classes all day and after dinner we were subjected to hazing until bedtime. Our days were crammed with classes that included physics, math, Morse code, and weather....
>
> The man who spent the most time with us was a black officer who was director of physical training, Captain Bracken. He was extremely tough on us and issued gigs for the slightest infraction. We were required to walk them off on the quadrangle of Tuskegee Institute – one hour for each gig, usually on Sundays after church services. Sometimes it caused us to lose our weekend passes entirely.
>
> It was a rough two months.[2]

Only four cadets – Rayford, White, Knighten, and George Knox – went on to graduate.

"The day before I graduated," Knighten said, "I was in a flight with Sherman White. I was flying a Stearman and hit the brakes too hard on landing and turned it over on its back – it went over very slow, boomp! My head was six inches from the concrete, and I fell out on my head, bang! Who picked me up but the general who was there for the graduation! The next day he gave me my commission."

In the first three classes, only twelve out of thirty had finished. To the students, this was proof that the Air Force was not in a hurry to form a black squadron. "It was such an expensive waste," said Jamison, "there were a lot of good pilots who didn't make it." Some cadets were not suited to fighter planes. White cadets could go to the Air Transport Command or to B-17 bombers. "We couldn't." In fact, there was only one place for a black washout to go — he became a buck private at Tuskegee. It was the ultimate humiliation.

To cut down the washouts, Parrish insisted that the fourth class be made up mostly of CPT graduates. Pearl Harbor had given added urgency to the training, and this class was an experiment to see if training could be accelerated. CPT grads skipped the pre-flight and primary flight phases and went directly into basic flight training.

Two were former civilian instructors at Tuskegee — Bill Campbell and James Wiley.

At twenty-six, Campbell was the oldest in the class. Though soft-spoken, he was a natural leader. "The top pilot in our class — in the whole 99th," Spann Watson declared. "I thought he was one of the most capable blacks who ever came through the Air Force — a brilliant, fair-minded man, who looked at all sides. You couldn't come up with a one-sided story and get it through Bill Campbell, because he was going to digest it with all the other information he needed. His family was all college graduates. And he was a hell of a flier. He should have been a general."

As for Wiley, "he was a natural-born pilot," Clarence Jamison said, "and a brilliant student of physics. He knew the engineering, he loved the mechanics of it." He was quiet, Robinson said, "but he was a brain."

Lou Purnell also joined the class.

I grew up in Cape May, New Jersey, so I've gone to school where I was the only speck of pepper in the salt shaker. My mother and father were both school teachers, and my father told me, "In order to appear equal, you've got to be twice as good." Mathematically that's wrong, but everyone in our race knows it's true.

When I was in high school I went to the airfield in Newcastle, Delaware and swept the hangar floor and cleaned greasy wrenches. On Saturdays and Sundays the instructor, Guy de Regaudier, would take me up. Soon he let me take over the controls, and from then on, it really bit me.

About 1938, I went to Lincoln University, between Philadelphia and Washington on old Route 1. Civilian Pilot Training was given at the college, and we'd drive to the field in an old Model-A Ford with isinglass windows all during the winter — and I mean it was cold as hell. But we had flying on our minds. I soloed in a Piper Cub. The instructor's pride and joy was a Taylorcraft, and if you were pretty good, he'd let you fly it, and then I really was bitten by the bug.

I heard there was an advanced course in stunt flying — we called it aerobatics — with a heavier plane and hotter horsepower, a bi-plane called a Waco. But being black, the only damn place we could fly this plane was at Tuskegee. I left with nothing but my bus ticket in my pocket and didn't know how the hell I was going to survive, but luckily I got a job in the laundry at the Institute.

There was a big group of cadets on campus, and we'd look at those guys, going to and from their classes. I'd sneak around the building and sit under the window. I absorbed the whole course by sitting under the window and listening.

Another cadet was Spann Watson:

My dad was a Carolina farmer, carpenter, millwright, and a station engineer, supplying power for big mills. That was an exceptional job for a black man in South Carolina at that time.

We left the cotton fields in 1927 when I was ten and moved to Lodi, New Jersey, adjacent to Teterboro Airport. Back in the country we'd see or hear an airplane a couple of times a year, but after we moved, there were nothing but airplanes flying around. We were so fascinated, the whole family would visit Teterboro Airport one or two times a week. They used to conduct flying circuses and triangular races with biplanes and high-wing planes — low-wings were ugly airplanes, and we'd laugh at them, but they'd win the races every time.

I never forgot anything I saw. My parents sent me to the post-office to buy a two-cent stamp, and it had a picture of the 'Spirit of St. Louis,' Lindberg's plane. Shortly afterward, on July 4, 1927, we were visiting Teterboro. There must have been twelve to fifteen thousand people. An airplane came over the airport, and I yelled, "That's the 'Spirit of St. Louis!'"

The announcer looked at me, and before those thousands of people, he said, "Heh, look, this little colored boy said that's the 'Spirit of St. Louis,'" and gave a big laugh.

The plane taxied up, and it *was* the 'Spirit of St. Louis.'" That was a key point in my lifetime. That announcer had embarrassed me before fifteen thousand people. He didn't say, "That little colored boy was right." I just stood there quivering. I never forgot that. I'm one of those guys, you laugh at me, I'll show you what I can do.

The people went completely wild. The crowd would have destroyed Lindberg and his plane, so they grabbed a bunch of men, including my dad, to push the plane down to a cleared space while this howling mob followed. My dad made sure each of his three sons touched the 'Spirit of St. Louis.' They opened a big hangar door and pushed it inside, and Lindberg escaped out the back door.

All the big pilots of the era came into Teterboro, and I saw them all — Frank Hakes, Jimmy Waddell, Lee Goldbeach. Amelia Earhart with her tousled hair was quite an idol, everybody loved her. Wiley Post, the one-eyed part-Indian who had a black patch over one eye, was flying around the world, racing, and making a big name for himself; he flew a big old 'barrel' airplane, the 'GeeBee,' that looked like a bumble bee.

I built model airplanes with rubber bands and sold them to other kids for a nickel. In a wind they would take off like a balloon. Flying school was completely inaccessible to us, so I wanted to be an aeronautical engineer. I went to Howard University, which didn't offer a course in aeronautical engineering, but I majored in mechanical engineering — maybe I could be a mechanic at least. Then I studied more and more and said, "Why the hell don't you fly?"

In 1939, the CPT came along, and the Pittsburgh *Courier* campaigned until they finally established a program at four or five black schools, including Howard. The school thought we were absolute fools to think white folks would let us fly airplanes, but Addison E. Richardson, who's about ninety now, of the school of engineering pushed it, and Howard got it.

There were ten of us, and Chief Anderson came to train us. He was unaffected and friendly, and he'd do anything to make you learn to fly. The better you could fly, the better he liked you.

Here we were, broke students, and not one Washington airport would let us fly from their field.

Finally, an airport at Hybla Valley, Virginia, which was going broke, agreed to let us fly. My younger brother had a '34 convertible and was kind of rowdy with it, so my dad told me to take the car to school, and that's how we all got to the airport.

Tuskegee had an advanced program with a Waco biplane, similar to a military trainer, and again Chief Anderson was there. Tuskegee had set a national record for scholastic achievement — this little black school beat all the white schools around there; *Time* magazine had a story about it.

Watson acquired a reputation for being outspoken, but as a cadet, "he was the quietest man you'd want to see," Knighten said. "he'd just sit there and grin. He got to be outspoken later on."

Before long Spann became "a man of strict opinions about the right thing to be done," Dryden said. "He insisted on meeting the top standards and was critical of people who were goofing off." Or, as Clarence Jamison added, "He just wouldn't take any crap."

Spann could not tolerate unfairness or injustice and spent his life swimming upstream against it. "We could all look up to Spann as a model," Wiley said. "He was determined. But he didn't restrain himself at all times and became a bit obnoxious to the leaders. If you're going to get ahead, you have to play ball."

Another cadet, Charlie Hall, came from Indiana. Spanky Roberts remembered him as "afflicted with a rare disease — he didn't know fear. A comparatively small individual, he was an outstanding athlete. I've talked to people who went to high school with him, and they said he threw his body into 240-pounders without thought."

Hall was one of Wiley's students. "A very good student, caught on quickly," Wiley said proudly. "I soloed Charlie Hall."

"He was an outgoing fellow," Lemuel Custis remembered. "Not like me — I'm an old stick in the mud. Hall was very ebullient. If you were around him for five minutes, you'd get to like him. Very jolly. Probably his only weakness was he'd bend the elbow a little too much."

"Charlie Hall was a great one," Jamison said, "got along with everybody. Get him at a party, get him high, he'd start singing dirty songs, and he knew all the verses. A life-of-the party guy, down to earth."

Willie Ashley was from Sumter, South Carolina, a graduate of Hampton University. "He was a very comical fellow," said his close friend and fellow South Carolinian, Robinson. "He knew everyone, and everyone liked him. He liked to have a good time, but was a very religious fellow. He was an only child, and he'd get attention — you know how only children are."

"A real down-home country boy," was Knighten's thumbnail sketch. "Old home-spun humor. Liked to run around, dance, always full of fun, knew a thousand stories."

"He was the funniest man I ever did see," agreed Watson — "a clown and a comic. Everyone loved him. What's he going to do next? And no woman got by him; he'd say, 'Who's going to fix me up?' You had to lock him up. But when you got him in an airplane, he was a different guy; he'd fly like hell."

Erwin Lawrence, another Clevelander, was just the opposite. "Very quiet," said Purnell. "If he stood in the corner, you wouldn't know he was there. He didn't have the knack of being a hail-fellow. His mind was on flying."

"Very handsome," said Dryden, "squeaky clean, never swore, very reliable."

Wiley liked Lawrence and was best man at his wedding. Jamison also thought highly of him: "Quiet, personable, loved the military. Determined and courageous, a typical 99th fighter pilot. Colonel Davis liked him quite a bit."

Graham Smith "was a real country boy, laughed at all our jokes," Knighten said. He stood barely five feet tall and could hardly see over the gunsight in his plane, hence his nickname, 'Peepsight.' (He also "looked like he was blinking all the time," Wiley said.) Smith carried a variety of cushions to increase his height in the cockpit.

Paul Mitchell, from Washington, D.C., was another one of the comics — "smart but funny," as one cadet said.

Faythe McGinnis from Muskogee, Oklahoma was "very good-looking," Wiley said, "a fine type person, with a lot of personality and flying ability."

A New Yorker, Percy Sutton, was another CPT alumnus. He shared a barracks room with Wiley and Campbell — they gave him an upper bunk. "He was very jovial," Wiley said, but just an "okay" pilot.

Training was rigid, remembered Purnell. "The red clay of Alabama clung to our feet like Elmer's Glue. If we got our shoes muddy, we were told to fall out of formation and come back in ten minutes with those shoes cleaned and shiny. Our washout ratio was sixty percent. At Maxwell Field up the road, where the white pilots trained, it was twenty-five to thirty percent. But it made us good pilots. It gave us the feeling that, hell, if we could get through, we must be damn good."

The previous graduates doubled as instructors. "Custis was a pain in the ass," Watson said with his customary bluntness. "Every little thing was wrong. But a great guy, and became a great leader."

Spann developed a personality conflict with Roberts, who almost washed him out − one more pink slip and Spann would have been gone.

> I was one of the top pilots, a professional from the word go. I thought we were doing a noble thing, and I went in thinking that everyone is going to do a thousand percent to prove we can be first-class and can compete with any squadron in the world. But it didn't exactly work that way. Other people had personal ambitions and didn't mind trying to eliminate someone who was a threat to them. Blacks have intrigues and cliques just like whites do. The 99th was rife with cliques from the beginning.

Davis remained above such intrigues. "There were a lot of problems he was unaware of," Wiley said.

One annoyance the cadets faced was obtaining whiskey for their cadet club. Pat Evans barricaded the roads from the wet counties, "but we got around that," Purnell said. Every Saturday they made a training flight to Columbus, Georgia, where they stocked up at the Fort Benning liquor store. "Pat Evans never knew the difference."

Purnell's biggest scare was not in the air but on the ground.

> I have a knack for imitating, and it nearly got me in trouble. The commandant of cadets was named Bob Lowenberg. He looked to be about seven feet tall, big as a barn door, with crewcut hair, which made him look ferocious, and this

big deep voice. When he'd come through the barracks, you could almost feel the quake of both his weight and his voice.

A week before graduation, we were off on gunnery practice in Florida. One morning, when things were quiet, I got outside the tents and in a big Lowenberg voice ordered all the men to get over here on the double. I got good response, because everyone thought I was Lowenberg. When we returned to Tuskegee, one of the officers told him, "I've got a man who can really imitate you."

One day at lunch Lowenberg came to the cadet mess hall. Naturally we all jumped to attention. He put us at ease and said he wanted to see Aviation Cadet L.R. Purnell immediately after the meal in his office. You can imagine how I felt, just three days before graduation: I thought it meant washout. I choked through the rest of the meal.

When I got to his office, he made me come to a brace [attention] and kept me in it for about five minutes. It was a hot day in June, there was no air-conditioning at that time, and sweat was running down my face and the small of my back. Then he popped the question: "I heard you can imitate me. This is a command performance. Start your act."

I couldn't move a muscle. At last he said, "At ease," and his voice changed, and he was really one of the nicest guys. We talked about where I was from, how I felt about the training, and whether I was ready for combat. Then he dismissed me. I went around to the side of his office to recuperate because my legs had given out.

Parrish was right about selecting CPT grads. Of twenty-eight who started, fourteen graduated on June 3, 1942 — Ashley, George Bolling, Campbell, Herbert Carter, Herbert Clark, Hall, Allen Lane, Lawrence, McGinnis, Mitchell, Purnell, Smith, Watson, and Wiley.

One who washed out was Sutton. In later years he would say he was dropped by error because someone read his medical records wrong. He remained in the 99th as an intelligence officer and after the war bought Harlem's Apollo Theater, became a millionaire and the borough president of Manhattan.

McGinnis was on his bunk, waiting to get married that afternoon, when they needed one more flier to make up an eight-ship flight. He said he'd go. But, as tail-end in the flight, when the group went into a loop, he was the last one to go into it, and he didn't come out. He got killed on his wedding day. McGinnis may have blacked out, Knighten believed, or he may have simply misjudged how much space he had left.

He was the first Tuskegee officer to die. His fiancee "was a sad picture for a long time," Watson said.

More trained enlisted specialists arrived (Arnold's nine-year training cycle had obviously been wrong). One enlisted man, Arthur Freeman, was Bessie Coleman's nephew. All were required to have at least two years of college, which of course was above the requirements for white mechanics, and, the pilots agreed, most of them were officer candidate material. However, as Harry Sheppard observed:

> At that time there was very low esteem for soldiers — black or white. A black soldier was even one layer lower.
>
> The Air Force completely underestimated the caliber of people whom they had so carefully screened. It thought we were black and ignorant and not capable of anything but the most menial assignments. I resented this. They were competent and dedicated. It takes ten to twelve people on the ground to keep one plane airborne — medical, operations, technicians, communications, security, administration. We lost some of our NCOs overseas; they lost their lives just like the pilots did.
>
> One of the draftees named Clayter bugged the captain to send him to school to be a meteorologist.
>
> The captain said, "What! Do you realize you have to have differential and integral calculus, you have to be able to create skew curves and compute these things?"
>
> He said, "Yes sir, I think I can make it."
>
> So the captain said, "Well, let him go, the worst thing that can happen is he'll fail and come right back here."
>
> Clayter did so well that they retained him to be an instructor — later they found he was a Ph.D. from the University of Chicago in mathematics. We rolled on the floor when we heard this.

Ambrose Nutt was a graduate of the University of Michigan and worked on the Ford factory assembly line because he couldn't get a job after graduation. He applied for West Point and was turned down. Then he got a job as an aeronautical engineer for the Air Corps and helped invent the high-speed ejection seat.

"You have to give strong play to the part played by the guys on the ground," Roberts declared. "They busted their tails to make sure that those in the aircraft had the best going for us. There wasn't a man among them who couldn't have gone to OCS. Many of those men did go on to become officers. They are lawyers, politicians, doctors now."

Although the white flying instructors were excellent, Carter said, "Those eyes were always upon you. It was very easy to become almost paranoid."

Roberts believed some of the students were nervous flying with whites. "One cadet, from Louisiana or Alabama, had been taught all his life not to perform with whites. He just couldn't land with his white instructors. But he was able to relax with me. With me in the plane with him, he shot perfect landings all day long.

"Some students I had to wash out," Wiley shrugged. "That was the time to catch them," before they faced worse consequences later. It was not an easy decision to make, however. "One guy was just about ready to be sent back. A nice guy, but not a good pilot, and Spanky was about to ground him."

He came to Wiley, saying, "Save me. I don't want to go home in disgrace.

"OK," Wiley said, "you fly with me for awhile." The cadet flew Wiley's wing, "and finally I got him to the point where he could turn right with me." He went on to graduate and flew many combat missions with the 99th. "He had almost begged me to let him stay, because he could do better."

As each class graduated, the new pilots checked out in some battle-weary, oil-leaking P-40s from the renowned 'Flying Tigers' of the China Theater. They were sometimes called 'Flying Coffins.'

Mac Ross had a close call on his first flight. Smoke began streaming from his engine, and the others called to him to jump, which he finally did, and became the first black officer to join the so-called 'Caterpillar Club.' He sweated that "maybe they'll start saying Negroes can't fly after all;" however, he was cleared of pilot error.

Custis approached his first flight with apprehension. "I was a bundle of nerves. It was a heavier plane than our trainer, with much more power. It was a hot day, and the plane had an air-cooled engine, so until you got off the ground, it was like being enclosed in an oven."

Alexander Jefferson, probably the smallest pilot to go through Tuskegee, remembered that "that old girl had a bad habit of pulling to the left as you were going down the runway for a takeoff. I would have to stand on the rudder pedal with all my 112 pounds to keep her from running off into the woods. The nerves in my leg would be quivering like crazy as we fought it out. I was determined to be a pilot, and this clumsy old plane was determined that I wouldn't."

Jerome Edwards' engine quit on takeoff. He plowed into some trees, banged his head against the gunsight, and was killed instantly. His best friend, Howard Baugh, accompanied the body home to his wife and two children.

"There was no two-seater version," said Baugh. "They just put you in the cockpit, the instructor knelt on the wing, you read the characteristics of the airplane and studied the cockpit, then he said, 'Go.'" Practicing a power stall, Baugh pulled the nose up. But instead of stalling, the plane climbed to thirteen thousand feet, then suddenly stalled, went into a spin, and "threw me around the cockpit. It took me six thousand feet to recover — it was a damn good thing I had a lot of altitude."

With its narrow landing gear, the P-40 was susceptible to ground-loops on landing. "You had to work on every landing; there was no relaxing," Sheppard said. "And chopping the engine or advancing the engine produced all kinds of torque to keep you busy in the cockpit. But the P-40 was a good aircraft. Tough. I was a prop specialist, and it had a Curtis electrically controlled prop. You could change the pitch on the blade with a control in the cockpit."

Said Custis: "I found out that if I followed the advice, 'Fly the airplane, don't let it fly you,' I mastered it. It was really like any other airplane, and I had no more trouble with it. "

Tuskegee had now turned out almost enough pilots to form a squadron and needed only a few more. Class Five produced them.

Willie Fuller was "a big, bearish fellow," said Roberts. "He was probably our tallest pilot, because fighter pilots were generally smaller."

On December 6, 1941, Fuller was in Florida playing in the Orange Blossom Football Classic against Florida A&M. On the way back home Sunday morning, December 7, he heard of Pearl Harbor. "The next day I made up my mind that I would see about getting into the Air Corps."

Meanwhile, he had his commercial and instructor's ratings. He was on the field in Tuskegee for a check-out ride to become a civilian instructor of cadets when a sergeant hailed him: "I just got authority to accept you into the Air Corps." Said Fuller: "I dropped my flying suit and took off."

A second man in the class was John 'Jack' Rogers. Watson called him 'Radical.' "We were the radicals in the squadron. When something was not as good as it should be, Jack and I would speak up — he'd say he'd kick your butt. He and I got the lowest appraisal ratings, although he got along a hell of a lot better than I did."

Like Jamison and White, Rogers had taken CPT at the University of Chicago. "He was my closest friend," Jamison said. "I got married when I graduated from Tuskegee, didn't wait for payday, and borrowed a couple hundred dollars from John. He always had money — and he was just a cadet."

Leon Roberts, a dentist's son from Mobile, was the youngest pilot to join the 99th. His brother, Cleon, was a mechanic with the same unit. "Leon was a ladies man — oh, a ladies man!" Robinson laughed. "That's what he lived for. He lived well, and he played a lot."

"But you could always count on him," said Dryden. "Call on Leon, and he'd do it. One day on a training mission Roberts flew under some wires and cut off the top of his rudder. We shouted, 'Bail out! Bail out!' But he flew back and landed. That took quite some airmanship."

The pilots waited and waited for orders — and flew and flew. There was a lake near Tuskegee with two bridges and a power line about twenty feet off the ground. "Yes, I've been under that wire," Knighten said. "That was part of the fun. We'd go under both bridges, under the power line, make a loop, and go under them again. The propeller would spray water on the fishing boats. We were dumb. We didn't know it was dangerous. We were young college man just having fun, just stupid. If we'd had any brains in our heads, we'd have quit. How we got through, I'll never know."

Some didn't. Walter Lawson was flying with Richard Dawson in an AT-6 advanced trainer when he tried to fly under a bridge and didn't make it. Dawson was killed; Lawson was found wandering, dazed, in the woods, the origin of his nickname, 'Ghost.'

Earl King rounded out the class, and the 99th had its full complement. Within two weeks Davis was promoted from captain to lieutenant colonel, and on August 24, 1942, he took command of the 99th Fighter Squadron, the first black squadron in U.S. history.

When Secretary of War Henry Stimson visited Tuskegee, the Negro press thought it strange that he had not had his picture taken with Davis, so a photo of Davis was quickly pasted next to one of Stimson and released to the press.

The infamous faked photo of Colonel B.O. Davis. Jr. and Secretary of War Henry Stimson when he visited Tuskegee.

Davis may not have been a natural seat-of-the-pants flier ("he made nice, slow easy turns," one of his officers would say), but all agree that as a commander he drove the unit to achieve. "Davis just commanded attention," Wiley said. "Whenever he came into the room, you knew B.O. was there; everyone became silent, no one said anything. He still has that bearing. He reminds me of what I think MacArthur was like."

Davis was rather aloof, said Jamison, "a typical West Pointer, spit and polish. It was hard to get close to him. I knew Davis from Cleveland; my family lived down the street from his. But you wouldn't know it from our relationship in the 99th. Now he's a little warmer than he was then. But he was what we needed at the time."

"He went strictly by the book," nodded Fuller. "He also played a mean hand of poker."

"Davis was respected by most and hated by some," said Felix Kirkpatrick, another poker buddy, "but it was because of the discipline he exacted that we were able to make the record we did."

Charles Bussey, who would later serve under him, called Davis "the most positive commander I ever had. He stressed the awful price of failure. He brooked none, and he got none."

Behind his back, Davis was 'the Whip,' 'the Thin Man,' or, usually, the time-honored Army appellation, 'the Old Man.'

Hannibal Cox, another future pilot, said: "You had a bunch of young and well-educated blacks to control and discipline, which was not easy to do. He did it. He was the epitome of an officer and a role model for us. He was the single greatest influence in my life, other than my father."

Roberts worshipped him.

Davis was very bright, ambitious, and self-controlled, which in my opinion was a result of his Academy days. His intensity to achieve made many people think of him as a martinet. That made him, to the outside observer, cold, and he's not; he's a very warm person. Many people have tried to build a competition between B.O. Davis and me, but I loved him with all my heart.

Davis led every major raid while he was in Europe. Usually we alternated, but if there were two biggies in a row, he'd take both of them. He considered the place of a leader to be out front.

I don't name my heroes in order, but if I did, he would be number one.

Davis named Roberts his Operations Officer, or second in command. Purnell admired him greatly: "the kind of guy you would go to hell with and for."

"A regular guy," nodded Fuller. "He knew his onions about flying."

Jamison agreed that Roberts was "a good leader," but added, "I wasn't cut out to be a military man at that time, and Spanky loved that rigid discipline."

He took up pipe-smoking, Knighten said, to give himself an aura of maturity with the younger pilots.

Erwin Lawrence was named assistant operations officer. Carter doubled as pilot and squadron maintenance officer.

The pilots were divided into three Flights of four planes each under Custis, Jamison, and Wiley.

Watson flew with Jamison. "He was a real decent individual and a good leader," though Spann criticized him for being "too soft on going to bat against some of the knuckleheads we had."

The 99th probably had the most training of any unit in the Air Force, but it had one problem the white units didn't: It didn't have experience. "We didn't have anyone to teach us combat," Dryden said. "We just did the best we could, based on what we thought we should do."

The 99th was ready to go, but the War Department wasn't ready for them. No overseas commander wanted them. Liberia on the, west coast of Africa was most often mentioned as a posting — the Liberian Task Force was a labor-oriented black organization. Meanwhile, white units were flying off to the wars, but the 99th trained. And trained. And trained. They trained for a year and went through three training cycles "until we were bored," said Jamison. "We had several hundred hours, which would have been unusual for white pilots before going into combat. We would try all kinds of maneuvers — snap rolls, whip stalls, spins etc. We were pretty good.

The pilots had dogfights among themselves, and rivalries were strong among the three Flights. "My Flight, C Flight, didn't have all the flair of some of the other guys," Jamison said. "But we told 'em, 'We'll kick your butts, A Flight or B Flight.' Whenever we went up, I'd head for a P-40 and dogfight. I'd take on everyone – Bill Campbell, Charlie Hall. Hall was a tough fighter. In dogfights, we'd go right down to the ground together. I couldn't get on his tail, and he never got on mine. Just like Wiley – I could not get the best of him. Wiley didn't get nearly the recognition some of the other guys got."

For Knighten, it wasn't all work and no play. "Ashley and myself would sneak out of the barracks and run to Montgomery. As soon as that sun went down, we were out the back window. We were going somewhere!"

"Are you out of your mind?" the others asked.

"We might get killed tomorrow," they answered, "but we're going to have fun tonight." On weekends they headed for Atlanta and the coeds at the colleges there.

Not everyone followed them. "Jamison was quiet and studious, one of the most studious guys I knew. You'd never catch him sneaking out like us."

Campbell was also more mature and thoughtful, Knighten said, "very thorough, never made any rash decisions. We were young, and he always acted older than us. He'd talk you out of some things and show you the best way to do things."

Still, the black squadron was a white elephant.

*   *   *

While the airmen waited, the Army ground forces were training two black infantry divisions, the 92nd and 93rd. The latter, wearing a French helmet as a shoulder patch, included the old Indian-fighting 24th and 25th Infantry Regiments. It was sent to the Pacific, but there was no intention to fight it; rather, the Division was broken up and assigned piecemeal to white units to be used as laborers, security, and truck drivers.

The 92nd, the 'Black Buffaloes,' trained in Fort Huachuca in the Arizona desert, possibly the worst hell-hole of all the

Army's posts. Their commander, Major General Ned Almond, was not well-liked, and the unit developed severe morale problems, which General Ben Davis, Sr. was sent to try to solve. However, the problems were still acute when the division embarked for Italy in 1944.

A black cavalry unit was sent to North Africa and was also broken up for labor battalions. Other African-American GIs built the Burma Road to China and the Alcan Highway to Alaska and later drove the Red Ball Express trucks in Europe.

Negro nurses, one percent of the nurse corps, didn't have black casualties to attend to, so they were sent to care for German POWs. Four thousand African-American women joined the WACs; while white WACs typed, black WACs worked in the laundries and mess halls.

Things weren't any better on the civilian front. North American Aircraft Company, makers of the P-51 Mustang fighter, had a policy of not hiring blacks, except as janitors. (Ironically, the P-51 was the plane the Red Tails would fly to their greatest successes.)

When an ammunition ship exploded at Port Chicago, California, three hundred dock workers were killed, most of them African Americans. Survivors who refused to return to the job were court-martialled for mutiny, and were defended by Thurgood Marshall, later a Justice of the Supreme Court.

*   *   *

Finally, in March 1943, the 99th received orders to North Africa. On March 25, the squadron went up for its final flight before going overseas. Earl King's plane hit the power line and crashed into a lake, killing him.

He was hastily replaced by Jim McCullin of the sixth class. A graduate of Knighten's high school in St. Louis, McCullin had starred in football. "He was quite an athlete," said Watson. "A short man, but he had tremendous strength in his hands and shoulders, the type of guy you'd want on your side in a fight."

On April 2, the Tuskegee Airmen filed onto their trains to begin their historic adventure.

Dryden remembered:

> We left after a week of high emotion, because we were
> feeling the grim certainty that some of us weren't coming
> back. There was going to be a dance that last night, and some
> nurses had arrived by overnight train from New York that
> same day. One of them had graduated from Harlem School of
> Nursing and had volunteered as an Army nurse that same
> week. She was tired and was going to retire, but the Chief
> Nurse told her, "Our boys are going overseas, and everyone
> on base is going to the dance at the Officers' Club," so she
> went with them.
>
> A friend told us, "You two New Yorkers ought to meet
> each other," and it was love at first sight.

Just before they left, Colonel Parrish stressed one thing in
his last address. "You have the future of the race on your backs.
If you don't succeed, there will be a catastrophic change in the
country's attitude. So do well!"

Jamison's brother, an Army lieutenant colonel, was also
boarding a train for the 92nd Division. They passed each other
somewhere in North Carolina.

The 99th crossed the Atlantic on a converted luxury liner.
As C.O. of the only combat unit on board, Davis was named
troop commander, the first time an African-American officer
ever commanded white troops. However, on their first morning
at sea, the pilots walked on deck to find a rope separating them
from the white troops. "But it didn't worry us," said Purnell. "We
were on our way to defend our country. We were flying. We had
done the impossible."

Davis eagerly looked forward to the test ahead. "The
coming war represented a golden opportunity for blacks, one
that could not be missed.... We owned a fighter squadron,
something that would have been unthinkable only a short time
earlier. It was all ours."[3]

5

Combat

North Africa and Sicily

The 99th arrived in Casablanca, on the Atlantic coast of
Morocco, soon after the Allies had driven Germany out of
North Africa and were preparing to invade Sicily and Italy.
Davis wanted his unit to look sharp. They disembarked in pink
and green dress uniforms, "like a proud squadron," Jamison
said.

It was their first look at a foreign land, and Purnell remarked on the "brown, chocolate soil" and "deep azure blue
skies." They arrived in a city of refugees, many of them Jewish.
Spann Watson called it the cleanest city he'd ever seen, with an
Arab at every corner to keep the block clean.

The fliers had all seen the movie, *Casablanca*, so they wrote
to their wives and girlfriends that they had been to 'Rick's
Place.' "I don't know how the censors let us get away with it,"
Watson smiled.

Davis and Roberts reported to General John K. Cannon, commander of the Northwest (Africa) Training Command, who gave them what Roberts called "a very cordial and warm" welcome. Then they proceeded to their airfield at the town of Fes, in the interior, away from the other U.S. units. The pilots shouldered full packs and began a ten-mile hike. "We should have been infantrymen," Purnell grumbled. Some were luckier. They rode in a forty-and-eight train — forty men or eight mules to a car — just as Roberts' father had done in France in World War I.

They arrived at Onediger, 'the River of Snakes,' near Fes and found a former Nazi airfield still littered with wrecked Messerschmidt fighters. They were invited to the mayor's house for dinner. There they met Josephine Baker, the ex-patriate African-American singer who had made a career on the French musical stage and had fled France after the Nazis marched in.

She did the translating, and when she grew tired, Colonel Davis took over. Fuller was impressed that there were no racial inhibitions. Frenchmen and Moroccans walked into the room and kissed her on the cheek. Later, performing at a theater before thousands of persons from all branches of the service, she threw a single flower into the audience while soldiers climbed over each other to get it. "It was quite a contrast to the American South," Fuller thought. "I began asking myself several questions."

The airmen were only the second black unit in the Army in North Africa. The 450th Anti-Aircraft battalion had fought with Eisenhower's ground troops. One G.I., boxer Kid Chocolate, lost both legs.

The other white units were supposed to come over and conduct indoctrination and training. "But I only saw them one time," Campbell said. "We were strictly on our own, off by ourselves. Enlisted men drew rations and gasoline from fuel dumps without any problem; they got along with the white sergeants quite well. But most of us never saw anyone but black people, so we didn't come in contact with that [racial] sort of thing."

Davis remembered the stay there as pleasant. Some white officers from the ship stopped to say hello, and the pilots of the 99th and the neighboring white fighter outfit met in sports contests on the ground and in friendly 'dogfights' in the air and strolled the streets of the town without incidents.

Meanwhile, Purnell had found a treasure, a bottle of 'America's favorite soft drink,' and deposited it in the squadron safe for the proper occasion to open it.

The men also received brand new P-40s. The plane could not out climb the German Messerschmidt 109 nor the Focke-Wulf 190, and did not have their speed or altitude. But it could outdive them and was superior on the turns. It could take a lot of punishment, which was important in ground support missions, and it had plenty of firepower – six .50-caliber machine guns, and a 1,000-pound bomb load. It wasn't a long-range plane, it was designed to come and go, like the 109.

With the new planes came a visit by a veteran P-40 pilot from the famous 'Flying Tigers' in China, Lieutenant Colonel Philip Cochran, better known to comic strip fans as 'Flip Corkin' of Terry and the Pirates. Roberts called him "one of the finest things that happened to us. He was the prototype of what fighter pilots looked like – around my height, five-foot-nine, sort of wiry but solidly built. Flip moved in with us, slept with us, ate with us, flew with us, talked with us, spent twenty-four hours a day with us for a week, and poured out information, lore, understanding, like a coffee pot that you turn up to pour out coffee."

One of the top dive bomb experts of the war, Cochran called his new charges "you young birds" and put them through a rigid flight exam – maneuvers, formation flying, and aerobatics – and pronounced them a natural-born group of dive bombers. Unfortunately, sighed Purnell, "that stayed with us. All our work after that was dive bombing. But we didn't care. We became very proficient at it, so what the hell?"

Cochran taught them that if a pilot was caught in the sky alone, he should make a quick tight turn to be sure no one was on his tail. Back in the United States, instructors had taught them to fly in V-formation, but because the enemy planes were much faster, Cochran told them to fly in a line abreast, so they could check each other's tails.

In case of attack from the rear, the leader called, "Break right (or left)," and each pilot "cranked his plane around 180 degrees in the tightest turn he could make, so they were all facing the enemy with six .50-caliber guns pointing toward them from each P-40. "The Germans hated those .50s," Watson said. "The Messerschmidts had 20-mm cannons, but they were too slow. In the heat of battle you could see the shell leaving the plane like a Roman candle, they didn't seem to be moving at all."

Cochran imparted another lesson. "If you push your rudder, you look like you're flying straight, but you're actually slipping to the side, not much, but just enough to fool the anti-aircraft guns on the ground. If they don't compensate, they miss you."

Cochran died in Pennsylvania about 1980. "No fanfare, no nothing," Fuller said. But to the pilots of the 99th, "he was one hell of a guy."

"He was like a nova," said Roberts. "He flashed on our horizon, affected us tremendously, and was gone. All I can say is, thank God for Flip Corkin — Colonel Philip P. Cochran."

On May 31, the 99th boarded forty-and-eight trains and moved a thousand miles east, across Algeria, to Cap Bon on the coast of Tunisia, barely a hundred miles from the coast of Nazi-occupied Sicily. They were attached to the 33rd Fighter Group under Colonel William 'Spike' Momyer.

Momyer, a big, imposing man who never smiled, had arrived six months earlier with seventy-five P-40s, of which twenty-one crashed while landing. When they went into combat in January, they quickly knocked down eight enemy planes. But, spurred by the triumph, Momyer sent them out too far from base, where the Germans were stronger. Losses were so heavy that in February the 33rd was taken out of the war to await fresh pilots and planes.

By the time the 99th arrived, Momyer had eight enemy planes to his personal credit, four in one day. When Davis and Roberts reported, he didn't return their salutes or stand up or say welcome, Roberts said. He merely looked at them and

(*l.*) Colonel Philip 'Flip' Cochran, a true hero to the Tuskegee Airmen. Cochran generously shared his knowledge with the fledgling fighter pilots after their arrival in North Africa. (*r.*) In North Africa, the 99th joined the 33rd Fighter Group commanded by Colonel William 'Spike' Momyer.

barked, "Well, I hope you've got replacements; I've been losing a lot of my squadron commanders."

Said Roberts: "His whole attitude spoke his distaste for us, the fact that he didn't want us."[1]

"When we first got to North Africa," Knighten said, "one Sunday a chaplain came, playing an organ and preaching, and there were four or five people there. Leon Roberts was so embarrassed, sitting there with his Bible, the rest of us all in town in Medina, running around. We teased him about it." The party boys − Knighten, Lee Rayford, and Sherman White − "would jump in a jeep and go to Tunis or somewhere like that. I didn't want to fly and get killed and not see the world."

On June 2, four pilots from the 99th − Campbell, Hall, Wiley, and Jamison − climbed into their cockpits to fly into combat as wingmen to the 33rd. Their assignment: to bomb the enemy island of Pantelleria. The first two, Hall and Campbell, paused at the head of the runway and gunned their engines to the cheers of the other pilots and crews. "I was scared," Campbell admitted later, "but I was determined to stay on my lead's wing if he carried me to the enemy's front door."

Wiley and Jamison were next. Wiley flew the wing for Momyer, who told him curtly: "You all boys, keep up."

Said Wiley: "I stuck right with him. He couldn't get rid of me, though I think he tried."

Jamison's counterpart also told him "get on my wing and stick with me."

"That's all he said. I'm sure I had more flying time than he had. I could handle the plane, no problem." Over the target, the lead pilot signaled to follow him down. Jamison stuck so close that when the other looked back, his eyes popped in surprise. When Clarence saw "those little black clouds of smoke, just a carpet four thousand feet below us, it suddenly dawned on me: That was flak — they were shooting at me! That's when it really hit me. Until then it had just been an exciting game."

The next day the four pilots led their own squadron mates on the identical mission. Still, Momyer ridiculed them and tried to embarrass them. He scheduled a briefing, then moved the time up one hour without informing the 99th, so that they walked in when the briefing was almost over.

On June 9, the 99th saw its first enemy planes. Six men — Jamison, Charlie Dryden, Watson, Willie Ashley, Sidney Brooks, and Leon Roberts — encountered twelve German bombers and twenty-two fighter escorts. Dryden recalled his baptism in his plane, 'A Train,' after the Duke Ellington song:

> I've been asked if I was ever scared in combat. Before I even saw a German, the thing I worried most about was being chicken, turning and running. I found out something about myself that day. I wasn't a hero, but I wasn't going to turn chicken and run from someone who was obviously trying to kill me.
>
> Ground control alerted us there were bombers approaching. When I saw the swastikas and knew that this wasn't play any more, those Nazi pilots' mission was to kill me. My reaction was, "I'm going to get him first." I knew then that, if I was going to run, I was going to run after him, not away from him.
>
> We all took after them like quail. The report later was that we scattered and broke flight discipline. It's true. But every one of us wanted to be the first to shoot down a German, that's why we took off.

Watson:

We were breaking left, and Willie Ashley lost control and spun out — stalled. When you lose speed, the airplane starts to spin, and he lost three to four thousand feet. You've got to go down, gun the engine, and pick up speed again. I was his wingman. I could have gone on with the crowd, but I had to stay with him. He recovered, and we climbed back into the fight, but we lost a lot of time.

Ashley claimed a probable kill, which would have made him the first black to score a victory. However, Watson questioned it. "I personally don't think it was possible, because we were trying to pick up speed and get back to the formation. We were pointing up, we weren't in position to start firing."

Momyer later charged that the 99th became disorganized, scattered, and showed no discipline. "He lied." said Watson. "There was no white man there who could have told him that, so there was no way he could tell if we had broken up. We certainly went out together, and we certainly came home together. For years we have been refuting that story. Eight German planes attacked us, we turned around and shot them like tigers, and they took off."

Two days later Pantelleria capitulated, thus becoming a footnote to military history. It's a truism of war that artillery and air power can soften a target up, but only infantry can actually take ground. Pantelleria, however, fell to air assault alone, a historic first. The New York *Times* military writer, Hanson W. Baldwin, reported it, but he neglected to say that the 99th had helped do it. The official history of the 12th Air Force also noted the significance of the bombing but failed to mention the 99th.

However, the area commander, Colonel J.R. Hawkins, gave the 99th their full credit. He sent "heartiest congratulations for the splendid part you played in the Pantelleria show." They had met the enemy and borne up well under battle conditions.

"After the first week in combat," Knighten said, "everyone was in chapel. When we crossed that bomb line [over enemy territory], we weren't heroes. I guarantee you, every guy was as scared as the next guy."

Early each morning they lay in their cots listening for Erwin Lawrence in his jeep coming to awaken the men for the day's first mission. "You listened to see if he went past your tent; if he did, you went back to sleep."

On July 2, the 99th escorted bombers over Sicily. The day was bright and cloudless as they joined some sixty other fighters from three white Groups and headed across the Mediterranean. They rendezvoused with the bombers, took up protective positions at their sides and rear, and continued on to the target area. As they neared the target, German gunners on the ground got busy, and the sky was soon filled with flak bursts and tracer bullets.

"You gotta be lucky," Knighten said. "You see all those flak bursts around you, one burst is all you need, and poof!, your airplane is disintegrated."

The bomber leader couldn't find his Initial Point (IP) for the final run over the target and went around again in a big circle. By the time he got back to the IP, the German fighters had scrambled — the 99th pilots could see them taking off from their dusty strips.

The bombers dropped their loads, went into a slight dive turning left, picked up speed, and headed back to Africa.

Knighten:

> That's when all hell broke loose. Somewhere up there, thousands of feet above us, in the sun where we couldn't see them, the Jerries were waiting, and suddenly their cannon bursts and tracer bullets were all over the place. We turned left after the bomb run, the Messerschmidts came down, and we all turned and shot at them. McCullin was flying my wing.

"When the smoke cleared, McCullin and Sherman White were missing," Watson said. "They were just gone."

"We don't know what happened to them," Knighten said. They were the first two combat fatalities suffered by the 99th.

"I wish I'd been a German with a Focke Wulf," Knighten said. "We were flying airplanes at 280 miles per hour; the Germans were flying 380 miles an hour. We were the defenders! Each of us went in different directions, chasing the attacking fighters or being chased by them."

Dryden was flying Campbell's wing when a pair of Germans bore down on them. He called, "Break right!" but Campbell apparently didn't hear. "Finally, I just flew into the attackers myself, and they broke off the attack." As instructed by Cochran, he immediately went into a tight turn to check his rear.

> Five hundred feet below me I saw a P-40 who had not one, but two, German ME 109s behind him. He was in a wide lazy circle and didn't know anyone was on his tail, so I dropped to his level and fell behind the second German and started spraying bullets at him. I saw them bouncing off him.
>
> Then I saw tracers off my own wing and turned around and saw a German Focke Wulf in position behind me. So I immediately tightened my turn; if he was fool enough to stay there, I would eventually end up on *his* tail. I was beginning to out-turn him, but as I kept looking over my shoulder, first I saw his cockpit canopy, then his nose cannon, and then the belly of his aircraft, and I knew *he* was picking up the lead on me. Sure enough, he started firing his machine guns, and I saw puffs of smoke coming out of the nose of his propeller. One round of 37-mm cannon hit my wing with a loud bang that shook my plane. I knew I was in trouble.
>
> Looking around the sky for some kind of help, I saw that the bombers had already started home and I could see the tails of the planes disappearing, but there were still dogfights all over the sky. Then I saw another pilot in the distance. He must have caught sight of me, because he peeled off and settled in behind the German and started firing on him.

It was Knighten. "I heard over the radio one of the planes calling for help. I looked out, and there, just below me, was one of our P-40s in a tight turn with German planes turning with him and shooting everything they had. Without thinking, I dove and started shooting. My tracer bullets must have scared them away, because they immediately turned right and climbed back up into the sun."

Dryden waved a thank you. "Then we got jumped in succession by two ME 109s coming up from low altitude. The Focke Wulf also came back; he had played dead until he saw an opening, then he attacked. My buddy, whoever he was, and I turned into them and fought them off for ten minutes, though it seemed like three hours."

Knighten:

> Dryden dove down to the ocean to gain speed and headed home. I started to follow him, but then I realized those Germans were coming back out of the sun, and I was their target! So I was sitting there with four German fighters shooting at me. All I could do was go into a right turn, count the Germans as they dove past me, and then turn back toward Africa and safety.
>
> But the Germans had other ideas. They climbed back up into the sun, and moments later they were coming down again, their machine guns blazing, cannons flashing. How they missed me, I'll never know. So for me it was another tight, tight turn, tracer bullets streaking past me, and counting those swastikas on their planes as they went under my wing and back up into the sun.
>
> At this point they must have been out of bullets or low on gas, because they leveled off and headed north, and I dove for Africa and headed south. Charlie was already safely home when I landed. Our months of fighter tactics training had paid off, with Lady Luck riding in both cockpits.

"Knighten was one of the hottest pilots we had," Dryden said gratefully. "Everyone acknowledged that. He was a hot rock."

Meanwhile, Buster Hall was making history. As quoted by Charles E. Francis in the book, *Tuskegee Airmen*, Hall described what happened.

> It was my eighth mission and the first time I had seen the enemy close enough to shoot at him. I saw two Focke Wulfs following the bombers just after the bombs were dropped, and I headed for the space between the fighters and bombers and managed to turn inside the Jerries. I fired a long burst and saw my tracers penetrate the second aircraft. He was turning to the left but suddenly fell off and headed straight into the ground. I followed him down and saw him crash. He raised a big cloud of dust.[2]

(*above*): General Cannon (r.) congratulates Charles B. Hall after he downed the 99th's first enemy plane. Lemuel R. Custis is to Hall's left and Wilson V. Eagleson to Cannon's right. (*below*): Charley Hall and the famous Coke.

The 99th had scored its first aerial victory.

General Eisenhower, plus the U.S. theater air commander, Carl 'Tooey' Spaatz, and General Jimmy Doolittle, the World War I ace, arrived almost immediately to offer congratulations.

Hall was awarded the Distinguished Flying Cross, the Air Force's top award. But Purnell told of another, perhaps even sweeter, award. Lou retrieved the Coke from the safe and from a town fifteen miles away got a block of equally precious ice. In the shade of a grove of olive trees the Coke, perhaps the only one in the Mediterranean Theater, "came to a well-deserved end."

The 99th didn't see another enemy fighter plane for six months. But they were kept busy with close air support of the ground forces in Sicily, the moving artillery that went ahead of the troops to soften up the enemy. "If they wanted a bomb placed on a target," said Roberts, "there was no question who they picked. We could throw bombs in the windows of a castle."

Bill Thompson, our armament officer, designed a way to put bazookas on the wings of the aircraft to give us a rocket-firing capability. I doubt if Bill would bring it up himself, but the ground troops couldn't get to enemy tanks effectively, and we couldn't do much with our machine gun bullets unless we caught them on paved roads, when we could skip bullets at them. But with rockets we stood a much greater chance. Bill Thompson is the guy who did it. He finished just as we got word from the United States that they had done it back there. But Bill did it in the field.

Purnell:

They gave us the dirtiest missions, dive bombing and strafing. Dive bombing, that was my specialty. At least four planes that I knew blew up as a result of strafing.

We were flying two or three times a day. We'd sit in our aircraft waiting for a red flag to take off, then we'd go up, come down, refuel, and go back up. Some of the guys would make four missions a day. I've talked to other squadrons, and that was unheard of. But if we broke under the pressure, that would have been all they wanted. We were really under a magnifying glass. They reported the least little discrepancy.

Some suspected that other squadrons dropped their bombs in the water so they'd be light and ready in case of attack.

Fuller:

Once or twice the white pilots made slurring remarks. For instance, one day it was pretty cloudy before we got to the target, so the 99th turned back. The next flight, all white fellows, flew through heavy clouds and two of their guys didn't come back. They said something about the fact that we turned around, but we said it was better not to jeopardize the pilots and hit the targets another day. All our pilots returned; they lost two guys. Frankly, we thought it was unnecessary.

When the 99th flew missions with white squadrons, they flew 'ass-end Charlie.'

Fuller:

That's the guy who gets the most flak. The Italians on Pantelleria had sent up flak, but it wasn't too accurate. But when we started going into Sicily, the guns were manned by Germans, and they put it where they wanted to put it. They used to try to box us in. You looked at the ground and saw guns winking: two shots in front of you, two behind you, one to the left, one to the right. You're boxed, my friend − look out for the next one. You're flying through it and smell the powder from the first shells. That's close! That's close.

On July 20, another Tuskegee Airman lost his life in an act of courage. When a man from another squadron was in distress in the water, Master Sergeant Edsel Jett jumped in to help him, even though Jett himself did not know how to swim. Jett was awarded the Soldier's Medal for heroism in a non-combat situation.

The average white fighter pilot was required to fly fifty missions, then go home. But because the only replacements for the 99th came out of Tuskegee, they had to fly seventy missions before they were rotated home.

The first four replacements were Howard Baugh, John Gibson, John Morgan, and Ed Toppins. When they arrived at Camp Patrick Henry in Newport News to pick up their ship, Baugh says, "Of course we had to be segregated." So the Army gave them a complete barracks to themselves. "Everyone else was jammed in double bunks in their barracks and lined up to go to the latrine."

Their ship was a Japanese luxury liner, The *Empress of Japan*, which had been caught in a U.S. port at Pearl Harbor. Once again, the black officers had to be segregated.

Baugh:

> They put us up on the promenade deck, and we had some of the best accommodations on the boat. All the others were sleeping in the hold and queuing up for the wash basin.
>
> After we had been out to sea a couple days, we went on the deck, socializing innocently, but there happened to be some white nurses who joined in the conversation too. The powers that be called the young ladies in and told them they were not to be seen talking to us. Of course they came and told us right away.
>
> At Casablanca we were almost on our own to try to find the outfit. No one had ever heard of the 99th. We found out they were up toward Tunis and got some rides on a C-47 and found out they'd moved to Sicily. We had to do this all on our own to get to combat. We joined them in Sicily in July '43. I don't know how we happened to find them, but we did.
>
> We were living in pup tents on the ground in an olive orchard and stayed there for most of the summer. Then we moved up on the northern shore of Sicily, near Mount Etna.

Two friends from Oregon, Bob Deiz and Sam 'Lizard' Bruce, arrived soon after.

Deiz received his first taste of flying from Tex Rankin, a stunt pilot of the '30s. "I was so young, they had to wrap a blanket around me to make me big enough for the seat belt." But he never had "a blind desire to fly."

> My mother taught me to play the piano when I was six. I always tell this story: We had two peach trees in our backyard with no limbs below six feet high. My mother picked them all

off beating me because I wouldn't practice. Later I went to the violin, but I couldn't stand it because I had a decent ear and knew when I was wrong. So I took up the trombone; however, we had six trombones in the high school band but no one to play bass horn. I took one home over Thanksgiving and by Christmas I was playing the bass horn.

In college Bob took up the cello and played in both the Portland Symphony and the Oregon University Band.

He also played football with his best friend, Bruce. Deiz was a running guard and he was also state champion in the 100- and 200-yard dashes. Another classmate, Jack Holsclaw, a hotshot third baseman, also went on to become a Tuskegee Airman.

In the summer of '38, Bob enrolled in Oregon's CPT Program. When the war began, the Navy recruited a special Torpedo Squadron from Oregon and Oregon State:

> I signed up and was all set to go until someone looked at my application and saw "Negro," so they turned me down. Later the squadron lost every man except one. I said, "The hell with it," tore up my draft card, and went to California. That's where the FBI caught me.

> The agent said, "You've got a good record, I'll give you two weeks to go back to Oregon and sign up for something." The head of the draft board, whose son and I had learned to fly together, said, "Bob, they're starting a Negro unit in a place called Tuskegee. If you'll sign up for that, I'll see that you're not called."

> By that time I was thinking real slick. I figured, "Well, there are thousands of black guys all over the U.S. who want to fly. It'll be ten years before I'm called." So I went down and volunteered. Damn if they didn't pick me in three months time.

> I didn't like going to a segregated unit because I didn't come from that environment. Some guys would sit around and say we had to do twice as much as the other guys to get half the recognition. But I didn't have any drive to prove myself.

> I already knew how to fly — and I don't mean flying on Sunday and taking the girls for a ride in your porkpie boots. I had about three hundred hours by then, so I didn't have any real trouble, except breaking normal rules and regulations

going through the cadet corps. I didn't give a damn like some guys. I've seen guys break down and cry like babies when they washed out. I didn't particularly care for fighters, but that was the only thing for black pilots to fly in those days.

From the day he arrived, Deiz pestered Roberts for a transfer, "because I was never interested in being a fighter pilot." He was continually writing letters to get into a twin-engine outfit. But of course there were none that would take blacks.

Bruce, on the other hand, was happy as a fighter jock and an enthusiastic party-goer. "Bruce was a super guy," Knighten said. "Didn't have a care in the world, always smiling. He flew with a Bible in a pocket in his leg. And he was a foodhound. We were flying, and he said he saw a patch of collard greens from the air and started toward the enemy lines looking for collard greens! We really loved him."

On August 11, Bruce was getting into position for an attack, when to his right Graham Mitchell developed engine trouble and veered into Sam's path. Bruce yanked his nose upward, just missing a direct collision. "I thought we missed," Bruce said later, but his propeller chopped off Mitchell's tail. Mitchell "never had a chance." He was killed, but Bruce jumped, and his 'chute opened with seconds to spare. His only injury was a sprained ankle.

Wilson Eagleson also arrived from the States. Harry Sheppard had known him as a cadet. "'Swampy' Eagleson," he smiled. "I never saw him with his hat on straight. He always had his jacket unzipped and his galoshes open and flopping." But Swampy could fly, as he was to prove before long.

For months the 99th had almost no contact with German fighters. "When we did see German planes," Knighten said, "we were one hundred miles per hour slower than they were, and they were always ten thousand feet higher than we were, unless they were stupid enough to come down. The first ones I saw were flying our wing. We said, 'Look at that!' When they'd break it off, we'd wave. Later on it got a little dirtier."

Deiz:

There were times we'd pass the Jerry going one direction while we were going the other. We wanted to drop our tanks and bombs and go after them and chase them all over hell. But we had this Colonel Davis, who wouldn't let us do anything but what we were supposed to do, and that was go over our target. So normally, while I was over there, we didn't have a chance to get at the German airplanes like the guys with the P-51s did later. Consequently, it didn't look good on our score sheets. However, the guys we flew protection for swore by us.

After the Allies invaded Italy at Salerno, south of Naples, some of the 99th enlisted men crossed the strait to begin setting up an airfield at Foggia, Italy. When the Germans counterattacked, they were rushed into the lines as infantrymen, Watson said. One sergeant was handed a rope and instructed, "If you hear the Germans coming, drag this anti-tank weapon across the road."

Once the Allies had a foothold, the 99th strafed and escorted bombers over Monte Cassino. This fortified medieval monastery, in rugged mountains, was holding up all Allied attempts to advance. Deiz was hit several times from ground fire — "holes in the wings, stuff like that," he shrugged.

Ernie Pyle, America's most popular war correspondent, wrote about the 99th in his best-seller, *Brave Men*. "Their job was to dive bomb and not get caught up in a fight. The 99th was very successful at this.... The dive bombers' job was to work on the infantry front lines, so they seldom got back to where the German fighters were."

Still, the brass was unhappy. Aerial victories remained the glamour statistic for fighter units, and white pilots were adding to their totals, while the 99th was not. "We stayed in Sicily, hundreds of miles from the battle zone," Watson complained. "Colonel Momyer knew it. He waited until all his squadrons had gained victories, then criticized us for not getting any."

"How could you get aerial victories flying ground support?" Purnell grumbled.

Hap Arnold dropped in on the 99th headquarters and tongue-lashed both Davis and Roberts. "I never felt so bad in all my life," Roberts said. "I felt like crying, and I could see that Colonel Davis was deeply hurt."

Soon after that Davis was called back to the States to take command of the 332nd Fighter Group, which was completing training. He turned the squadron over to Roberts, with Custis as Operations Officer.

The new commander offered a contrast in styles, replacement pilot Dick Macon said: "Spanky Roberts was one of the great leaders of the 332nd. He had a much more effective rapport with the men than B.O. Davis. B.O. was kind of like the boss, he didn't fraternize. But Spanky could fraternize with everyone, and they still gave him their respect as the leader." In the air, "Roberts was fearless. There must have been many things that scared the hell out of him, but he always chose the most dangerous missions to lead the squadron."

Purnell and Dryden were selected to return with Davis to become combat instructors. Dryden flew his last combat mission over Salerno beachhead September 16, his birthday. Then he was grounded pending transfer home. He recalled:

> Sidney Brooks was assigned for a mission and got in his plane and cranked it up, but it didn't check out, so he jumped out of his plane and jumped into mine. The squadron had already taken off, and by the time twelve aircraft had gone down the runway, it had stirred up a lot of dust, the sun was getting low on the horizon, and visibility was pretty bad, just the worst conditions.
>
> Jamison and I were sitting around, watching them go, when we heard his engine sputter — hrrrp, hrrrp. All eyes were on him.
>
> Brooks apparently decided to abort and turned downwind. He had enough altitude, but apparently he couldn't see the ground. There was a brick fence at the end of the strip. When he saw he would over-shoot, he raised his landing gear and went in on his belly.
>
> But his belly tank with gas was hanging below him. We were screaming at him, "Jettison your tank! Jettison your tank!" Of course he couldn't hear us. I'm not sure I would have done anything different if I'd been in the plane. It wouldn't have occurred to me to drop the tanks. I would have been concentrating on getting the aircraft down.
>
> When his fuselage hit the ground, the tank bounced around like a football. Then it sheared off and left a vapor

trail of fumes. Fire raced along it until it reached the airplane, and all of a sudden the plane went up in flames. He jumped out, and we ran up, caught him, and tackled him.

Knighten was also there. "Brooks pancaked in in a big burst of flames and jumped out, his flying suit on fire. Someone patted the flames out and he laughed, 'Ha-ha-ha, they almost got me that time, didn't they fellows?'"

"He was taken to a British hospital," Dryden said, "and when we went to visit him, he was conscious. His hands were burned, but he dictated a letter to his wife, Lucille, and Jamie wrote it for him. He felt good and said, 'Get me my clothes, I'm getting out of here.' But they made him stay there that night.

"Next day we went to see him, and he was dead! He had suffered secondary shock and smoke inhalation.

Dryden and Purnell flew home on a B-25 bomber, along with several white pilots. At each stop, said Lou, they went out together "carousing."

"One pilot in particular was on the same wavelength I was — we thought the same things at the same time." When they landed in Florida, they waited for transportation to their quarters.

All of a sudden he acted strange, as if he didn't know me. He kept looking down, kicking at an imaginary stone. He extended his hand to me but kept looking to the side. As the vehicle came up and the headlights swept across his face, I could see his lower eyelids full of tears. The vehicle took him and the other bomber pilots to the BOQ [Bachelor Officers Quarters]. When a jeep came for us, it deposited us in a boarding house. There was a brass bed and something I hadn't seen since I was a kid — a wash stand, bowl, and pitcher — and a bare light bulb hanging down from the ceiling.

Next morning my friend told me, "You know, Lou, here we are in the good old USA, the country we've defended, and you can't even go to the same places I can. How do you feel?"

I was so astounded, I couldn't answer. I don't speak for the whole group, but if there's bitterness carried within a person any length of time, there's a good chance he could burn himself out within, while the object of that hate will be unscathed. I could pound this into the heads of young people nowadays, but their heads are much thicker than ours were.

Dryden immediately called his girlfriend before visiting his parents. "I'll go with you," she said. They were married in the chapel at Tuskegee.

Purnell headed for the bright lights of New York for some action.

When I got to New York, I had a writeup in a couple of papers, and I was in the Theresa Hotel. There were three things I wanted — well, four, really — a good big pitcher of cold milk, because they didn't have any over there; a nice soft bed, and a good shower bath. I was upstairs enjoying those — I think I stayed in the shower until I was wrinkled. I was all ready to go out on the town when I got a call from the girl at the desk downstairs to say I had a visitor. I put on my uniform and, the minute I stepped out of the elevator, there was Hubert Julian. I can still see him today. He looked just like he did when I was a kid.

He immediately went into his act. He strolled up and down, looking around at his audience. "Is this any way to treat a returning war hero?" he said in a loud voice. "He should be out on the town. Don't you know how to treat a celebrity? Give him the keys to the city!" He ran his hands in his pockets. "Here — here's the key to my car. Return it when you wish, tomorrow or whenever you're finished."

I felt like two cents. I could have shrunk down and hid in the pile rug. Julian just wanted to be seen, to make a big impression.

"My car is right outside," he said.

I just said, "Thank you very much." When I got outside, there was his car, a great big black Cadillac — "six rooms and a bath," I called it. It had a parking ticket on the windshield for parking near a fire hydrant. I guess he didn't think anyone would give him a ticket. I got in and turned the key. The gas tank registered empty. What he was after, I thought, was gas. He knew I would like to go up and down Harlem with this car and pick up gals. I took it around the block and parked it back in the same place and gave him his keys. He berated me for that right in front of the people in the lobby. He said I didn't know how to accept things graciously and his offer was like casting pearls before swine.

After he lost his audience, he extended an invitation to come up for breakfast in the morning. He living in Morningside Heights, a brownstone house. When I arrived at his home, I could have cried. Not a damn thing in it. No furniture in the living room, the dining room had nothing but one big oak table, the kitchen was bare except for one table. And he was standing there in his satin smoking jacket and monocle. I couldn't smell any bacon and eggs anywhere, so I left. I really pitied the guy. He was living in another world. He was playing the part of a king in an empty, cold house.

Meanwhile, a bombshell hit. *Time* Magazine reported rumors that the 99th's days might be numbered. Momyer had forwarded a report calling the 99th unsatisfactory. He said they hadn't learned to fight as a team, broke formation when attacked, chose undefended targets instead of defended ones, turned back from one target because of bad weather while white pilots went ahead, and asked for rest when other units didn't. In short, Momyer wrote, the 99th didn't show the "fighting caliber" or "aggressiveness" necessary to make good combat pilots.

"Naturally your formation would scatter," Purnell retorted. "You can't dive bomb in formation. They said we were scattered by the enemy. Hell, we were already broken up — you're not going to fly a pattern so they can fly in there and shoot the hell out of you."

Wiley:

For anyone to put me in his gunsights and call me incompetent was just a dirty lie, and I'd have told him that to his face. I was as good as anyone in the field. I was as tenacious, I was proud of what I was doing, and I did it well. And I resented that even the War Department considered us an "experiment." Here I was, fighting for my country, and I was just an "experiment!"

But you have to remember the time. The South controlled much of the Air Force, and the commanding generals were mainly from the South.

Momyer's superior, Brigadier General Edwin House, concurred that "the negro type has not the proper reflexes" for combat. Major General Cannon endorsed it, and Lieutenant General Spaatz added his opinion that the 99th should be reassigned to rear area coastal patrol. In Washington Air Force chief of staff Hap Arnold agreed.

The Great Experiment appeared to be over.

6

Triumph at Anzio

Davis hastened to the Pentagon to save his unit. He told the brass that the 99th, himself included, had arrived in Africa with no combat experience at all. He agreed that there had been some lack of confidence and mistakes on the early missions but with experience, confidence had increased. He himself may have been conservative, he admitted, because he knew the crucial importance of the experiment and did not want to lose "the whole ball game in a single operation." Davis pointed out that his men had operated for two months with few replacements, while white units received regular replacements. The 99th had only twenty-six pilots, compared to as many as thirty-five for white squadrons, forcing his men to fly up to six missions a day without a day off. He concluded that he would put the stamina and aggressiveness of his fliers up against those of any comparable unit.

Arnold now backed up Davis, so General George C. Marshall, chairman of the Joint Chiefs, ordered a comparative study of all P-40 units, and agreed to take no action until the report was complete. Davis had saved the great experiment, for the moment at least. But, he wrote, Momyer "had come within inches of destroying the future of black pilots forever."

Meanwhile, back in Italy, Spanky Roberts almost faced a court martial.

> I was called in by a colonel, who talked to me for hours about a night cover mission for parachute drops in Italy on the darkest night of the month. I told him as nicely as I could that the plan stank: The 99th would be wiped out; we couldn't see to land.
>
> "What if I order you to fly this mission?"
>
> "If you do, I would refuse it."
>
> "Well, I'm going to order you."
>
> "Well, I'm going to refuse."
>
> I went back and told my operations officer to be ready to take over; I would either be shot or sent to the U.S. Neither of those happened, however.

The squadron was moved to the ex-Nazi field at Foggia on the East coast of Italy and was put under a new Group, the 79th, commanded by twenty-nine-year-old Colonel Earl Bates. "Bates was the first commander who greeted us as I felt a fellow American should be greeted," Roberts said. "No snide implications; he just expected us to do our job. We had a marvelous time in that organization."

"A super guy," Willie Fuller agreed. "Used to come over and get briefed with us and fly with us. A hell of a guy."

"You had princes, and you had bastards," Wiley said. "Bates was a prince. He came over to us and welcomed us aboard and made us part of his Group. We got promotions through Bates; he wrote recommendation letters for us. And he wrote letters that were read aloud to all his squadrons — that he was very happy and to keep up the good work."

Bates sent his other squadrons and the 99th on missions together in support of the British Eighth Army and named 99th pilots to lead some joint missions. Morale quickly improved. Said Roberts: "General Davis, Colonel Parrish, General Cannon, Colonel Cochran, Colonel Bates — these are my heroes."

On one joint mission, Bates and Roberts spotted a camouflaged train in the snow-covered Apennine Mountains.

He and his wingman took one end of the train, I and my wingman took the other end to immobilize it. The rest of the squadron went in and did terrific damage while our elements stopped the enemy ground fire from doing any damage.

But there's no record of that train officially. If the mission is recorded, they may have recorded it under Bates, not the 99th. There were all these people who didn't want us to succeed.

The 99th kept busy strafing and dive-bombing and breaking in its new men.

C.C. 'Curtis' Robinson joined them as a replacement.

I went over on a Liberty Ship. About a hundred and ten ships were in the convoy — eleven across and ten deep. We were in the first line, fourth row from the left. Every night we'd come under attack from U-boats. They knocked out the first two ships on our side, so we ended up in the second row. A day and a half out of Gibraltar, the ship alongside of us lost a steering gear and rammed us at seven o'clock one morning and knocked a hole in the ship just below the water line. The water rushed in and, of course, we rushed out of our bunks. We had no place to sleep, so they put us in the officers' quarters upstairs and we used the officers' mess. That was of some concern to the white officers there.

We were disabled for a while and the convoy left a destroyer back with us. They were able to pump the oil from one side of the ship to the other to make us list less. The destroyer left us when he saw that we weren't going to sink. The last attack from a sub had been about three nights back, so I guess he thought we were safe. We crept along toward Gibraltar at about four knots and it took three days and two nights. That was scary.

Robinson landed in Sicily and took a month to find the 99th, which had moved to Italy.

The commanding officer, Spanky Roberts, "had a great ego," Robinson said. "But he could back it up. He was very bull-headed. If he was wrong, he was wrong all the way. He wouldn't back down. You had to prove to him that he was wrong."

Lemuel Custis "was a little older than most of us, very diplomatic, a real gentleman," Robinson said. "Roberts was very close to him."

Robinson considered another Flight leader, Clarence Jamison, "a little, quiet fellow, very nice. You wouldn't know he was in the room if he didn't speak. Jamie would laugh at a joke, but that was about all. Smiled all the time. I saw him last year [1995], and he looked like forty years ago, hasn't changed at all."

Erwin Lawrence, the Operations Officer, was "tall and good-looking, quiet and efficient."

About a month after arriving, Robinson was reunited with two of his roommates at Tuskegee, Leonard Jackson and Albert Manning. "My best buddy over there — my bunkmate, was Jackson. They called him 'Black' Jackson to distinguish him from Melvin 'Red' Jackson, who came along later with the 332nd. "Funny thing about Jackson: Flying calls for a lot of coordination and Leonard couldn't even throw a baseball or play ping pong — nothing. But he could fly the hell out of the plane."

Manning "was more mature, more practical," than the others, although he was about the same age.

Elwood 'Woody' Driver was 'The Brain.' "He was top of his class in college in New Jersey, graduated when he was nineteen or so and volunteered for the Naval Air Corps. They accepted him — until they saw who he was." Driver was twenty-two, about three years younger than the other pilots. "He was a playboy and wanted everyone to like him and he never forgot a name."

Another rookie, Howard Baugh, was "a sweetheart. Soft-spoken. would listen to everyone and would give his opinion if it wouldn't hurt anyone. The colonel liked him because he was quiet and efficient. You asked Howard Baugh to do something, it was done!"

Ed Toppins loved to play poker, Robinson said, "and he'd bluff you in a minute with nothing. Money wasn't worth very much, because you couldn't spend it. If we were playing draw, he'd throw fifteen dollars in the pot and everyone would fold, and he'd come out with fifty dollars." In the sky, Ed "was a brave and gutty guy. Loved to fly, and loved to fight."

"Toppins was a very gung-ho pilot," Baugh agreed, "very aggressive, almost a daredevil."

Freddie Hutchins loved to spout 'folksy' sayings, such as, "the blacker the berry, the sweeter the juice." He was "a jovial fellow," according to Charles Bussey, who knew him in Italy later. Hutch was from Georgia, had learned to "roll with the punch," and didn't let discrimination bother him, Bussey said.

Robinson became wingman to Charlie Hall, already celebrated as the first black to score a victory. Baugh joined Wiley's A Flight, along with Peepsight Smith. "Howard Baugh and I socialized quite a bit," Wiley said. "I bought a Bianchi motorcycle with him. We each paid ten dollars, and we'd go out together in Sicily and look over the countryside." They brought it with them to their new base in Italy.

Wiley also found an abandoned Italian Fiat fighter plane. After his mechanics put it in flying shape, he used it as a mail plane and for other errands for the squadron.

Another replacement, Clarence Allen of Mobile, arrived in October. He "was sort of a playboy," Spann Watson remembered. "His old man seemed to be wealthy, at least from our point of view. He had had some seaplane training − it cost money to take lessons then. He attended most of the good schools and got kicked out of them. He was a rugged, hard liver."

On January 2, the 99th lost one of its new men, Baugh said. "John Morgan landed down wind, down hill and couldn't stop the airplane, and it ran off the end of the runway into a ditch and killed him. I made it a point to stay away from airplane accidents. No point in going to see them. It wouldn't help him, and it wouldn't help me."

Soon after that the squadron moved to Capodicino near Naples, and life became hot in a hurry. The Battle of Anzio, when the Allies launched a second invasion, south of Rome, was the turning point for the 99th.

With the winter weather, "we really couldn't fly much more up in the mountains," Wiley said. The Allies were planning a major invasion at Anzio on the west coast to link up with General Mark Clark's Fifth Army which was moving slowly up from Salerno. The 99th was detached from Bates' Group and sent to Capodicino, joining the 324th Fighter Group, which turned out to be another happy command relationship.

Fuller flew with the second wave of the invasion. "We could look down at daybreak and see the ships unload and hit the beaches. There seemed to be no resistance, and they put all their vehicles and tanks in straight military lines. Beautiful. Made a graphic picture from the air.

"Then about the fourth or fifth day the Germans pulled out their Big Bertha artillery piece and started shooting. All those vehicles disappeared in a hurry."

Wiley:

> The Germans were up in the hills peppering the beachhead and the transports out in the harbor. They peppered my plane, too — at one point there were nine holes in it. Our problems came from the flak and the ground fire from the Germans. We had to be very careful about flying without sufficient altitude, at least five thousand feet. We had a lot of targets — hitting the German positions up there and flying almost continuous cover over the beachhead. There were cargo ships in the harbor, and they had to be protected. The Germans were very tenacious; they wanted to push the Americans back into the water.
>
> The 109s came down from above Rome, and the invasion forces needed protection from them. Therefore, we were flying close support in the hills around Anzio and flying cover for the invasion. But many of the Germans were relatively new pilots, they weren't as good as the older ones we'd seen.

Hall led a flight over Anzio, and a few days later prepared to lead another.

Robinson remembered:

> It was my first flight there and Hall came to see me one night: "Look, when you take off, as soon as you see those mountains, you start to weave. If you fly straight, the German gunners will knock you out." Well, we took off. Our formation was a line abreast, one hundred yards between each plane. The Germans had many more planes than we did. Five minutes later I could see the mountains, so I started to go like

this [his hands describing a skateboarder going back and forth up the walls of an inclined court].

We got over to Anzio and I could see a group of planes, about thirty of them, about twenty miles away. I started to call out, but said to myself, "These guys must see those planes because they have been here before," so I didn't say anything. I was still weaving. Soon they were on us and we went in it. I dropped my belly tanks, but I forgot to switch to internal tanks and, with all that weaving, my engine cut off. My stomach was upset with all the maneuvering and I threw up right in the cockpit.

By the time I switched tanks, everyone else had gone. The Germans turned and hit the deck, but I couldn't catch up. When we got back, everyone laughed like that was the funniest thing in the world. That was a joke Charlie pulled on me.

We were very much outnumbered by the Germans, who sent up sixteen or thirty a flight; we sent up eight planes at a time. I usually flew in the mornings, and the Germans usually came in the mornings, so I saw quite a bit of action in that rickety old plane.

The P-40 could out-turn anything flying, but our top speed was 280, the Germans' was about 365, so we could never start a fight, we had to let them start it. We just sat and waited for them."

Then came perhaps the most crucial date in the entire war for the Tuskegee Airmen – January 27, 1944. As Roberts put it: "For the first time we were given the responsibility of knocking Jerry down to protect the beachhead."

Early that morning, about 8:30, under clear skies Jamison led three Flights of twelve pilots, mostly rookies, who ran into fifteen enemy and waded into the fight.

Jamison described it.

The radar ground controller said there were bogeys [unidentified planes] coming in very high, twenty thousand feet or so. We were at twelve thousand. The British Spitfires were supposed to be up there, but I don't know where they were, and we couldn't climb that high to get to the Germans, so we held our altitude and dropped our belly tanks. I signaled our guys to arm, and we headed toward the Germans.

The enemy planes screamed through the American formation. "We really didn't need any aircraft identification," Deiz said. "The German planes were flying so fast, you knew they were German, they weren't ours." The P-40s had only one chance to catch the foe. "We'd take a heading to intercept them, and for maybe ten seconds, as they leveled off, our air speeds were about the same. If you could get on the ass of one, you had a chance to do something."

"The only way we could get to them was to gain extra speed from a dive," Baugh said, "so we dropped fuel tanks and dived down on them. Instead of zooming back to altitude, they stayed low to hedge-hop back to their friendly territory." It was a fatal mistake.

Jamison:

> I did a 180 — a split-S, we called it[1] — and came out going in the same direction the enemy were going and above them. I had timed it just right luckily, and was right on the top of one of the German flight leaders. We were about one hundred feet apart, two hundred feet above the ground, and I looked right in his cockpit. Everything was happening so fast.
>
> Ashley and I were right on the tail of this guy, almost too good to be true. They were just determined to get back to Rome, they weren't about to stay around and dogfight. I gave him a blast with all six machine guns in my wings. ["Hits were registered on the right wing, and chunks flew off," the official report said.]
>
> Then my guns jammed. I know I hit him, he was smoking, but I don't know if he went down or not, so I got credit for a damage.

According to the official report, Ashley "jumped a 190 on the deck and chased him to within a few miles of Rome. The enemy craft first began to smoke and burst into flames."

Deiz spotted a 190 below and off to his side at about 750 feet. "I just pulled in behind him," he said laconically, "and let him have it. That's all." A portion of the enemy cowling flew off, and the plane went into a steep dive. It crashed and burned in a yard near a house.

Baugh and his wingman, Clarence Allen, maneuvered behind a 190. "I just pulled the trigger," Howard said. "He just flew into the ground, almost belly-landing in a cloud of dust. We flew right on over him, pulled a left turn, and went right out to sea. The whole thing was over in about a minute." The two shared credit for the kill.

Baugh spotted another 190 and, the official report said, fired three-second bursts into him. "Tracers were seen going into the plane, and small fragments flew off from the wing and tail."

Leon Roberts also chased a 190 on the deck. "Roberts was a natural," Jamison said. "When he flew my wing, I felt secure with him out there. He got on this guy's tail. He must have been a young pilot since he had a faster plane, and could have outrun us, but when the bullets went by, he'd twist and turn instead of pouring on the speed and pulling away. Leon said he'd give him a blast, correct a little bit, and finally hit him in the wing. He flipped over and went into the ground."

Ed Toppins got a third plane. "Toppins was a very gung-ho pilot," Baugh said, "very aggressive, almost a daredevil." He fired a short burst into a 190 on the deck. The plane hit the ground and exploded.

Jack Rogers and Elwood Driver "caught another 190 heading in the general direction of Rome. As the plane was smoking excessively and diving into the ground at about fifty feet, it was probably destroyed as claimed," the squadron report declared.

George McCrumby "spotted a 190 on the deck, picked a lead, and commenced firing at point-blank range. Sections of the horizontal stabilizer and rudder flew off. One 190 is claimed as damaged.

"Henry Perry caught an FW 190 coming out of a dive and raked the enemy ship head-to-tail at about three hundred yards. Pieces from the canopy flew off. The plane seemed to flutter ... fell off on the wing and headed to the ground. A damage is claimed."

Back at the airfield there were seven victory rolls.[2] Five enemy planes were destroyed, including the one shared by Baugh and Allen, plus one probable by Jamison, and four damaged.

In five minutes the 99th had made up for five months of frustration.

That afternoon Custis led another flight and ran into another large flight of 190s and Messerschmidt 109s coming down from Rome.

"We had a lot of experience by then," Custis said, "and most of the good German pilots had been sent to Russia because they were desperate on that front. The German pilots at Anzio must have been young guys who didn't have experience; they didn't know how to veer or take evasive action. They were sitting ducks." Custis himself wouldn't describe the action, but the official report had this to say:

> Captain Custis spotted an FW-190 on the deck. Several bursts were fired at close range, and the plane crashed in a creek.
> Lt Wilson Eagleson caught an FW diving on the tail of Lt. [Erwin] Lawrence. He came in at 90 degrees and closed to 200 yards. The 190 burst into flames and hit the ground.[3]
> Lt. Charles Bailey caught an FW-190 heading in the general direction of Rome with a 45-degree shot. The pilot was seen to bail out.
> Lt. Lawrence probably destroyed an FW-190 with a difficult shot almost from the side. Eagleson saw the FW roll over and dive for the ground, smoking excessively.

The results: three destroyed, one probable. It brought the day's total to nine destroyed and two probable.

One plane did not return, however. Deiz' friend, Sam Bruce, was last seen pursuing two Focke Wulfs. What happened next is veiled in mystery. Robinson said Sam tried to bail out but didn't make it; "we're not sure who shot him down."

Spanky Roberts gave this version.

> Sam Bruce was shot down deliberately by a South African. While he was in his 'chute, the South African strafed him and killed him. The 99th was ready to declare war. The South Africans never contacted us, although they did contact the American headquarters and said it was a mistake.
> The Americans who knew about it began to have a changed attitude toward us, because even the worst ones didn't envision killing their own. They felt they too had been betrayed by an ally. There was no great outpouring of words

or people hugging us, but there was less "Damn you, go to hell" and more "We're in this together."

Some veterans of the 99th said they knew nothing about such a report. Others heard the report, though none can verify it and most can't believe it. Wiley said flatly, "I doubt it." There were a lot of tales out about Sam Bruce, he admitted, but there was so much anti-aircraft fire, and that was how he died. Knighten also couldn't believe a Spitfire would come down thirty thousand feet to shoot at him. Knighten, himself, said he never encountered "personal problems" with any Allied pilots.

However, as Custis shrugs, "There will always be an element of doubt" about exactly how Bruce met his end.

The next day Charlie Hall led another victorious flight which included Deiz and Knighten. The report recorded: "FW 190s at four thousand feet approached from the north, our formation at five thousand feet dove on them. As the enemy turned away, one of them was shot down by Captain Hall ... closing in at three hundred yards. The 109 was on the deck and burst into flames and crashed on the ground.

"Captain Hall [then] caught a 190, firing dead astern, closing in at two hundred yards, with short bursts."

At that point Robinson had his biggest scare of the war. He was diving on an enemy and had just opened fire when another plane suddenly flashed in front of him. It was Hall, blasting away at his prey. "I just knew I'd hit Charlie," Robinson said, "but luckily I missed." He watched the German spin and crash into the ground. It was Hall's second victory of the day, his third of the war.

Deiz, the reluctant warrior, suddenly became a quiet tiger and scored his second in two days. Whether the death of his friend, Bruce, was a factor, is not known. Deiz described his second kill laconically: "One of them got in my way. We were at about four thousand feet, mixing it up in a dogfight, and my leader made a turn when a Focke Wulf saw him and pulled in behind him. I don't know whether he saw me, but all I had to do was level my wings and there he was. Just a short burst, and that was it." The pilot bailed out.

Peepsight Smith also got one. According to the report, he chased a Focke Wulf and caught it with a difficult 50-degree shot from the left-rear, like a quarterback leading his receiver. "The aircraft veered out of control about twenty feet from the ground and burst into flame."

The total for the day: four more enemy craft destroyed.

In their first six months, the 99th had scored only one kill; it now had thirteen in two days, plus two probables. "We poured the hell into them," Spanky Roberts exclaimed. "We laid to rest forever the word that blacks couldn't fly."

Charlie Hall was suddenly a star. "He was a 'tutor' on the banquet circuit," Robinson said. "He was quite good at it. Different units would invite him over to the mess hall and he'd take me with him. He'd speak and we'd have a great meal."

"Hall was a very quiet guy until he got those three victories," Knighten said. "Then he suddenly became a know-it-all about everything. Sudden stardom did it to him; he actually started strutting. Before that, he was just our buddy, running around with the rest of us."

On February 5, Elwood Driver scored a victory.

On the same mission, George McCrumby was hit by ack-ack and went into a dive. "The plane was spinning," Jamison said, "and his body was flying around inside the fuselage." McCrumby tried to bail out but was blown back inside by the prop blast. Then he tried from the other side of the cockpit but got only half-way out, where he dangled until, only a thousand feet from the ground, he finally fell free. He grabbed for his rip cord and gave a yank. Nothing happened. He yanked five more times before the 'chute finally opened in the nick of time, depositing him in a cow pasture. When he got back to the base, Jamison said, "his eyes were completely bloodshot from his face being beaten against the inside of the fuselage."

Meantime Jamison, the Flight leader, was having trouble of his own.

It was low-level stuff, right above the ground. We were badly outnumbered. I had six guns, but they jammed, and a Focke Wulf got on my tail and I couldn't shake him. He must have sensed that my guns were gone. He was so close I could see the tracer bullets going by my plane and could see his 20-mm cannon shells exploding on the ground in front of me. He'd line you up with machine gun tracers, then let the cannon go.

I had no idea where I was; I just knew I was heading back to friendly territory. I burned up the engine, and it quit right above the ground. It was too low to bail out, so I made a crash landing, sliding across a farmer's field, wheels up.

Some Army Rangers came and got me and told me I was in no-man's land. They showed me a farmhouse and said the Germans were using it as an outpost and they thought the Germans were going to come out and get me. I had to spend the night on the ground. Flying in the air was nothing, but being on the ground and hearing the artillery and feeling the ground rock was a different war for me. I wasn't cut out to be a ground soldier.

Clarence Allen was also shot down, but he, also, evaded the Germans and got back to American lines.

Two days later Leonard Jackson and Clifton Mills scored victories, bringing the squadron's total to seventeen in the Anzio campaign. In the same period the three white squadrons of Bates' 79th Group downed thirty-two enemy. The 85th and 87th squadrons each brought down fifteen planes and the 86th, two.

General Cannon sent the 99th his congratulations. Even Hap Arnold admitted the unit had done a "very commendable job," adding, "my best wishes for their continued success."

After Anzio, Davis wrote, all criticism of the 99th was "silenced once and for all."

"If we had failed," said Custis, the whole history of Air Force integration would have been changed. "But we didn't go into it to fail."

Time magazine reported: "Any outfit would have been proud of the 99th's record. Its victories stamped the final seal of excellence on one of the most controversial outfits of the Army.... The Air Force regards its experiment proven [and] is taking all qualified Negro cadets it can get."

7

The 332nd

Tuskegee had grown to a military city of whitewashed barracks and classrooms, turning out replacements for the 99th and pilots to fill out three new squadrons — the 100th, 301st, and 302nd — for the 332nd Fighter Group.

One of the first of the new generation was Melvin 'Red' Jackson, the son of a gardener from Warrenton, Virginia. He remembered that "the segregated school system didn't offer very much, so my father paid teachers to teach us at home." Melvin was nine when the Depression hit, and the family could no longer afford the teacher. "A cousin came down from New Jersey so she could get some food — we're talking about rough times — and she taught us."

Jackson's family was fair-skinned. "As times got tough my mother's sister moved to California and wrote my father, 'Why don't you come out here and live as a white man?' He just laughed; his community was his home, and his home was his life. I had no interest in passing; it never once occurred to me to do it. I had too many friends and was enjoying my life."

A year later Jackson's father had a stroke. The boy quit school to go to work at the age of ten and then went back to a one-room school for a year. In high school a teacher encouraged him to go to college, and Melvin worked summers in one of President Roosevelt's New Deal CCC (Civilian Construction Corps) camps and winters in the WPA (Works Progress Administration) for thirty dollars a month.

Eventually Jackson saved enough to enroll in Virginia State College to study agriculture, working on the school farm and as a part-time janitor. He also boxed on the college team. ("He was tough as nails," said Harry Sheppard.) "College was everything I ever wanted," Jackson said. But when the Air Corps opened its doors to Negroes, he decided, "This is exciting, you can fly — and it's free! I'll join.'" He had to wait a year until he got orders to report to Tuskegee in March 1942. He was twenty-four.

In all, twenty cadets reported. "They washed out as many as they could and graduated as few as they could," he said, "but I didn't worry about it." In the end only four graduated, including his college friends, Howard Baugh and Terry Charlton. "They washed out a lot of good pilots."

Among those who enrolled in the next class were two future squadron leaders, Bob Tresville and Ed Gleed, plus the man who would become the Red Tails' hottest pilot, Wendell Pruitt.

Pruitt was a dashing figure. A St. Louis native, he was the youngest in a family of ten children, sang in the glee club, built radios, repaired automobiles, and learned to fly in CPT at Lincoln University. "He was easy-going, never cared about anything," a fellow student and future Red Tail, Arthur Pullam, said. Pruitt played guard on the basketball team. "You had to be ready for the ball any time, because you didn't know when he'd throw it."

Chris Newman met Pruitt in Civilian Military Training camp in Ft. Riley, Kansas. "He was an eager beaver, always ramrod straight while the rest of us were lazy and sitting around." But later, as a pilot, Newman said, Pruitt's attitude was "sort of carefree. He was daring, and he had a little bit of the rogue in him. He didn't mind breaking regulations with his flying and did things the higher authorities didn't approve. He was the best we had in the skies at that time. On the ground Pruitt was a quiet, unassuming man. He just flew loud."

"He didn't mind taking a few chances," said Ed Gleed, "doing things the average guy wouldn't do."

Pruitt had the glamour and flamboyance of a typical fighter pilot. "A good-looking guy, the girls were crazy about him," Bernard Knighten said.

"He was a flashy guy," another future pilot, Jimmy Walker, said — "a hot rod, a ladies' man, but a hell of a pilot. And he knew it."

Charles Bussey, who later flew with Pruitt, agreed that he was a leader, athletic and good-looking, but Bussey felt he was shy with women. "He couldn't handle girls. They were looking for glamorous boy friends, and maybe they just overwhelmed him." Pruitt flew all the time. "Sunday morning, when all the guys were trying to get over their hangovers, he was out flying." He had a distinctive, flashy style. "You could see an aircraft flying by, and you knew it was Pruitt in it."

The second of the triumvirate, Tresville, was an Army brat, son of an old Buffalo Soldier band leader in the 24th Infantry Regiment. He was also the first black West Point graduate since Ben Davis and was obviously groomed for a high position in the 332nd. Tresville was tall and handsome, "strictly military but a real smart guy and real gung-ho," one classmate remembered. "A very fine man, a beautiful man, a gentleman," agreed Jackson.

"But he was a mechanical pilot," said Gleed, "and he had a hard time soloing. The average expected time was six hours; I don't think he soloed until twelve hours. Anyone else would have washed out."

Tresville was put in command of the 100th Fighter Squadron, the first one formed after the 99th. "He was my idol," said Walter Palmer, who joined the squadron a month later. "He knew how to mingle with us, but was still able to command our respect."

The third man of the trio, Gleed, "was super cocky" said his fellow pilot, Harry Sheppard, and probably the most colorful cadet to report to Tuskegee.

Gleed:

My grandfather was a slave. He came out of West Virginia as soon as the Civil War was over and came west to Lawrence, Kansas. The guy never had an education, he could hardly write his own name, but he became a produce dealer, buying chickens, cattle, eggs, and hogs, and died at the age of ninety-nine.

I was born in Lawrence, November 3, 1916. My old man hit the skids when the stock market broke down, and when I was in the fifth grade, he and my mother divorced. My mother took my brother and me to Tuskegee, where she was going to teach home economics. That was my first experience with out-and-out segregation. We were in a Jim Crow car and saw white deputies bringing black prisoners on the train with their hands shackled.

My mother sent us back to an aunt in Lawrence to finish high school, and that's where I got my next taste of segregation. There was one movie in town we just couldn't go to; in the others we had to go upstairs in the 'chicken roost.' We even had a separate colored basketball team in high school.

After high school I went to Kansas University. I hesitate to say I was self-made, but my mother gave me a total of fifteen dollars during my college career. The only thing my dad gave me was his old Peerless roadster when he bought a new Phaeton to go out to the 1932 Olympics in Los Angeles. He never gave me anything else but the little gas I could drain from his gas pump and a small sum for working for him on weekends and in the summer. I put myself through college waiting tables. Most of the waiters at the sorority and fraternity houses were black.

I got thrown out of university swimming pools twice, along with another fellow who was a physical education major. Swimming was a required subject for him to graduate, but they ended up giving him credit for it rather than allowing him into the pool. The famous Phogg Allen was basketball coach. His favorite saying to us was, "You can come out for the team, but you ain't gonna play." Yet later he was the one who sought out Wilt Chamberlain and brought him back from Pennsylvania. Ironic.

I graduated in 1937 and got a work-scholarship to Howard University law school. I worked in the library in the afternoon, then worked to twelve o'clock at night waiting tables out in Chevy Chase.

Then I took off and went hoboing to New Orleans, riding on top of coal cars. I got on the wrong train up in the hills out of Bristol, Tennessee and damn near froze to death. In Chattanooga I got picked up by a railroad cop and got put in the county jail. At three o'clock in the morning a Negro deputy sheriff awakened me and asked me where was my family. I said I didn't have any folks, so he gave me a good meal, took me to the bus station, and bought me a ticket. I cashed the ticket in and hoboed the rest of the way.

In New Orleans I unloaded bananas, then I got a job as messman on a United Fruit boat and made two trips through the Panama Canal and back, making forty-five dollars a month. I was working as a scab when they had a strike, and I got my head busted open twice.

I ended up in a San Francisco drydock. Where to go? I had a cousin in Los Angeles but didn't know her address. So I hoboed down the road in three days, couldn't find my cousin in the phone book, and lived in a flea-bag hotel near Union Station for about two weeks, hustling, and rolling drunks at night. The hotel room was occupied in the daytime by two other guys, and a friend and I occupied it at night. These other guys were up to really serious trouble; finally they got picked up, and they took our clothes to jail with them. If I'd gone on like them, I'd probably be in jail, too, or dead by now.

I said, "We've got to get out of here," and we started walking across town. We'd walked four or five miles when one of those believe-it-or-not things happened. At a drugstore I saw an attractive young woman reading a letter. She was holding the letter down so that I could see the hand-writing, a very distinctive hand-writing. I said, "Aren't you Lolita? Isn't that a letter from Aunt Ellender?"

She stared at me! My middle name is Creston, which I detest. She said, "Yes! ... *Creston*?!"

I got a job with Bing Crosby working a big circus party. He put up big tents over his tennis court and had an all-night bash for a day and a half. Shortly after that, his first wife, Dixie Lee, had an operation, and they were looking for a temporary chauffeur for four weeks. I was bumming, not doing too much, and it sounded like a good move, so I took it.

Then I went to work for Bob Hope as a butler in his house in North Hollywood, a house that Clark Gable had once owned. I did that for eight weeks until I got ticked off at his mother-in-law. For several days straight she'd say, "I left something out on the back porch." I'd go out there and couldn't see anything but dirty clothes in a wash tub — she meant she wanted me to wash her laundry. So I said, "You didn't hire me. Go upstairs and get Mr. Hope and tell him I want my money." He begged me not to quit, said, "Come out to the studio, be my valet."

Instead, I hit the road again, to Tuskegee to see my mother. Damn near froze to death again in Texas in the Panhandle. I stayed in Tuskegee three months and met Captain Ben Davis and his father, later Brigadier General, B.O. Davis, Sr.

Then I went to North Carolina with two other guys in the photography business. It was one day pork and beans, the next day steak. So in 1940 I went back to Kansas University law school.

I registered for the draft, and that's the first time I had ever been called black. For some reason, that was a blow. I said, "What's this 'black?' Do I look black?"

This was 1941. War clouds were rumbling. A letter from my mother said, "They are getting ready to start an experiment here to train Negro flyers, and Captain Davis is going to be the first one. I thought you'd be interested."

The only contact I'd had with airplanes, my dad had a ten-acre plot behind his store, and barnstormers would use it to land in. I'd been up twice, open cockpit, and I kind of liked it. I figured I would much rather fly to war than fight in the trenches. Then I got a brainstorm, this great big light bulb — I can get into aviation easier if I'm on the inside rather than the outside. So I enlisted in the Army.

I was sent to Fort Riley, Kansas to the Ninth Cavalry, a black unit with all white officers. The famous Ninth and Tenth Cavalry were two of the major Negro units retained between World War I and World War II. I immediately put in my application for aviation cadet training.

There were only four black sergeants there to teach us, and I was immediately made an acting corporal. I'd been there less than three weeks and had barely learned to ride myself. We started getting raw draftee recruits, who had never been over ten miles away from home in their lives. Seventy-eight percent were absolutely illiterate; only half of the rest could sign their names. Three days later they sent us one hundred wild-ass horses from Arizona, supposedly broken. They weren't. Trying to teach these recruits how to ride wild horses! We killed a few horses. Some we never broke.

I was drawing twenty-one dollars a month, was made acting sergeant, and put in for NCO school — I was putting in for everything.

In the meantime I was contacted by guys in civilian clothes asking a whole lot of questions. They were from military intelligence, and they were interviewing me for the counter-intelligence police, which was just being built up.

Meantime the Ninth was called out for maneuvers in Louisiana and Texas, and during a three-day lull, the troop clerk said, "Heh, you get that letter?"

"What letter?"

"You're supposed to be going to Washington, D.C."

I stormed up to troops headquarters, and reluctantly the first sergeant found the letter. The rascal made me walk over to the main highway to catch a bus to Shreveport. I had about four dollars in my pocket.

In Washington I was reassigned to military intelligence and was trained to go to Liberia under cover as a road construction engineer and check out clandestine German radios. We worked with FBI guys dressed in covert top coats — I spent all my clothing money and then some.

I went back to Fort Riley on furlough, just to say "hee hee" to the old cavalry troops, when the troop clerk said, "Oh, I've got a letter I've been meaning to send you." This was the letter calling me to aviation cadet training.

I was sent to Tuskegee in April 1942. They had hazing of the new dummies, but they were afraid to touch me, because I walked in there in my covert top coat. Word had gotten to somebody that there's something strange about this guy.

We had a class of twenty people. In fact, only eight graduated. But I didn't have any question in my mind I could fly — I soloed in four and a half hours.

The two white officers in charge of primary flying school would give check-rides to see what you could do. If you couldn't hack it, they would catch you. One was Captain MacGoon. Everyone was deathly afraid of this guy: "When MacGoon takes a coon for a check-ride...." (We used language among ourselves that we'd fight about if anybody else used it.) I didn't even take the twenty-hour check-ride, didn't take the forty-hour check-ride. MacGoon gave me the sixty-hour check. Didn't have any problems.

The last check-flight was a night cross-country flight to Chattanooga and back by way of Atlanta. The only night navigational aids they had back then were light lines. At intervals of fifteen to twenty miles there would be beacons turning around, giving coded flashes. There were about five light lines going into Atlanta and several going out the other side.

There was a dance that night, and in my eagerness to get back, I cut the corner of Atlanta to pick up the light-line going back to Tuskegee. But I missed the damn light-line and hit the one going to Birmingham instead. I didn't know where I was, so I cut back and really got into trouble. I picked up another light-line, but it wasn't going where I thought either.

I was looking at the big E on the gas gauge. The low-settling fog that hangs over swamps had started building, and I had just made up my mind that "you've had it, pull up and bail out of this damn thing," when I spotted a small field, so I started down through the fog. I pulled back on the throttle, pulled back on the stick, jumped on the brakes, and stopped three feet from this little weather shack. I got a farmer to let me call the base, and two instructors came and got me. I didn't damage the plane, but needless to say, I missed the dance.

Captain 'Mother' Long was in charge of advanced training and chewed my ass out. I knew I was through. I had to write 150 times "Lessons for How Not to Get Lost." The next Monday at the start of advanced training, Mother Long told the class, "Several of you will probably not be here when we complete training." And he looked straight at me.

We had just finished the fourth week when I got called out of class. A lieutenant said, "Cadet Gleed, you're supposed to read up on the P-400."

"P-400! I never heard of it!"

It turned out to be a P-39 Aircobra. He said, "They're going to bring three here, and you've been elected to fly one."

"What?"

"Yeah, they're going to have a cadet and an instructor fly them."

My mind started spinning a thousand ways. The plane was brand new to me: You let the gear down with an electric switch; it had two .50-caliber machine guns and a 37-mm cannon that fired through the nose cone and dripped oil all over your pants. The engine was behind you, and there was always something going wrong with the doggone thing. While all this was going through my mind, he said, "You better get on up to the mess hall, get something to eat, and come back."

But I couldn't eat. Overhead I heard these strange-sounding planes coming in. There were masses of people around the flight line to observe this exhibition — they probably all figured I'd wash out.

When I reported to Mother Long, the crew chief took the plane's door off, and I squeezed in with my parachute. I was frightened enough, so I went to get another 'chute to try to get the butterflies out. I finally got the monster cranked up and got it onto the taxi strip. It was bedlam from then on.

The nose-wheel locked, and the damn thing spun around twice. But I got a takeoff, and everything went just as if I'd planned it. I went up and had a whole lot of fun in it. I did a couple rolls, then got nerve enough to do a snap roll, then decided to land. But when I dropped my gear, for some reason the darn plane was sinking and sinking. The trees were coming up looking at me. I poured more coal, more coal, pulled my gear up, and climbed back up. The tower was screaming, but I couldn't hear half of it. Mother Long was out of his mind.

I made a 360-degree turn, and it was almost the same thing. It wasn't until the third pass, after I'd settled my nerves, that I realized I was stalling that thing, holding the nose too high. This time I came round and made a smooth landing of it.

Next the white instructor went up. He held the nose way back when he landed, dragged his tail and damaged it. The guys said, "No way you're going to wash out after this." But *I* damn near washed me out!

The performance made quite an impression on Gleed's fellow cadets. Gleed graduated first in his class. Felix Kirkpatrick, who later served under him, said, "If we wanted to give someone an accolade, we'd say, 'He's the greatest thing since Gleed.'"

The 99th had by now been completely trained and sent overseas, and we were still putting out pilots. What the hell do you do with them? They established our squadron, the 100th, to take the overflow. Then they formed the 332nd Group with three squadrons — the 100th, 301st, and 302nd. At first we were flying P-40s, then they decided to give us P-39s. I'm the only guy who had flown one, so one day in June 1943 I found myself being told I was now the squadron commander of the 302nd as a second lieutenant.

Bussey remarked: "I like to tell young men that our squadron commander, a lieutenant colonel's job, was only twenty-six years old. Ed Gleed was a natural pilot. In a foot race or a fist-fight, Gleed was your man."

One of the next classes included Walter 'Moe' Downs, a high school teacher from Tahoma, Mississippi. He remembered a flight with one instructor who was demonstrating crash landing techniques and added so much realism to the lesson that they actually did crash. They ended up upside down, hanging from their safety belts, in an Alabama swamp.

A member of the next class, Woodrow 'Woody' Wilson Crockett was the product of a two-room school in Arkansas. His mother taught grades one to four, his father, five to eight. Their own educational levels were unknown, but they somehow got teaching certificates. (His mother eventually received her college degree at the age of sixty. "She was determined to get it," Woody said.) but Crockett decided that "an eighth grade education wouldn't make it in this world." When a colored high school was opened in Little Rock, one of the many Paul Lawrence Dunbar High Schools in the country, "black kids from all over the state descended on it," including Woody.

Crockett went to junior college and dreamed of becoming a PhD in math. But he dropped out of school because he didn't have the six dollars a month tuition. "Those were tough times. About 1940 things were tight!" Crockett enlisted in the Army's black 349th artillery battalion, which was set up despite fears that the artillery was too technical for blacks. It had all white officers and was the fifth black unit in the Army after the two cavalry and two infantry divisions.

> My first sergeant thought I should go to West Point, but they said I was too old. Then they said I should go to Officer Candidate School (OCS), but only the infantry was open to black officers. I would have been the first black to attend Artillery OCS, except that this announcement showed up on the orderly room wall: "Be a pilot and earn $245 a month." A lieutenant's regular pay was $125 a month.
>
> So in August 1942, I arrived in Tuskegee. We were the first class to expand from the normal twenty per class. There

were thirty-five in our class, including fifteen who had previous Army experience. After nine weeks we were left with only fifteen. I read a book by Hap Arnold and Ira Eaker that said they washed out seventy-five percent of the cadets they took in — this was white boys. The 'washing machine' was going, and after bivouacking two years at Fort Sill, I was properly motivated to be in the upper twenty-five percent. The others criticized me for not going to town. I told them, "I didn't come here to go to town;" I was looking at that $245 a month.

"In the cadet corps we had some terrible math problems," C.C. Robinson remembered. "Most of us had to study like the devil, but Crockett had no problems. I think he tutored some of the other guys."

Woody was already married when he reported, although cadets were not allowed to have wives. "I didn't say a word," he smiled. "That's how I escaped the bullet."

Wilmat Sidat-Singh, an All-American football and basketball star at Syracuse, was also in the class. He came off the Washington, D.C. police force.

Another class member, Alfonso Davis, was an old Buffalo Soldier, a cavalry trooper from Fort Leavenworth. "A gung-ho soldier," Crockett said, "a straight arrow."

Meanwhile Harry Sheppard had made staff sergeant, applied for flight training, and joined the cadet corps in October 1942, in class 43-E ('E' standing for May, the fifth month and graduation date). It was the largest class thus far, with twenty-one grads.

One of them was Bussey, "a big-chested gung-ho guy," in Crockett's words. He was born in 1921 in Bakersfield, California, "a disgustingly prejudiced place at that time," Charlie recalled. "Even in kindergarten I became aware that there was something wrong, that I wasn't treated like the white kids, the oriental kids, or even the Mexican kids. I resented it bitterly."

Bussey's father had served in France, and his grandfather, an ex-slave, had fought in the Wilderness with Grant, on the western plains, and in Cuba. He carried three arrowheads in a pouch and one more in his neck. The old man, in his eighties, in a tattered army coat, drove a rickety buckboard wagon, and six year-old Charlie used to climb up beside him to listen to tales of the old days.

My other granddad had been a Methodist minister and had graduated from college back in 1887. He built churches in Bakersfield, Riverside, Pasadena, and Santa Monica. A very close relative of my father founded Voorhees College in South Carolina before the turn of the century, and I had an uncle who became the first black Supreme Court judge in California.

Prior to the Depression, my dad was a railroad mail clerk, he carried a pistol and rode with sacks of mail. But the Civil Service was different then, so when the Depression hit in '29, this became a white boy's job, and Dad had none.

Times were hard from then on. I'm not one of those people who talk about the good old days. The hell with them. I'd hate to go through them again. I worked in the fields from the time I was nine or ten, picking cotton, corn, all kinds of fruits. I got paid damn little, cotton went for one and a quarter cents a pound then.

When I was seventeen, a friend and I rode freight trains all the way to Detroit. In Ogden, Utah there was a wheat harvest on, and we bucked hundred-pound bales of wheat. We were there about ten days and made thirty dollars — that was big bucks. Around Lincoln, Nebraska we worked shucking corn for about three dollars a day, room and board. So when we got to Detroit, I had fifty-seven bucks, a king's ransom, it seemed at the time.

Then we went up the St. Lawrence and out to sea on a "rust bucket." I'd never seen the ocean before. I shoveled coal eight hours a day, the toughest way to make a living. About four hundred miles west of the Azores, the ship threw a bearing, and we were towed in by another ship, so we laid around the Azores about ten days, did some drinking, and the little money I had earned was soon spent. We stowed away on another ship heading back to Norfolk, hopped freight trains, and hoboed our way home.

I realized that stoking boilers by hand is a hard way to make a living, so I finished high school and went to Los Angeles City College for two years. College cost five dollars a semester, and I had a hell of a hard time raising that five bucks.

I applied to the U.S. Army in the middle of '41. Of course I was treated with the utmost discourtesy. I was disgusted and wrote to Eleanor Roosevelt, who responded within three days and told me there was a program for black fliers in Tuskegee and apologized for the segregated nature of things. As a result, in September 1942, I had an opportunity to go to Tuskegee for flight training.

It was exciting — flying was tremendously rewarding, and there were new people, very fine, high-type people, some with masters' degrees. I was one of the few who didn't have a college degree, which was consistent with my age, but it made me sort of a pariah.

However, the town of Tuskegee itself was not a good place to be in. They had a sadistic sheriff named Pat Evans, who loved hassling black soldiers, and we got hassled at every opportunity.

Sheppard recalled Bussey as aggressive and straight-forward. "There was no hesitation about anything. And he was outspoken; he gave you his views on whatever the subject was, without hesitation. A lot of people didn't like him because of that. But he and I 'bought' each other, warts and all."

Their classmate was Felix Kirkpatrick, the ex-West Pointer.

The thing about it was, I didn't plan to go to West Point; it just happened by chance. I had finished my first year in the Armour Institute of Chicago, now the Illinois Institute of Chicago; at that time we thought it was second only to MIT. There were three of us blacks in the institute, although it was almost unheard of then for blacks to choose engineering, because they had to go to South America to get a job. My credits in math were very good, and one of the students suggested, "Why don't you go to West Point?" Congressman Oscar De Priest got me an appointment, and before I knew it, I was in West Point under a 'dog ticket,' that is, they waived my entrance exam because of my credits at Armour Institute.

You have to know something about the West Point tradition: They're very clannish in the Army. As commandant of cadets they had a lieutenant colonel whose father had been governor of Virginia. The southern boys at that time were bitterly against blacks, and they were in a position to put us under the silent treatment. If one of your classmates was too friendly, they made it so difficult for him he wished he'd never seen you.

I had a room built for four, but I lived in it by myself. Going to church was a formation, something you had to make; I was in a pew by myself.

I was given demerits on a systematic basis. They'd tell someone, "Go over there and gig Mr. K.".... "Mr. K., straighten your hat." I'd put my hand up, and my hat was already straight, but when you saw the gig sheet, it said, "Hat on head crooked." I was always walking the yard on punishment tours until my classmates called me 'the iron man.' The main idea was to keep you away from your studies, but I was in the upper third of my class.

B.O. Davis was a first classman when I was a plebe. He came by my room and said, "Don't worry, they can't afford to dismiss you because of demerits." But DePriest was no longer in Congress, so I no longer had a sponsor and no one to turn to.

In six months I was on my way home.

When you're young, you're very resilient, you bounce back. The only effect it really had was that it interrupted my school, and I never did go back to full-time formal schooling. I went to work for the Pullman Company in Chicago as an electrician in the yard.

After leaving West Point, Kirkpatrick visited the Chicago *Defender* office to see editor Enoch Waters, and Willa Brown was telling Waters of her difficulties in recruiting students for Civilian Pilot Training. "Well," said Waters, "what about Felix here?"

"That," Felix said, "is how I started." At twenty-seven he was the old man of the class and in fact had to get a special age waiver.

"Kirkpatrick was one of the funniest guys I ever met," Sheppard chuckled. Even hearing Felix say grace in the dining room sent Sheppard into uncontrolled laughter until the cadet captain made Harry eat his meal under the table.

Still another member of the class was Johnny Briggs, a close friend of Pruitt in St. Louis. At a reunion of Tuskegee Airmen, Briggs strode through the hotel lobby in cowboy boots and Stetson hat. "I wonder if he takes that hat off to take a shower,"

Sheppard smiled. "And he had the shiniest shoes. I don't care what the weather was, his shoes looked like finish on a cabinet. Used to wear jodhpur boots, and the gleam would put your eyes out."

Classmate Clemenceau Givings "was the epitome of a fighter pilot," remembered Walter Palmer, who came along later. "And he always had something to say on any subject. When Clem was around, everyone was in good spirits."

Jimmy Walker was a very religious man, Sheppard recalled. He was born in South Carolina but moved to Baltimore to attend high school because there were no black high schools in his home state. He went on to Hampton Institute, Virginia, where he studied the building trade and attended CPT. He would graduate number-two in his class at Tuskegee.

The base was still segregated. The PX cafeteria was divided in half; some thirty to forty white personnel ate in one half, and from four hundred to five hundred blacks ate in the other half. At lunch the black line stretched half-way around the block.

Off base things were as bad as ever. When a bus driver told the 'niggers' to move to the rear, Milton Henry gave him "a few choice words," and the driver went for his pistol. Luckily a party of British cadets leaped between them, pushed Henry off the bus, and persuaded the driver to drive away. If those Brits had been American whites, one pilot said, Henry "would have been a dead man."

But, Sheppard emphasized, "the quality of our instruction was superb. I have *no* question about that. Some of those people may have been prejudiced, but as far as that flight training went, we got top-notch training. There are some people who would like to paint a picture of discrimination in the cockpit. No, that didn't occur in my case, nor in the case of anyone else with whom I received my flight training. I don't believe in embellishing our story. The story has merits of its own; we don't have to embellish it."

The training was tough, "but we absorbed it like sponges." Shep didn't have any interest going off base. For one thing, his pay had dropped from ninety-six dollars a month as a staff sergeant to seventy-five dollars as a cadet. After deducting his allotment home, there wasn't much left to spend.

For another, "you were looking for an encounter with the law enforcement people who were always baiting you, hoping you'd make a mistake." On a trip to Atlanta he and fellow cadet Melvin Brooks bought bus tickets to return to Tuskegee.

> The MPs would stalk through the stations, looking for excuses to break your head. An MP spotted me and put me under arrest.
> "Come with me."
> "What's the deal?"
> "Don't ask any questions." The guy took me to Camp McClellan and booked me.
> "What are the charges?"
> "Impersonating an officer." They locked me up! I guess he felt real proud of himself.
> The next morning they released me.
> I had been the class captain, and I lost that. I had to meet a board. Brooks was about to pass out laughing; I could see his shoulders shaking as they asked the questions. I sweated being thrown out, but was restricted to base pending graduation.

Sheppard's kid brother, Herb, was a sergeant in the Army. "He came up from Camp Rucker, Alabama to see me graduate. He rode on top of the bus with all the duffel bags. I flew him back to his base."

Sheppard, Kirkpatrick, Bussey, and Walker were assigned to Gleed's 302nd. Crockett went to Tresville's 100th.

Just a month behind that class, another formed. One of the cadets was Charles McGee, who had learned to fly with white students in CPT at the University of Illinois.

Another was Walter Palmer, Charles Dryden's cousin. As he wrote in his book, *Flying With Eagles* (1993), his parents had come to Harlem from Jamaica. His father, an elevator operator, also played trumpet in the Salvation Army band, which Walter followed proudly through the streets. Moving to the Bronx, he grew up in "a virtual League of Nations." Most of his friends were Orthodox Jews, and he earned a few pennies on Friday nights lighting their candles, which they were forbidden to do. Walter played stickball in the streets and hiked six or seven miles to the Polo Grounds to see the Giants. He entered

New York's only aviation-oriented high school and worked as a delivery boy in the lower East Side garment district.

Palmer was training to be a police officer when Pearl Harbor hit, and he rushed to volunteer for cadet training, then waited nine months for the call.

On January 8, 1943, all classes were halted to mark the death of Doctor George Washington Carver, a professor at Tuskegee for half a century.

Finally in June the class graduated — twenty-four of the original fifty-plus. Palmer's fiancee traveled from New York for their wedding, and the sun "came out in all its glory." Palmer and Al Lewis wore their new lieutenants bars for the double wedding at the chapel. Palmer then took his bride up for a spin, showing her a loop, a snap roll, and an Immelmann. It knocked her glasses off. "That was an expensive flight for me," he sighed.

After graduation the new officers checked out in the P-40s, 'the Flying Coffin.' Sheppard was practicing loops when the instructor told him, "You're going up to eight thousand feet and stick the nose straight down. Then point it straight up and take your hands off the throttle. If you touch the controls, the airplane will stall."

"Well," Sheppard gulped, "that was kind of hard to do!" He did loop after loop, hoping each time to be allowed to pull out. "No, not this time," the instructor ordered. "Finally I started to run low on fuel. My hair was standing straight up."

Oscar Kenney's plane plummeted into the ground. No one ever knew why. After the funeral Shep and each of his classmates received a letter from Kenney's parents, "urging us to perform our patriotic duty so that Negro people could share fully in the freedom for which we were fighting."

The next class was also distinguished. Its most famous graduate was Daniel 'Chappie' James, the former flight instructor. West Pointer Ernie Davis, who was also in the class, was half the size of James, Bussey said. "He was very mild, very learned, very sharp. You'd never think of him as a fighter. For some reason Ernie and Chappie got into a little fisticuffs, and Chappie came out quite the worse."

James "wasn't the outstanding person in that group, not by a hell of a shot," Bussey insisted. "We had many more people who were much more accomplished than he was. But he got the breaks." Too big for a fighter pilot, James went on to fly bombers, thus missing combat in Italy.

James' classmate, Lee 'Buddy' Archer, another of the DeWitt Clinton high school triumvirate, came to Tuskegee from the 369th National Guard regiment, the famous 'men of bronze' of World War I. Archer was a typical New Yorker, Red Jackson recalled, aggressive in speech, but a popular mixer socially, and he played a deadly hand of poker or blackjack. In Italy, Archer teamed with Pruitt as the hottest duo in the Group, and no man in the outfit received credit for more enemy planes destroyed.

Archer's classmate, William 'Chubby' Green, was "one of the finest pilots I ever knew," Lee said. The two became close friends.

A third member of the class was Pruitt's roommate, Bill Melton.

> I was an army brat from the old, old segregated army. My father was in the medical corps. They had one medical company assigned to each of the four black regiments scattered around the country and the Philippines. I was born in New Mexico and entered school in New York when my father was assigned to West Point. I grew up around Tucson — Fort Huachuca — and my father is buried there. I got pretty good training as a child; I was in church every time the church door opened. I lived very near the airport and used to ride my bike out there when they had these barnstorming air shows and wore my Boy Scout uniform so they'd let me in free. That's when I met Ernst Udet, a World War I ace, who could do unbelievable things. I became instantly fascinated with aviation.

Melton's best friend was Elmer 'Chubby' Taylor. "I called him Mussolini," Bill said. "He looked like him, bald, gregarious, full of humor. He was from Pittsburgh, educated, sophisticated, but he had a weight problem, and the physical training instructor had him sucking a lemon all day long to lose a few pounds, just like boxers do."

The 332nd now had filled all three squadrons and moved to Selfridge Field, Michigan, outside Detroit for advanced combat training.

Two P-47 Thunderbolts were sent to tow targets. "They were tail-dragging types with heavy radial engines," Gleed said. "No one was qualified to fly them, so who gets selected? Me, although I'm the commanding officer."

The students doing the shooting were in P-40s that were even older and more un-airworthy than the ones the 99th had trained in. They still had the sharks' teeth of the 'Flying Tigers' painted on their noses. Wilmat Sidat-Singh crashed into Lake Huron, and though he bailed out, he was never found; some speculate that he got tangled in his parachute and drowned. "He was a hell of a nice guy," said Sheppard. "The entire Group was struck with grief, because he was one of our first losses."

Detroit, 'the Big D,' with its nightclubs and pretty girls, beckoned to the single guys, who headed for the Adams Bar and the St. Antoine nightclub. Clem Givings exhorted them: "Hair conked, shoes shined, and running to St. Antwine." Palmer took his wife to town and passed Sergeant Joe Louis, the heavyweight champ, coming toward them. The champ threw him "a snappy salute."

The airmen found that Jim Crow was as alive in Michigan as in Alabama. While they were there, Detroit suffered a bloody race riot, and the black officers' weapons were confiscated and they were confined to base, surrounded by a guard of white troops. The citizens of Iosco County made it plain that they didn't want the black fliers any more than the people of Tuskegee had. "The town fathers wanted the U.S. government to close Selfridge," Sheppard said. "The government and some senators came to our rescue and really gave the town hell."

The base was just as bad, said Bussey, "maybe worse." A scandal broke out when the first base commander, Colonel William T. Colman, shot his Negro jeep driver. Some reports say Colman was drunk. Dick Macon of the 332nd thought it stemmed from a triangle involving the colonel's wife.

Coleman was replaced by Lieutenant Colonel Robert Selway, a Kentuckian and a West Pointer, who ran the base much as Colonel von Kimble had earlier run Tuskegee.

Said Bussey: "His job was not to give us training but to see that we didn't use the Officers' Club or swimming pool; that was his biggest concern." Selway was backed up by the commanding general of the First Air Force, a World War I ace and two-star general, Frank O'Driscoll Hunter, who had "a filthy mouth and a hatred for blacks."

"It was separate," smiled Johnny Briggs, "but it was far from equal. We had our own barber shop. Our PX was a make-shift PX in the barracks, where you could get cigarettes, chewing gum, beer, that sort of thing. The Officers' Club was off-limits. That was up in Michigan! You wouldn't think that would be, but back in those days, that's how it was."

Meantime, as with the 99th before them, the 332nd found that no one overseas wanted them. So they trained endlessly. Keen rivalries developed. "The 302nd 'Hellions' were the cockiest," Gleed maintained forty years later. "We built up an esprit. We thought we had the best pilots. I still consider it that way."

Sheppard agreed.

> We had a dynamic bunch of guys. I think we were the most closely-knit bunch. We studied together, we fought together, we suffered together. We were a unit. There was a camaraderie you often didn't find in white units.
>
> Pruitt was a hell of a nice guy, a fun guy to be with. Always imaginative, especially in the air. I just loved to fly behind him in a string of six planes. When we were up doing our training thing, we'd engage in mock combat and 'rat races' — that's follow-the-leader. He'd peel off, heading straight for the ground, then pull up. We'd fly under the bridges at Port Huron. Everyone loved to fly with Pruitt and admired him.

Gleed, Pruitt, Archer, and Chubby Green soon became a foursome. "We'd fly together every time we had a chance, even if we weren't scheduled to," Archer said. "We considered ourselves a natural group. At one time Ben Davis was going to court martial all four of us because of the way we flew together. We were trying to fly acrobatics in formation, and that was not done. He thought it was a risk we should not be taking. If something happened, it would reflect badly on the Group."

Sheppard and Palmer brought their brides and lived in the same motel. Whatever one tried in the air, the other tried to do better. "We were happy-go-lucky kids and just loved flying," Palmer said. "I was only twenty-two, mind you, and I just thought flying was the greatest thing in the world."

Flying under bridges was great sport, even though Richard Dawson had been killed trying it at Tuskegee. "They were kind of high," said Sheppard, "thirty to forty feet above the surface; we had plenty of room — you just didn't want to arrive there at the same time someone was coming the other way."

The next step was to try it at night, Palmer said. "It would really test your instrument skills. Better know your altitude and hope your instruments were correct!"

"I'm not going to lie," admitted Alexander Jefferson, "I think all of us were scared when we did it. But you just didn't show the white feather."

Soon they were not only trained to a fine edge, they were over-trained and bored. It led to some dangerous antics. 'Moe' Downs said that one day they dreamed up a game of 'peek-a-boo' with a train. "We'd fly straight at the engine and then pull up. To enliven things, we did all kinds of loops just in front of the engine." Of course they got a stiff chewing out.

Palmer pulled another escapade.

> We heard that the Tuskegee football team was going to be playing in Detroit against West Virginia, another all-black school. I was assistant Flight leader, and I said to the group, "We'll fly down to Detroit and buzz the game," because we knew some of the members on the team. We made a cursory pass at the field at about five hundred feet, and the other three members of the Flight said, "OK, we're heading back home."
>
> I said, "That's ridiculous. We made this whole trip down here for one cursory pass? No way! I'm going to go down and let them know we're here." They went on back, and I came down to about a hundred feet or so and checked to see if there were any telephone wires or anything. There was nothing in the area, so I came over a third time below the level of the stands, and as I was pulling up, I did a slow roll. When executed properly it is a beautiful maneuver, and this one was executed to perfection.

Who happened to be at this all-black football game? Colonel Selway, who didn't like blacks flying in the first place! I don't think I finished my slow roll before he got on the phone and said, "Have the pilot of plane E-5 grounded, and let him know he's going to be court martialled!"

By the time I got back to the field, they brought a military vehicle to take me back down to Detroit to be court martialled. I got rumors from my friends, who said Selway planned to have me expelled from the Service as an example. Of course I was sick, because here I had just graduated two or three months before, and now I was going to be thrown out of the Service. I had made my wife and parents so proud, and this would bring disgrace on all of them.

While awaiting trial, Palmer was confined to the bachelor officers' quarters, and nights without his wife, Nita, were lonely, so one weekend she snuck into his room, which was separated from the others by temporary dividers. She hid in a locker until the coast was clear, then they tiptoed into bed. Unexpectedly the officer across the divider, Virgil Richardson, had not gone home that weekend. While the couple snuggled, Virgil called out that he had a good book Walter would enjoy and tossed it over the divider. Wrote Palmer: "I don't know whether he suspected anything or not."

At the court martial, my commanding officer, Captain Tresville, testified in my behalf, and so did my Flight commander and my Operations Officer. The question was put to them: "Would you take him in the squadron if he gets out of this court martial?" They said, yes, they would. As a result, I'm sure, I was just given a fine of seventy-five dollars a month for three months. I was also relieved of my job as assistant Flight commander. But shortly thereafter I got it back because my commanding officer liked the way I flew.

Meanwhile, the War Department was still trying to decide what to do with the unit. General MacArthur's air chief didn't want them in the Pacific; the British didn't want them in the British Isles, nor even in British islands in the Caribbean, and the Danes vetoed Greenland. "We went through three training cycles. The troops were growing restive," Sheppard said.

Hitler is kicking their butts, and here's a force of trained combat pilots, and they're fooling around with this racial trivia. We really looked forward to getting into combat. We were on a keen edge, like tempered steel. But we lolled around. You can overtrain and become dull. I'd been reading about the German 190s and 109s, like a boxer sizing up his opponent, and we wanted to get overseas and see what the Luftwaffe had for us.

At last orders came down: They were going to Italy.

While they waited, they flew. Most white cadets went overseas with forty hours. "I had 145 flying hours in the P-40 and 125 in the P-39," Crockett said. "So I felt I was red-hot when I hit Naples."

Just before they were to move out, three more replacements arrived for the 302nd — Roger Romine, Hubron Blackwell, and George Haley. They had to catch up fast. "We had those poor rascals strapped to the P-39 from the time they arrived," laughed Sheppard. "Their day was just jammed from dawn to dusk. Oh, they pissed and moaned." Haley memorialized it in a poem:

> The 302nd worked like bees
> To get their outfit overseas,
> But none worked as long and hard as these —
> Romine, Blackwell, Haley.
>
> With frigid feet and fingertips,
> Horseshoe spine and aching hips,
> Commanding colonels still plan trips
> For Romine, Blackwell, Haley.
>
> When "each and every" off to town
> To some sweet pad to lay him down,
> Up in the sky still duty-bound
> Are Romine, Blackwell, Haley.
>
> If one dared take that evening date,
> By dawn he'd be in awful shape.
> But still they'd strap him to that crate —
> Romine, Blackwell, Haley.

"Operations thinks it's best
Because of weather take a rest,
But you three take a ground school test" —
Romine, Blackwell, Haley.

Flight leaders change throughout the day,
Let missions vary as they may,
From dark to dark in their ships stay
Romine, Blackwell, Haley.

Blessed peace, oh praise the will
That brings release from plans to kill.
Dear God! Tonight there's "dinghy drill"
For Romine, Blackwell, Haley.

Sheppard took pity on them. "I'll take one of them," he volunteered. "I'll take Haley." And Haley became Shep's wingman for his entire combat tour.

At last, in December the 332nd was on its way to Hampton Roads, Virginia, its embarkation point.

Lou Purnell decided to go back with them. "At Tuskegee I was given a group of cadets to train, two of whom froze on controls while I was teaching spins and recoveries. After you stall, you make precisely two complete 360-degrees and kick out. I was counting three and four turns, and the ground was coming up right fast. You don't know when you're coming out until you break the strangle hold of that kid in the back seat. Right then I decided to go back to combat, where it was safer."

At Camp Patrick Henry, Virginia, Bussey found the whole camp "just riddled" with signs saying 'Whites Only.'

Directly across the street from our area was a movie that said 'White Troops Only,' and the PX said 'White Troops only.' The nearest PX for Negroes was two and a half or three miles away. I got a belly full of it. I just said, "The hell with this crap. I'll raise some troops, and we'll all go to the movie." When the troops showed up, I pulled the sign off the building, and we all bought tickets.

When we left the movie, a few fist fights broke out between the black and white soldiers. Later on it got more serious. They had issued us guns and ammunition that day, and the guys started firing at random up in the air and caused quite a bit of consternation. The MPs arrived, but when they saw the situation, they chose not to act, so my squadron commander, Gleed, sent me down to put a stop to it. I went with a couple of enlisted men, and it was kind of scary, believe me. But finally we got the thing put down.

"Some of those bullets must have come pretty close to headquarters," said Purnell, "because we could hear them whistling overhead." The next day soldiers went through the area and took all the signs down. "Beginning that morning we could go to any damn theater we wanted to. That's one good thing we did before we left. The rules of segregation at Camp Patrick Henry were changed. Changed forever."

That's when Charlie got his nickname, 'Big Bad Bussey.'

They had one last job to do, Kirkpatrick said. On the ferry going to their ship were two more large signs, saying, 'Whites Only' on one side of the boat and 'Colored Only' on the other side. "Bussey was on one side and pulled down one sign, and I was on the other and pulled down the other one."

The 332nd was on its way.

8

Naples

The P-39

The 332nd was on the high seas when news of the 99th's triumph at Anzio reached them. "All we heard was about those black pilots who shot down eight planes in one day," Crockett said.

They spent a month on the Atlantic in a convoy of eighty Liberty ships, using speed to outrun enemy U-boats. Thirty officers were crammed into a twenty by thirty-foot space. Charlie Bussey said, "We were sleeping on the floor." For amusement, musical instruments were brought out. They also played a cutthroat game called 'dirty hearts' — the loser had to drink a pint of water. "When you had a long losing streak," said Bussey, "you were in deep trouble."

Arriving at the toe of Italy, they were trucked to an airfield at Capodicino outside Naples. "They told everyone to be prepared, we were in the war zone, and to dig fox holes," said Charles McGee. "One night a German Heinkel III bomber flew over Naples, and we were all out there watching the show with the searchlights on — until one of the planes made a run down our own airstrip, dropping frag [fragmentation] bombs, and damaged twenty-seven aircraft. Of course everyone hit the fox holes."

"No one realized how dangerous anti-aircraft fire was," Walter Palmer said. "We'd shoot up little chunks of metal about the size of a poker chip or larger. One came down through our tent."

The next day, McGee said, "folks were out there digging those fox holes three times deeper!"

McGee was soft-spoken and much admired by the others. "I wouldn't call him reticent," Sheppard said, "but he wasn't one of those voluble, effusive fountains of knowledge you couldn't shut up." McGee was also a physical fitness bug and led the calisthenics for the Group.

Woody Crockett found a jeep driver to see the sights of Naples. That night the Germans bombed it. The Army had smoked it with chemicals to obscure it from the German planes, and the driver couldn't find his way down the street. "Then Vesuvius erupted, so the Germans had no trouble locating the city. I don't think they could have had a better beacon." For weeks afterward, the pilots had to fly out to sea to avoid the huge cloud of ash before beginning their patrols.

Palmer had a taste for opera, which he apparently shared with the Germans, who had not bombed the Naples Opera House, so Walter spent his days off there listening to arias. C.C. Robinson of the 99th also took in the sights. "The opera changed every week like a movie; we'd go every Sunday — I got to be quite an opera buff. There were a lot of museums, and I must have visited the Vatican five or six times" to see the Pope. And, he admitted, he also enjoyed "a lot of girl-chasing, what guys in their twenties would do."

The fliers formed tent groups within their squadron rows.

Sheppard gave a rundown on some of the major ones in the 302nd: "Bussey lived in 'Poker Flats.' There was always a poker game going on, and they were the roughest poker players you would ever find. Before each game Weldon 'Baldy' Groves would close his eyes in prayer, which would invoke Bussey's anger; he thought Groves was praying for celestial help.

"The 'Chargin' Misters' tent — Dudley Watson, Milton Brooks, and Edwin 'Evil' N. Smith, and Roger Romine. "A very caustic bunch. They challenged everybody about every subject on earth."

Sheppard's tent was 'the damned handicrafters.'

> We used crates to insulate it. Jimmy Walker, a product of Hampton Institute, was adept at tools, and we were always hammering and sawing at night, and you could hear us throughout the area, much to the disgust of our neighboring tents, who used to complain vociferously.
>
> There was always something going on. We'd give short sheets, and if you were lucky enough to get a metal cot, we'd very delicately balance it so when a guy sat down it would collapse.
>
> Gwynne Peirson was from the Berkeley area. He had attended college, had played a lot of semipro baseball, and had a cryptic sense of humor. He was a hell of a good pilot, smooth, dependable. He always wanted to get in our tent. One day he popped his head in while George Haley was eating an apple and said, "You guys got anything to eat in here?" That's why we called him 'Hungry' Peirson.
>
> We had nicknames for everybody. We had four Smiths. Luther Smith was called 'Quibbling' Smith — he spoke too rapidly. Another guy stayed up all night carousing, so we called him 'Dissipatin'' Smith. Another Smith told fantastic tales about everything; we called him 'Fantastic' Smith. Edwin N. Smith had kind of a mean demeanor, although he was a good man. We called him 'Evil' N. Smith. Lewis C. Smith of the 99th was from Des Moines, Iowa. He always had a half-smile on his face so he was known as 'Smirkin'' Smith.

As often as he could, Sheppard, a pianist, and Lawrence Dixon, a jazz guitarist, got together in the day room or the Club.

Another musician of note, Henry Pollard, had played saxophone in Jimmy Lunceford's dance band.

Roger Romine was an individualist who also loved good music and wrote poetry.

Sheppard recalled:

He negotiated with Italian workmen, and they made tiles out of pressed wood shavings and concrete, almost like concrete blocks. He built this damn hut all by himself. The other guys were teed off because they were all in tents, and Roger had built himself this unauthorized hut, his palace, and he was quite happy. Except the tiles were flammable. He was in there reading on the bunk, had nothing on but his shoes, and the stove exploded and set the hut on fire, and he ran out. All he had on was a pair of shoes and carrying his book and his .45.

After that he moved in with the Chargin' Misters.

Meanwhile, the Air Force study ordered in September had not been completed, and the 332nd was given the innocuous task of coastal patrol. "It was an intentional insult to me and my men," Davis wrote. But he bit his lip and dutifully hunched his six-foot body into the small cockpit of his P-39.

Lucky Lester of the 100th Squadron spoke for all the pilots:

A fighter pilot flying coastal patrol was like a brain surgeon being a physician at a Boy Scout camp: it was just about the most boring mission you could perform.

And the P-39s were dogs if I ever saw one, rickety old things, just lousy airplanes. It had the engine behind the pilot and a shaft with the cannon ran between your legs and shot out through the propeller spinner. It was good-looking, it had doors on it like an automobile, but it had very funny flying characteristics because the center of gravity was off because of the engine placement. It was lousy for air-to-air combat but pretty good for ground support because of its heavy shielding underneath. I didn't mind the airplane too much, because I could fly it. But there were a lot of pilots who were scared to death of it.

Nobody liked the P-39. Crockett said:

It was a little faster than the P-40, but it couldn't turn. You could change you heading, but you couldn't change your direction, it just mushed. And I didn't like running interference for a big engine behind me. If you were tall, you had to put the seat down all the way to the bottom. I'm five-foot-eleven, almost the limit, so I had to press my head down to get inside the door. There is no P-39 Pilots' Association today — apparently no one thought very much of it.

Sheppard:

We got the P-39s back from Russia and England, some of the old Lend-Lease planes we had sent them. They very gleefully gave them back to us when we got to Italy. I never did trust it. It had very poor aerodynamic characteristics in combat situations; it didn't like sudden changes in altitude or direction. In a real tight turn where you're pulling streamers off your wing, it had a nasty habit of snapping into a spin, which was quite exhilarating.

It was known for killing people. The cannon sat between your legs; if you ran into something, that was the first thing you hit. The engine was behind you, so it would come forward, the guns would come back, and if your ordnance man wasn't too sharp about the head space, the aft part of the gun could change your whole social life forever.

They designed the cockpit last: "Oh, we gotta put a guy in there!" The P-39 was not a great airplane to get out of. It had a door on the right-hand side, like a car. If you had to bail out, you had to pull a lever which pulled the pins out of the door, and the air stream would take the door off. Then you had to dive for the wing to keep from being hit by the tail.

Clemenceau Givings, my classmate from Hampton, Virginia, drowned in Naples harbor when he got tangled up in his 'chute.

Chris Newman of the 100th had several near-death experiences in the P-39. He wanted to have a look inside Vesuvius and flew over the smoking cone. Suddenly his engine started sputtering — the sulfurous air had little oxygen — and he immediately headed out. "If I'd gone down a little deeper, I might not have made it."

On his second flight, Newman made a night-landing without seeing the ground.

I was on the last mission of the day, flying Othel Dickinson's wing. The ground controllers sent us out to sea to try to find a May Day [a downed flyer]. We flew a search pattern and didn't see anything, but they said, "Well, can you look a little longer? We hate to lose a pilot."

When we finally got back, it was dark and when it's a blackout, you don't realize how little you can see. The airfield put a light straight up in the air like a beacon. I didn't know what it meant or where it was in relation to the field, but I started looking for the ground and pulling back on the stick. I got it all the way back to the stop, but if you're too high, one of the wings may stall before the other one. I knew I should be touching the ground, but it seemed like an eternity before I hit. The landing broke the nose gear, and I slid on down the field. Thankfully there was no fire.

The third time, Newman forgot to put his wheels down on landing. "I sat down on an external tank and, BOOM! All I saw was fire. The door was supposed to fall off, but it didn't." He finally kicked it off and fell onto the wing. "I had first-degree burns on my face and third degree burns — where you're kind of 'cooked' — on my leg. I was in the hospital about two and a half months."

As squadron maintenance officer, Sheppard had no plane of his own. "I had to fly them all, test hop them. If something was wrong as reported by a pilot, I test-flew it the same day or flew it on the next mission." He grew bored with the constant patrols.

Haley and I buzzed the Isle of Capri. We came down and flew right over it, skinning the island. Crazy fighter pilots — they called us 'bubble heads.' We didn't know it was a British rest camp for war-weary guys back from the battle line.

We got a hiding. Gleed says, "Look, you two guys are always into some kind of mess. Well, I'm going to keep you busy." He gave us dawn, lunch, and dusk patrols. That meant we took off before the rest of the guys while they were eating breakfast. Some of the barrage balloons were still up, which gave it a kind of hairy aspect. And landing after sundown wasn't good, because the anti-aircraft people are on edge, and they challenged us several evenings with lights — it's a good thing we knew the code of the day. You had a little telegraph key, and the lights on the side of your fuselage or wingtips would flash, and they used that for recognition. I couldn't even remember whether I was giving the right code or not, I was so damn nervous. Those British gunners could *shoot* and we were at low altitude anyway.

Palmer, who had almost been cashiered for buzzing the football field, apparently hadn't learned his lesson. He was Johnny Briggs' wingman.

We always did a lot of buzzing around − well, that's the nature of fighter pilots to buzz. Johnny had an outgoing personality. We didn't mingle socially, but he flew with such smooth motions, I figured I could improve my flying by flying his wing; we flew as many as six hours a day together. Johnny and I always flew a tight formation − we flew so close they used to call us 'the P-38 boys.' The P-38 was a twin-boom fighter with one wing and two fuselages, and when you saw our two P-39s together, it looked like one P-38, we flew that tightly.

Briggs:

Palmer was really sharp, he was doing all the work. I'd pull up, and he'd stay right in there with me. When we came back from a mission, the crew chiefs and ground crewmen would want us to buzz the field, and stuff would blow over the damn tents and everything. We'd circle around and come back and buzz it again, then we'd drop wheels together and touch down together. No, there was no one else like Briggs and Palmer.

The commander, Robert Tresville, told me, "Briggs, the next time you do that, you're going to be grounded." The very next day we did the same damn thing. Sure enough, he said, "You're grounded! Go to your tent."

I went to my tent and lay down on my bunk. An hour later the Operations Officer, Jug Turner [second in command], came up and said, "Briggs, we're short-handed, we need you on a mission in the morning." So that didn't last too long.

On February 15, the 332nd encountered enemy planes for the first time.

Melton of the 302nd recalled:

I was the first guy in the Group to encounter the enemy, a severely damaged Junker 88 bomber, while on patrol at the mouth of Naples harbor. They used to come over at a very low altitude and take pictures; they'd be low enough to throw wakes in the water with their props. They were always there a certain time of day, and we used to sit out there and wait for them. I thought I'd get one, but that old 37-mm gun jammed on me. The P-39 was a notoriously underpowered airplane, especially at sea level, so the Junker got away.

Going over as we did, we didn't have combat returnees to lead us, and I learned more in the first three or four hours in combat than in all the prior months. One white pilot recommended hanging our dog tags over our gunsights to tell our position with reference to the ground in case our instruments got shot out — whether we were skidding, whether our wings were level. That became a ceremony. My crew chief would take my tags off and hang them over the gunsight. (I also had a good luck charm, some Pompeian jewelry I'd bought as a souvenir, some porno stuff.)

Every inch of that Anzio beachhead was bracketed by that damn German 88 gun up on higher elevation. It was one of the damnedest weapons ever invented. They used it for anti-aircraft, and it was murder. Once I got hit by AA [anti-aircraft] fire, and my engine coolant temperature shot up. They had told me what to do in case I got hit in my radiator: Reduce all my power settings, drop my flaps, slow the airplane down to 170 mph and just wait until the gauge dropped. I couldn't have learned this from any black, because none of them had had this type of experience. This was taught to me by a white fellow I don't even know.

Woody Crockett's wingman was Earl Sherrod from Columbus, Ohio.

Sherrod was a hotrod; he always needed excitement. I had to do something outstanding every day just to keep him alive. Around Anzio we were flying, two guys low and two high. We made the Italians jump out of their sailboats, we were that low. And he almost ran into a big rock out there. He complained when he got back: "You like to killed me."

His biggest claim to fame was January 22. General Clark and his Fifth Army was stuck on the Volturno River for a long time and couldn't link up with the Anzio beachhead. When he finally linked up, Sherrod was over Anzio and his belly tank was leaking, so he went to Anzio to get refueled. They put him in a foxhole and refueled him, then they put the film of the linkup in Sherrod's plane, and he flew it back.

In March, President Franklin Roosevelt visited the Theater, and the Allies sent every plane they had into the sky. "They didn't want any enemy planes even *close* to him," Crockett said.

But Gleed was impatient for more action.

Sheppard declared:

> Gleed was a kind of happy-go-lucky guy, but in my estimation, he could be guilty of some rash decisions. A quick mind, but he had a typical fighter pilot's mentality: Let's do it without any thoughts of consequences. Gleed was a go-getter: 'Heh, let's go; let's do the job.' The methodology might leave something to be desired. He was a good leader, but he was kind of brash — bordered on foolhardy, I thought. Pruitt was somewhat that way too, but he had a little more skill to go with his foolhardiness.

Gleed and Tresville, the CO of the 100th, tried to stir things up a little without telling Davis. Gleed described the plot:

> Bob Tresville and I dreamed up a 'Cook's tour' a sixteen-ship formation of P-39s. We plotted to go out to sea, get up above Anzio and maybe stir up some enemy aircraft and get some kills. We'd done about three of these missions but never ran into any airplanes. The Old Man, Colonel Davis, found out about it and chewed Tresville out: "Bob Tresville! You, above all!"
>
> Bob sent another mission up. Then I sent another one up, and it turned out to be a disaster. I did one of the dumb things I never should have done — took my Operations Officer, Pruitt, with me on the same flight. You shouldn't both be on the same flight. My plane acted up, and I had to turn back, so he took over and went on as planned.
>
> He wound up around Rome when they were running low on fuel, so he took a straight line home. Instead of going out to sea, he came straight over Anzio down 'Flak Alley.' Those Germans had 88-mm anti-aircraft almost like rifles, peppering

you. We had two or three planes shot up; one had to crash land.

Walter Westmoreland had to bail out. He broke his leg and lost his plane.

That did it. The Old Man found out about it, came up there, said, "You prepare court martial papers against Pruitt."

I said, "I don't see how I can do it, sir. I was the one who scheduled the mission and flew on part of it myself."

"I want those papers prepared, and have them to me by noon!"

I said, "I just flat can't do it."

Ben had a way of being very impressive. When he was a student flying with an instructor, Ben had had an accident and banged his forehead on a gunsight, and it left a scar. Whenever he'd get really worked up, that scar seemed as if it pulsated. He barked at me: "*Lieutenant!*"

I said, "Sir, I can't help but say again, I should be the one to be court martialled." Well, that didn't help matters.

He said, "I want you off this field by twelve o'clock tomorrow! You're no longer commander of the 302nd Fighter Squadron."

Sure enough, I was off to the 301st Squadron, flying Tail-End Charlie.

"Davis damn sure let all the guys know that anyone he caught 'hot dogging' or using bombers for bait like some of the white squadrons did, he'd court martial them," Bill Melton said. Gleed paid the price. "But he stuck by his buddy, Pruitt."

He was replaced by Melvin T. 'Red' Jackson of the 100th. Jackson recalled:

Colonel Davis didn't inform me — he had a big tent, and I never saw him. Tresville said Colonel Davis asked him for a recommendation. The 100th was the senior squadron, had a West Point man in charge, and had more of the older people, so it would be natural for Davis to go to the squadron with the greatest age and experience, and Tresville said, "I recommend Jackson."

The squadron areas were a hundred feet apart, and I just walked on over to the 302nd. I knew everyone there, and everyone knew me. We had all trained together, we all ate in the same dining hall.

Jackson was a natural choice in point of seniority as well as in command ability. He had graduated at least two classes ahead of any pilot in the 302nd.

Sheppard found Jackson a contrast to Gleed.

Jackson's style was unhesitating, but the result of having put a little forethought into it. He would never give up, he had dogged determination. If the assignment was to attack the entire Reich on our own, he'd go ahead and do it. But first he'd think about ways to do it and what would happen after. There was nothing rash about Melvin T.

"A very even-handed, calm, judicious, capable man," Melton agreed.

Bussey called Jackson one of the most outstanding men in the 332nd. "Red was a tremendous man. He had very red hair and wild blue eyes. An exceptionally good flier, a real fine boxer, and a brilliant man academically."

The 332nd lost two of its enlisted men in this period. Master Sergeant Bill Harris was crossing the flight line in a weapons carrier and drove into the path of a plane taking off. The pilot never saw him, and Harris was decapitated.

Eugene Pickett, one of Sheppard's classmates at Chanute Field, was found dead around Naples. "I think he was murdered," Sheppard said. "There didn't seem to be a good investigation. The Military Police at that time were not black-indoctrinated; whether a black got killed or not was irrelevant to them."

The deaths hit Sheppard hard. He worked long hours with the mechanics on the flight line, and Harris had been his line chief.

Meanwhile, social mixing with white units was a sore issue. Some didn't run into overt racism. While the others stayed home and played poker, Bernard Knighten of the 99th, said:

I'd go to town and hound the bars. No racial things happened to me, but I didn't look for those things, the bars were open to everybody. I ran into a bunch of Australians, and believe me, they were real gems.

Capri had an R&R camp and a big hotel, but we weren't allowed to stay there. The Negro pilots stayed right across the park in the home of King Victor Emanuel — two Negro pilots and ten servants.

They had a dance at the white hotel, and a captain stopped us at the door, said, "There are white nurses here." We just walked off. We weren't torn up about it, we assumed that was the way it was; we weren't the aggressive type at that time. There were four hundred pilots there, and we couldn't get a dance anyway, so it didn't bother us one bit.

"Our guys got along well with the Italians, especially the girls," Gleed said. "This made the white GIs pretty unhappy. There were any number of incidents. The white GIs reportedly told the Italian girls to stay away from Negroes, that they all had tails."

Purnell of the 99th:

We were well accepted by the Italians after they found out the tales that had been spread about us weren't true. Our rest camp was nothing more than a glorified mansion — ballroom, pool table, several nice bedrooms. But one night we really pitched a good party with a band and girls from the University of Naples — good quality girls, really hand-picked, no whores; our Special Services officer made sure of that. We were really swinging when we heard gunfire outside. We looked out, and the whole place was surrounded by infantrymen on R&R [Rest and Rehabilitation], just returning from the front.

Immediately we called the MPs, but it looked like they were on the side of the infantrymen. So we called the British MPs, and they cleared the whole bunch of them out, infantrymen and American MPs alike.

Purnell went back to his old unit, the 99th, which continued operating independently, flying P-40s out of Capodicino.

They put us on the task of trying to knock out 'the Anzio Express,' a gun mounted on rails, one of the biggest in Italy at the time. It would come out and bombard our lines and air fields, had a hell of a range, then it would disappear into a mountain, and no one was able to get that thing. We dropped our bombs in every opening we could see. We marked off squares about a quarter of a mile wide and a quarter of a mile long, and we hushed that damn thing up."

Heber Houston was a gawky county boy, Spanky Roberts said, "and I do mean country. Probably the most unsophisticated individual you ever saw. But absolutely tenacious. He became a part of the aircraft." He was shot down two or three times over Anzio. The other pilots laughed that every time they saw him he was either making a crash landing or coming back to base in a truck. He just climbed in another plane and took off again.

Clarence Allen was also shot down for a second time behind enemy lines north of Rome and hid in a cave, C.C. Robinson said. Before long, German soldiers were setting up a machine gun at the entrance, and for almost an hour, Allen remained hidden until they left. After dark he crawled out and at sunuup discovered that he had crawled into an enemy bivouac area with German troops moving about, eating breakfast, and shaving. Once more Allen laid low until the Germans moved out. He finally reached friendly lines.

The Allies broke out of Anzio in April, and Rome fell soon after that. The 99th moved north of the capital and continued escort and dive-bombing.

Roberts finally was given relief and sent home.

He was replaced by Erwin Lawrence, according to Robinson. "He almost got everybody killed. A British officer had given the briefing and said, half jokingly, 'On your way back, why don't you stop by Cassino and take a look?' There were a lot of anti-aircraft guns scattered around, and no one really wanted to go down there, because you were almost bound to be hit. But we went down and, hell, everybody got shot up."

On another mission, Baugh recalled:

> I was dive bombing some gun positions in the Po Valley, and the anti-aircraft fire was thick. I remember seeing tracers going by my airplane. I'm going almost straight down as fast as I could get the airplane to go, 550 mph — in that airplane, that was fast. I remember very distinctly wondering, "Why did I ever take up flying?"
>
> I had one wingman, Smirkin' Smith, shot down on another mission. Smith saw a truck on the road, and I said, "You go down, and I'll follow you." He put a five hundred-pound

bomb in the bed of the truck, right behind the cab. Then we saw a convoy on the road. You should strafe across the road, but we strafed down the road to get more shots in, and they hit his airplane. He flew up a couple of thousand feet or so and bailed out and spent the rest of the war as a prisoner of war.

The Theater Commander, General Mark Clark, thanked the 99th for its support of his ground troops. General Cannon, the 12th Air Force Commander, called it one of the best ground support outfits in the theater. Even Tooey Spaatz requested more black units be sent to his command, and Air Force Chief Hap Arnold himself sent congratulations.

Meanwhile, the Pentagon study was finally released. It cited "no significant differences" between the 99th and other comparable squadrons in the Theater.

General Ira Eaker, the Allied air commander, also told Davis his 332nd had made "a magnificent showing." "They fight better against Germans in the air than they do on the ground support missions," he wrote and added that he had bigger things in mind for them.

Eaker was facing a crisis. He had been engaged in a long debate with the British over strategic bombing. British night bombing had proved inaccurate, and American daytime bombing had led to horrendous losses from enemy fighters. In February alone 114 bombers and 1,000 crewmen had gone down. More than three hundred men were lost in a single raid over Ploesti [oil fields in Rumania]; sixty bombers and six hundred men perished in one raid over Germany.

One problem was that England-based Spitfire escorts had a short range and could barely deliver the bombers across the Channel before abandoning them to the Messerschmidts. The P-47s had somewhat better range, but still couldn't escort far into Germany. The promised P-51, with a range of almost a thousand miles, could be the answer.

But that led to another debate, over deployment. The chief of the U.S. fighter Groups, Major General Frank O'D. Hunter, argued that the fighters should fly ahead of the bombers, sweeping enemy planes from the skies, which would give the fighter pilots opportunities for more glory. But Eaker protested that it would also leave the bombers to face the enemy alone; he insisted that the fighters stay with the bombers at all costs. Hunter was sent home to the States.

The 332nd could help solve Eaker's problem. "They were wasting three squadrons," complained Jackson. "We had seen one German Junkers 88 bomber the whole time we were over there." But could Negroes stand the intense cold of high altitude flying?

With his own career on the line, Eaker called Davis to his headquarters and told him what he needed.

"Needless to say," wrote Davis, "I jumped at the chance."

Along with the Anzio triumph, this was the other most important development in the history of the 'black air force.' So on May 31, the 332nd left the 12th Air Force and joined the 15th Strategic Air Force. "Morale," Davis says, "was soaring."

Briggs and Palmer celebrated with one last burst of hubris. Palmer described it:

> On our last mission before transferring, I said, "Johnny, don't forget to give them a good closing when we come in." We were going to "cut the grass" on the field — we got down about two or three feet off the ground and flew the length of the field. I was almost scratching his fuselage with my wingtip.
>
> At the end of the field there was a fence about eight feet tall. All of a sudden Johnny looks over to verify that I'm in real tight, gives the old signal, and jerks his plane up. That's rough on the guy that's flying his wing. But I hung with him. When he pulled it up, I pulled it up. Back down on the ground, I said, "Johnny, why'd you jerk it like that?"
>
> He said, "You know how close we came to hitting that wall?"

Davis, who had been watching the exhibition, just shook his head.

"No question about it," Palmer declared, "the 100th was the best squadron in the Group; we had real close camaraderie." As for himself, "I knew I was as good or better than any fighter pilot in the skies with me."

And Eaker wrote to Arnold: "These colored pilots have very high morale and are eager to get started."

9

15th Air Force

The P-47

June 4, the day Rome fell, the 332nd eagerly moved north and east to a new base at Ramatelli, closer to the bomber targets. It also received a new plane, the bigger, heavier Republic P-47 Thunderjet, nicknamed 'the Jug.' "It was like switching from a VW Bug to a Buick Roadmaster," Palmer said.

Purnell didn't particularly like the plane: "You needed a step ladder to get into it and a map to find the instruments. It was like trying to fly your bathtub at home."

Kirkpatrick agreed. "It was a big heavy thing. We could barely get it off the ground loaded with belly tanks and ammunition."

All the other Groups in the 15th Air Force had P-51s. The 47s were "hand-me-downs" from the 325th Group, Sheppard said, but "it was a fine hard-hitting airplane." He named his own ship 'Thor,' the god of thunder, and roared off.

The snub-nosed P-47 didn't look as sleek as the P-39, but Davis welcomed it with its eight .50-caliber machine guns, five hundred-pound bomb loads, and heavy armor protection. It could outfight, outclimb, or outdistance any other plane in the sky, he declared. And "it took a lot of beating."

Briggs agreed. The P-39 had been water-cooled, and a hit in the coolant system would knock it out. But the P-47 was air cooled. "If you got shot in the engine with small arms, no problem, it would bring you back home."

It was perfect for strafing. "Everyone who had to strafe thinks the Big Jug was best," Crockett said. "It could take a beating, you could knock off a cylinder. It had eighteen feet between landing gears [so there were no more fears of ground loops]. It had more room in the cockpit than any other airplane." He conceded it was heavy, "but the P-47 Club claims more victories than any other aircraft. It was a beautiful plane."

When the new planes arrived, they had to be tested. One volunteer was Clarence 'Lucky' Lester, recently arrived in the 100th from the States. The son of a chef, Lester grew up on Chicago's South Side, where his mother was a nurse and close fried of Janet Bragg, the aviation pioneer. He played football for West Virginia State, a black college — "I thought I was a hotshot football and basketball player in those days." After Pearl Harbor he applied for cadet training along with three other blacks and twelve whites. "I was the only one fortunate enough to pass."

In face and physique, he bore a strong resemblance to baseball star Willie Mays. The other pilots remembered him as a "cool" pilot, happy-go-lucky, who was always joking and kidding around. They called him 'the Chicago Kid' or 'Lucky.'

One thing everybody asks me is, how did I get the name Lucky? I had the name before I even sat down in a P-47. I was younger than the others in the 332nd. I was twenty-one when I got overseas in April 1944. Most of the other fliers were three or four years older, and they all treated me like a kid. They called me Lucky because I was lucky playing poker.

The name carried over into flying. I flew a total of ninety to ninety-five missions, and I never got a bullet the whole time I was in combat and never had an accident. I did have a couple of close calls, however. I was just plain lucky.

Those days weren't like it is today, where you go up in a two-seater and learn to fly with the instructor in back with dual controls. In those days you sat down and read what they called a TO, or Tech Order, which told you how the airplane flew. You memorized where all the instruments were, and the instructor gave you a written test: "What would you do if this happened? What would you do if that happened?" Then they put you in the cockpit, blindfolded you, and said, "Touch the air speed indicator," or "Touch the oil gauge." That was your orientation. Then they put you in a parachute and off you would go — it was sort of survival of the fittest. I'd never been in the P-47 before, had no idea of what it was like, but away I went.

You didn't have a lot of power in those planes, but I was doing pretty well until I tried to do ten loops in a row. I executed about eight or nine loops, but when I tried to fly through the next one, I knew I wasn't going to make it. The airplane began to shudder going straight up and did a hammerhead stall. It slid back down tail-first, then flipped over like a hammer striking a nail and started spinning upside down. In the normal spin, you apply the rudder opposite to the direction of the spin, but that doesn't work when the plane is upside down. In fact, they really don't teach you how to get out of an upside-down spin.

The standard operating procedure is, if you get below five thousand feet and you don't have the plane under control, you are supposed to bail out. So here I was in this horrible maneuver — I had never seen anything like it in my life. The instruments were going crazy, some of them had actually broken. I said, "Well, I'm past my five thousand feet, it's time to get out."

I reached up to pull the T-handle, which was supposed to release the canopy. I pulled, and nothing happened — the T came out in my hand. So I unbuttoned my seat belt, braced myself against the instrument panel, and tried to open it by hand. I was upside down, with everything spinning wildly, and I couldn't get the canopy open more than a couple inches.

All of a sudden it dawned on me that I wasn't bouncing off my head any more, I wasn't pulling any more negative G's. I said to myself, "Centrifugal force must be taking over."[1] The plane was in a tight spiral, but it was a controlled maneuver. It could be that just changing my position changed the flight characteristics enough to flip it over; we just don't know.

Anyway, I sat back down and started pulling the plane out of the spiral. I pulled out at about five hundred feet off the ground, directly over the field, and came roaring across the runway at about three hundred miles per hour. I pulled up, came around, and made a routine landing. They all said, "That was some kind of maneuver we were watching! What was that?"

I said, "Oh, that was just your usual hammerhead stall."

Later on I told my tentmate what had happened. He said, "Boy, you're just as lucky as ever, aren't you?"

One P-47 was donated by students of Chicago's St. Alphonsus Catholic school, who raised seventy-five thousand dollars to buy it. "Since I was from Chicago, the obvious thing was to give that airplane to me, Lucky Lester. I wrote my mother and told her, and she called the school and told them her son was flying it. They ended up giving out souvenir postcards with my picture and the airplane they had bought. I still have a postcard in my scrapbook.

Crockett recalled, "Earl Sherrod challenged Lester to a dogfight, and Lester ran him all over the skies. Sherrod came down pulling his jacket over his head, because everyone was watching them. Lester licked him real good."

One of the latest replacements with the 302nd was Frank Pollard, the former jazz musician. He had been with the squadron only three weeks when he was killed in transition training to the P-47.

On June 2, the 332nd suffered another death. It hit Bill Melton especially hard. "A very dear friend of mine, Chubby Taylor, had to bail out of his airplane when it caught fire. When they found him later, his 'chute had never opened."

On June 9 – three days after the Normandy invasion and five after the fall of Rome – the 332nd flew its first top cover mission. With the restricted range of the P-47, the unit could not accompany the bombers on their long-range bomb runs over Europe. "We had trouble getting much past the Po Valley," Red Jackson remembered. So they turned the handicap to an advantage.

"The Germans had found out very early that the P-51s and P-38s were escorting the bombers deep into Germany, but we had neglected the short hops." The Luftwaffe expected that, close to home, the bombers would have no fighter cover. Jackson decided to surprise them.

> The very first mission we were out on we were lucky. I saw about thirty 109s coming down from my right. They weren't looking for us, they were looking for nice pickings on the bombers, and we had forty American P-47s just sitting there waiting for them. They started attacking the bombers the very moment we saw them. Skipper [Davis] called, "Go get them," and the 332nd waded into the fight.

"The Germans didn't know who we were because we wore goggles," Sheppard smiled. "If they had, we might have given them the cultural shock of their lives."

Jackson was flying with his wingman, Chubby Green. "He was one of the youngest pilots, but an excellent pilot. A pilot depends on his wingman to protect his tail, and he'd stay right on my flank." Davis also insisted on Green for his own wingman whenever he flew with the 302nd. Jackson once asked Green what his biggest aspiration in life was. "To be the best damn pilot in the world," Chubby replied.

As soon as Jackson heard, "Go get 'em," he said, "I peeled off with Green following and fell in behind the second enemy aircraft, which was coming down in string formation. Having a faster plane, I overshot him, but Green and Bussey, who were behind me, shot him down."

Actually, Bussey said, "I shot down the airplane that was on Green's tail," but officially neither one got the victory.

Pruitt of the 302nd got the first enemy plane. His wingman, Gwynne Peirson, a new replacement, described it later in a Tuskegee Airmen newsletter. He found himself isolated without a wingman and spotted Pruitt, also alone, jockeying for position on the tail of a 109. Peirson "pulled up in line abreast off his right wingtip. I motioned him to move on the German fighter and indicated that I would cover his tail."

Pruitt's own description: A "flock" of ME 109s were attacking a flight of B-24s from five o'clock. "Each enemy made a pass at the bombers and fell into a left rolling turn. I rolled over, shoved everything forward and closed in on a 109 at 475 mph. I waited as he shallowed out of a turn, gave him a couple of two-second bursts, and watched him explode."[2]

According to Peirson, the enemy plane "poured out heavy smoke, and the pilot quickly bailed out."

Frederick Funderberg also got two victories. He spotted two ME 109s four hundred feet below and dove, guns blazing, as pieces flew off one enemy craft. Pulling up sharply, he found two more 109s heading toward him. He pointed his nose straight into them and fired a burst at one, which exploded.

Jackson, meanwhile, pulled out of his dive and started to climb. "I noticed a 109 headed straight down at me, blazing away with all his guns. My plane seemed to be dragging on the climb, and I realized I hadn't dropped my wing tanks. Probably, in the busyness of combat I hadn't pulled both release pulls. A full tank weighed me down and gave me trouble in the first encounter." When he finally remembered the tanks, they still refused to come off, so Red applied a water booster for extra speed and pulled away.

Below him were the Alps with a layer of clouds on their peaks, so he headed for the safety of the clouds and finally shook off his tanks. "As I broke through the clouds, I found my pursuer waiting to shoot me down. He made a pass at me, but somehow he missed, and I fell in behind him. He began weaving from side to side, but every time he turned, I gave him a short burst of fire. On the fourth burst, he started to smoke, and his canopy came off in two pieces." The pilot jumped, and Jackson circled him until he suddenly realized he was directly over an enemy airfield. "I dove down on the deck and headed for the Adriatic Sea." Once over water, he climbed back to altitude and cruised home "happy over my victory."

The 332nd lost one man, Cornelius Rogers, who never made it back.

As the victorious pilots roared back over their field, a technical representative from Republic was briefing the Air Force brass on the P-47. Pruitt's crew chief, Staff Sergeant Samuel Jacobs, recalled: "I remember the major standing atop a munitions carrier telling us 'boys' all about the 'flying bathtub' and how it should never be slow rolled below a thousand feet due to its excessive weight. No sooner had he finished than the planes returned from their victorious mission. "Down on the deck, props cutting grass, came Lieutenant Pruitt and his wingman, Lee Archer, nearly touching wings. Lieutenant Pruitt pulled up into the prettiest victory roll you'd ever see, with Archer right in his pocket, as the major screamed, 'You can't do that!'"[3]

Pruitt was the 'maverick' of the 332nd, said Robert Pitts, the Group intelligence officer. "He was the only pilot that B.O. Davis, Jr. never seemed able to severely reprimand. The men on the ground and particularly his crew chief really loved the guy. He knew the guys that kept him flying would like to see a little show now and then." After the other pilots had landed, Pruitt would put on a show for them. "He would circle the base, tip his wings, go into a chandelle [a steep, climbing turn] and a couple of rolls. After about ten or fifteen minutes of beautiful flying, he would come in for a perfect three-point landing. Any other pilot would have been chewed out by the Boss. To my knowledge Davis never said one word to Pruitt. He was probably — no positively — the most popular pilot in the 332nd. Next would be Lee Archer." Besides being excellent pilots, "they both had time to give advice to a novice."[4]

"We got five victories on our first mission," Jackson said. Thereafter the Germans quickly "moved those planes out of the Po Valley and put them back deep, and we didn't see any more for quite a while after that."

The Jug just didn't have the altitude or the fuel capacity for long-range escort.

As Lester said:

> We'd meet the B-17s at twenty thousand feet, but they would invariably want to keep right on going to thirty or thirty-two thousand because the higher they got, the more protection they would have from ground defenses. Our P-47s struggled to get to twenty-eight; we could go to thirty thousand, but the plane became sluggish and started wallowing around in the sky.

And the Jug used too much fuel. It would only let us go out at the most for three hours; then we'd have to turn around and come back. Other Groups had P-38s or P-51s with longer range, and the action didn't start until after we had to turn back. We would hear the other pilots on the radio, talking about the dogfights.

According to Alexander Jefferson, the P-47's wing tanks "were guaranteed to incinerate at the slightest mishap." On his first day with the 332nd, Jefferson watched a P-47 take off. "He got thirty or forty feet and nose-dived in. The result was just one massive ball of fire."

The Jug was, however, a workhorse at the gritty but essential jobs of dive-bombing and strafing and was used to soften up southern France for the coming Allied invasion.

Meanwhile what had happened to Gleed?

I got orders to go to North Africa. I didn't know what it was all about, but when I got there, a lieutenant colonel said, "Oh, you're the new test pilot."

"What!"

"Yeah, we're badly in need of test pilots."

"Uh-uh."

"Well, you'll learn pretty fast."

They'd bring new aircraft over to Europe disassembled, then re-assemble them. We took them up and tested them, then some of our guys from the 332nd came down and ferried them back. Like an idiot, I was taking them out every night, and when the word got back to the Old Man that Gleed was living in high cotton in Casablanca, he demanded that the 15th Air Force send me back to Italy. I came on back and got instructions from the Old Man to be on the mission the following day.

On June 22, the 332nd suffered its first big tragedy when it lost three men on a strafing raid to Genoa. Tresville of the 100th led the flight. His assistant flight leader, Crockett, recalled: "We had three squadrons, twelve airplanes each — thirty-six airplanes. We hit the deck after leaving Rome and were supposed to fly fifty feet above the water or lower, with the radios off. That wasn't very smart. The water was glassy in the early morning, and, smart as the Germans were, and with their radar, you could hardly sneak up on those guys at that range anyway."

They flew in a whiteout with no horizon visible, skimming the waves, their wingtips almost touching. Each plane flew just below the man to his left until the last man was almost touching the water, which he could barely see in the fog. Bill Melton recalled: "We were all about to switch to internal tanks when the two lead planes went into the water, one right after the other." Sam Jefferson crashed into the waves and exploded. Earl Sherrod, in Crockett's third flight, was next to hit the water. He scrambled onto his wing, ripped off his 'chute, and began inflating his life raft. His buddy, C.B. Johnson, peeled off to check on Sherrod, and he too hit the waves; he couldn't open his canopy in time and was quickly swallowed by the sea. Unaware of these tragedies, the flight droned on toward the northern Italian coast and their objective, southwest of Genoa.

Crockett:

> There was a mountain range by the coast and a lot of clouds below the peaks, and we couldn't get over the mountain tops. Three or four other units tried it and never made it to the target. I looked at Tresville, and he had maps all over the cockpit. He may have been a little cocky — West Point instills in you that you must succeed, and sometimes fellows try to do that at all costs. But at some point you have to back off when the odds become too great.
>
> It should have been a target for bombers anyway rather than fighters down at sea level. Or we should have hit the coast way down southwest of Genoa. Instead, we went into the harbor and never got to the target.
>
> I turned around and headed for Corsica to refuel because we couldn't make it all the way home in the Jug. I started climbing up and pulled out my maps. My wingman said, "Why are you looking at your maps over water?" I'm a former field artilleryman and a good math student, and I held my heading 142 degrees back to Corsica for thirty minutes, and we were two of only four or six airplanes that landed at the air strip. I said, "There's nothing wrong with my navigation, kid."

Tresville himself went into the water on the flight back. Some speculated that he might have become disoriented.

With Tresville's death, his operations officer, Andrew 'Jug' Turner, took over as squadron commander of the 100th with William Mattison as Operations Officer. Crockett moved up as Mattison's assistant.

Turner, the son of a Washington minister, was a student at Howard University when he volunteered for Tuskegee. Even for a fighter pilot, Turner was small. "He was very businesslike," Crockett said, "and loved to play bridge and poker. He could turn that airplane tighter than anyone. I attributed that to his short stature."

"Tresville was an eager beaver," said Chris Newman. "He was very aggressive and outgoing, much more than Turner. Turner was conservative. Maybe that's why Tresville didn't live and Turner did."

The next day the 332nd made a strafing run to Yugoslavia, when they scored a dramatic first for the Air Force in Europe. Peirson was again flying Pruitt's wing. He was surprised that Pruitt had chosen him. Perhaps Pruitt remembered the last dogfight, when they had teamed up. Peirson thought there may also have been a second factor: "Three days earlier, June 22, I had crashed on takeoff and completely destroyed my plane. It may be that Pruitt wanted me to get back into the air before I lost my nerve." Peirson described the mission in an article in the Tuskegee Airmen *Newsletter*.

It was low altitude, fifty feet, radio silence. Intelligence said there was a large contingent of enemy troops expected in a section of Yugoslavia; we were to strafe the troops with four planes.

We became targets of heavy ground fire. Freddie Hutchins' right wing tank dropped, but his left tank wouldn't fully release. It was set on fire, with flame streaming behind him, and it caused him to lose speed, so Larry Wilkins stayed with him. Pruitt and I moved ahead at tree-top level, but we were forced off course and never made contact with the ground troops.

Pruitt was on my left, and we made a low left turn to return. Flying over Trieste we crossed over houses on the waterfront and dropped even lower to just above the water, when we spotted a German destroyer a few miles ahead, crossing directly in front of us, left to right. We were already in range of the guns and would be exposing our undersides to gunfire if we turned left or right. We would also be unable to use our own guns, and it would slow us down.

Pruitt's flight path took him just to the stern of the ship. Peirson was flying directly toward midship and opened fire: "Tracers showed my first burst was falling far short, kicking up nothing but water. The next burst struck at the ship's waterline and started to walk up the side." All Peirson could see was "black smoke and flame. I pulled back on my control stick and climbed just enough to clear the smoke" as the ship rolled over and sank in the waves.

Back in Italy he found a few jagged holes on the underside of his wings with no exit holes on the top. He theorized that they were caused by fragments of the exploding destroyer.

Later Peirson's gun-camera film "looked like Hollywood," Sheppard said. "The ship blew apart just aft of the bridge as if it had been staged in Hollywood," Sheppard whistled. Post-war divers later identified it as an Italian torpedo ship from the Nazi submarine pens in Yugoslavia. Peirson had evidently set off one of the torpedoes.

The feat was almost unprecedented. In the Pacific in 1942, the Battle of Midway had been a victory of U.S. planes over Japanese ships. But in the Mediterranean, "the Navy took a little while to confirm that an aircraft had the nerve to sink a vessel," Sheppard smiled.

It was the Group's last, and most glorious, foray in the Jugs. The most brilliant chapter in their history was about to open up with a new and even better plane.

LTC B.O. Davis
Commanding Officer

Clarence W. Allen - 99

Lee A. Archer - 302

Howard L. Baugh - 99

Charles V. Brantley

John F. Briggs - 100

Sidney P. Brooks - 99

Roscoe C. Brown - 100

Charles M. Bussey - 302

William A. 'Bill' Campbell - 99

Hannibal M. Cox - 99

Woodrow W. Crockett - 100

Alphonso Davis - 99

Charles DeBow - 301

Robert M. Deiz - 99

Elwood T. Driver - 99

Charles W. Dryden - 99

Joseph D. Elsberry - 301/99

James H. Fisher - 301

Willie H. Fuller - 99

Edward C. Gleed - 301/302

George E. Gray - 99

Charles B. 'Buster' Hall- 99

George J. Iles - 99

Lt. Melvin T. Jackson - 302

Daniel 'Chappie' James, Jr. - 477

Clarence C. Jamison - 99

Alexander Jefferson - 99

Elmer D. Jones
C.O. AAF Service Det.-99

Felix J. Kirkpatrick, Jr. - 302

James B. Knighten - 99

Erwin B. Lawrence - 99

Clarence D. 'Lucky' Lester - 100

Andrew D. Marshall

Richard D. Macon - 99

James L. McCullin - 99

Armour G. McDaniel - 301

Charles E. McGee - 302

Christopher W. Newman - 99

Walter J. Palmer - 100

Wendell O. Pruitt - 302

Louis R. Purnell - 99

Lee Rayford - 99

George S. 'Spanky' Roberts - 99

John W. Rogers - 99

C.C. Robinson - 99

Mac Ross - 332

Harry A. Sheppard - 302

Graham Smith - 99

Edward Thomas - 99

William R. Thompson
Armament Officer

Edward L. Toppins - 99

Andrew D. 'Jug' Turner - 100

Spann Watson- 99

Luke J. Weathers - 302

James Wiley - 99

Robert W. 'Bob' Williams - 100

Bertram W. Wilson, Jr. - 100

Class 42E was perhaps the smallest AAF class ever to graduate. *(back)* Lee Rayford, George L. Knox; *(front)* James B. Knighten, Sherman W. White.

Class 42I members: *(l. to r.)* Nathaniel M. Hill, Marshall S. Cabiness, Herman A. 'Ace' Lawson (99), William T. Mattison (100), John A. Gibson (99), Elwood T. Driver (99), Price D. Rice, and Andrew D. 'Jug' Turner (100).

Class 42H members: *(standing)* John H. Morgan (99), Richard C, Ceasar, Edward L. Toppins (99), Robert W. Deiz (99), Joseph D. Elsberry (301); *(kneeling)* Samuel M. Bruce (99), Wilmore R. Leonard, James L. McCullin (99), Henry Perry (99).

Members of Class 42K, Tuskegee AAB. *(l. to r. top)*: Milton T. 'Baby' Hall, Robert B. Tresville (100), Peter C. Veerwayne, Wendell O. Pruitt (302), Romeo M. Williams; (bottom): Edward C. Gleed (302), Richard O. Pullum, William W. 'Wild Bill' Walker.

(l. to r. top): William R. Melton, Jr. (302), Maurice R. Page (100), Lowell C. Steward (100), Jack D. Holsclaw (100), and Buddy Lockett (100).

(l. to r.): Samuel Lynn, Fredrick D. Funderburg, and Othel Dickson.

The original 99th Fighter Squadron: *(l. to r. bottom)* Herbert E. Carter, Lee Rayford, George S. Roberts, Commanding Officer Col. B.O. Davis, Jr., Lemuel R. Custis, Clarence C. Jamison, and Charles B. Hall; *(middle)* Walter E. Lawson, Spann Watson, Allan Lane, Paul G. Mitchell, Leon Roberts, John Rogers, Louis Purnell, James T. Wiley, and Graham Smith; *(top)* Willie Ashley, Charles Dryden, Erwin B. Lawrence, William A. Campbell, Willie H. Fuller, Richard Davis, Sidney Brooks, Sherman W. White, and Richard R. Bolling. Absent from photo - James B. Knighten.

Class 42, 99th Fighter Squadron pilots prior to their departure for North Africa in 1943. *(l. to r. bottm)*: Charles B. Hall, George R. Bolling, Herbert V. Clark; *(middle):* Paul G. Mitchell, Spann Watson, Willie Ashley, Louis R. Purnell, Erwin B. Lawrence; (top): Allen Lane, Graham Smith, William A. Campbell, Faythe McGinnis.

99th in Italy, *(standing)*: Herber C. Houston, William N. Alsbrook, Wilson V. Eagleson, Charles P. Bailey, George S. Roberts, Alva N. Temple, George E. Gray, Clarence W. Dart; (kneeling); Clarence Jamison, Charles W. Tate, Henry B. 'Herky' Perry, and Leonard M. 'Black' Jackson.

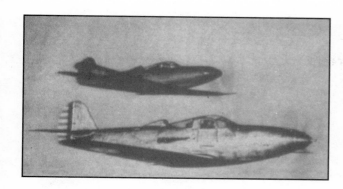

P-39

P-40

P-47

The B-17 (*l.*) and B-24 (*r.*), both carry markings of the 5th Wing, 15thAAF, the bombers escorted by the Red Tails.

P-51

Spitfire

ME 109

FW 109

ME 262

301st pilots enjoying a bit of R&R. (*l to r*) Carl B. Carey, Charles L. White, James H. Fischer, Samuel L. Washington.

10

Walterboro

Meanwhile the returning veterans of the 99th were engaged in another war, a war at home. It was actually a civil war between two armies of American soldiers, each of which had sworn to die for the ideal of America as it saw it. Neither army was prepared to give quarter. But, said Spann Watson, "in the military, we started integration right up there in Selfridge."

After the 332nd left for overseas, the base continued to give advanced training for the new men coming out of the pipeline from Tuskegee. The training squadron was commanded by Lieutenant Colonel Charles Gayle, a white officer, and included Clarence Jamison, Charles Dryden, Bill Campbell, James Wiley, Ghost Lawson, and Spann Watson.

Watson had applied for the Eagle Squadron, the all-white unit of American volunteers in the Royal Air Force." I thought they would integrate one black, but they just ridiculed me, and that was that."

The squadron was soon joined by the cadre for a proposed new unit, the all-black 477th Bomber Group. It would include a future four-star general, Daniel 'Chappie' James; a future Secretary of Transportation under Gerald Ford, William 'Bump' Coleman; a future mayor of Detroit, Coleman Young; and a future mayor of Los Angeles, Tom Bradley.

The 332nd's old nemesis, Colonel Selway, commanded the Group. Wiley remembered him as "a pompous person, always surrounded by his white commanders. All of us black guys were just 'crew members.'" The base commander, Colonel William Boyd, was also white. Major General Frank O'D. Hunter, who had lost a policy struggle to Ira Eaker in Europe, had been sent home to command the First Air Force, the next echelon above Boyd.

There were several irritants at Selfridge. For instance, black officers were not allowed to occupy officer's housing on base. But the main battle was the same one the 332nd had fought — the Officers' Club.

Although Army regulations said all Officers' Clubs must open their doors to any officer on base, Selway ruled that the Club was for whites only and told the blacks to wait until a separate club was built for them.

Said Wiley: "The Officers' Club, Lufberry Hall, was the usual plush Officers' Club. But we were told to stay out."

Our so-called club was a room at the end of our barracks with a pool table and a bar. Most of the guys were putting their lives on the line, or had already put our lives on the line, and we said, to hell with this." Foreshadowing the civil right sit-ins of the 1960s, the black officers decided to go to the white club anyway.

Dryden:

> On New Year's Eve 1943, I was on leave in Detroit with my wife when a group of three pilots went to the main Club — they thought there would be more guys, but a lot of them chickened out. The three were ordered not to come back. It would be unwise for the same ones to go back and disobey a direct order in time of war.
>
> That would be tantamount to treason.
>
> The next night some others of us decided to try again.

That morning on the flight line when I was suiting up to fly, Lieutenant Colonel Gayle told me, "I hope you understand that, as the ranking first lieutenant, I expect you to keep these guys in line and make them understand Army policy."

I said, "Yes, sir."

That night we decided we would go to a movie, and when it was over, we'd amble over to the Club and go for a drink or two so it wouldn't look like a conspiracy. But when I looked round, only two other guys were going in the door with me. Colonel Gayle and Colonel Boyd, the base commander, were the first two persons I saw inside the door. Colonel Gayle's face turned as red as a beet, and he said, "Goddam it, I thought you understood."

I said, "I understood, but I don't agree. It's the Officers' Club, and we're officers." We were "guard-house lawyers," and we knew Army Regulation 210-10, paragraph 19-C, which obligated us to support the Officer's Club. That was pretty clear.

Colonel Gayle almost had a fit. "You leave this club right now!" It was a direct order, so we left.

The next night a different group did the same thing.

Jamison recalled:

I had flown sixty-seven missions in combat, I was a captain, and I think I was the senior black officer on the base. I'd go over to the Club with the others, and a white captain would say, "You can't come in." He was embarrassed because I'd been overseas getting my butt shot at. But we went on in anyway, stood around a while, and then left. At least we'd made the point. We did that for two or three nights.

The Air Force brass, nervous about race riots in nearby Detroit, charged that the whole thing was communist-inspired. Bill Campbell denied it: "Nothing could be further from the truth. The problems we had were strictly racial."

When the Pentagon got wind of the crisis, Dryden said, "The Inspector General from Washington arrived to interrogate us — General B.O. Davis, Sr. spent twenty to thirty minutes with me. I was thrilled to get a chance to spill my guts." About a week or

two later, both Colonel Boyd and Lieutenant Colonel Gayle
were relieved from command. We thought we'd won a victory."

However, General Hunter called the officers to an assem-
bly. An aide called "Attention!" and down the aisle strode
Hunter, in a black mustache and trailed by his entourage.
"Gentlemen," he snapped:

> This is *my* airfield. As long as I am commander of First Air
> Force, there will be no racial mixing at any post under my
> command. There is *no* racial problem at this base, and there
> will *be* none.
>
> You're not ready — colored officers are not qualified to
> lead anyone. The policy of the Army is the same as the rest of
> the country, and that policy will be enforced to the letter. Are
> there any questions? If there are any questions, I will deal
> with the man personally!

"We were thunderstruck," said Alexander Jefferson, a brand
new second lieutenant who had just arrived from Tuskegee. "He
stood there and looked at us, and we looked at each other." His
aide called "Attention!" again, all snapped to their feet, and
Hunter strode out of the hall with his aides in tow.

"We black officers were immediately restricted to the base.
They locked the gates, cut off the radios, phones, and all
communications."

Dryden:

> Two days later the fighter pilots were exiled by train at
> night. The black press and our relatives didn't know where we
> were going. *We* didn't know either. We crossed into Canada,
> where we saw a couple of stations with French names, then
> headed down the Mohawk Valley, through New Jersey and
> Washington, D.C., and raced through Virginia, North Caro-
> lina, and South Carolina. The next day we looked out the train
> windows and saw Carolina pines and GIs with carbines stand-
> ing every hundred feet on both sides of the train.
>
> We didn't know what the hell was going to happen. The
> Japanese Nisei had been interned in California; we thought
> we might be interned too. As it turned out, it was an air base
> far from public scrutiny or attention.

They were in Walterboro, South Carolina.

Meanwhile, the 477th had been exiled to Godman Field, Kentucky, outside Fort Knox, the Army's tank school.

Campbell noted wryly: "You can draw your own conclusion why. Some people thought, 'We'll get them down there where they keep blacks in their place.' That was one of the conjectures, and it makes sense."

Dryden:

> In later years, I found out General Arnold wanted to deploy the outfit to the island of Antigua in the Caribbean so we would be far from the black press, although that fell through.[1]
>
> All our planes had been flown down from Selfridge — none of us was allowed to ferry the planes. We lived in beat-up World War I barracks.
>
> We immediately tried to integrate the theater. There was a rope down the middle, and the guys cut the rope and 'checker-boarded' the theater, some sitting here, some there. The theater manager, a tech sergeant, refused to start the film until the officer of the day ordered us all out, and we went back to the barracks.
>
> The base commander told us in no uncertain terms that he was going to enforce the segregation laws. I guess we acquiesced with the letter of the law, but the spirit of the law got me in trouble.

Campbell:

> By that time the Army had come out with a regulation that you couldn't segregate government facilities by race, so the white officers went down town and formed clubs. They built a nice club for us about a mile from the base, where there wasn't much chance for us to come in contact with whites. I stayed there about two and a half months and volunteered to go back overseas.

Dryden:

> To me, the low point was seeing German prisoners of war who could use the white side of the PX cafeteria while we

couldn't. I was so furious, I lost my self-control; I was going to show these crackers I could fly.

The next day I demonstrated how to attack a machine gun tower. There was a water tower in town about ten stories high, and our flight path took us right across the home of the mayor of the city. You can imagine a quiet sleepy Sunday morning with four P-39s at full power roaring across town.

One of Dryden's students, Dick Macon, also buzzed the church, for good measure.

Another student, Alexander Jefferson, was also on the 'bombing' run. He remembered Dryden as "an absolutely fantastic guy, very out-going with a dynamic personality, and a great instructor." Jefferson had arrived in Tuskegee in April 1943.

I was a "big" 117 pounds. You had to be 118 to be accepted. The guys at the recruiting center told me to go downstairs, buy some bananas, eat all I could, drink some water, and come back. I did. I weighed in at a little over 118.

I think there were ninety fellows originally in the class. When we finished, there were about twenty-five. I don't remember much about primary training except getting up, running, and, oh, those pushups. I remember soloing, bouncing about five or six times as I landed, scared to death. Anybody who says he is not scared on that first solo is a damn liar.

I can say that I successfully ground-looped everything I flew up to the P-40. Anybody who ground-looped in primary was out; by some miracle or other, I stayed in. Man, they check-rode me regularly. I even had the infamous MacGoon check-ride me. It was well known that a check-ride by MacGoon was the end of your flying career. It was one hell of a check-ride, but I miraculously survived.

I went to Selfridge in January 1944, and was on the train to Walterboro. I was also on the flight that buzzed the tower. The whole class was in on it. Dryden got court-martialled. Why I didn't get court-martialled, I'll never know. One classmate, MacIvers, was given a dishonorable discharge — why he was selected to be an example is not clear. I went overseas the next week.[2]

Dryden:

I was given a general court martial and dismissed from the Service. But I was granted a second trial because my rights had been violated when one member of the court was heard to say they were going to throw the book at me, which is a prejudicial statement.

After the court martial, Major Campbell, one of my buddies, was seeking volunteers to join the 477th to be sent to the Pacific. I was so fed up with the South and Jim Crow, I said, "Take me! Please!"

Spann Watson remained an instructor with three or four other blacks and twenty-three to twenty-four whites.

The best training the fighter pilots ever got, they got at Walterboro. We put aside the race battles and put out good pilots. We had some of the most sincere people. I didn't see any sloughing off in training black people for combat. Lieutenant Colonel Joe R. Williams, director of flight training, turned out to be a great guy. The only thing, they asked us not to 'brace' the white cadets [that is, to hold them at attention].

Hugh White, Carl Ellis, 'Mr. Death' [John Whitehead], Yenworth Whitney were the best in my flight. You could do anything with them. Let me pick four or five pilots, give them a hundred hours in a P-47, I'll lead 'em, and I'll compete with you in everything — dogfight, formation flying, anything!

Whitney looked like a little mouse, looked like he was about seventeen. But no matter what I did to confuse him and throw him off, he would end up sitting on my wing like a mouse, looking right at me.

White had one of the most spectacular women. This is something that's never been written about. The great Tuskegee experiment brought the most sensational black women from everywhere in the country, looking for husbands. We had jumped in pay from $21 to $250 a month, with esteem, respect, and beautiful uniforms. The most beautiful, most educated women anywhere flooded Walterboro. No matter where you'd go, you'd see one of these outstanding women, most of them college girls. From New York, Chicago, Los Angeles, you name it, they found out about Tuskegee.

It turned the social structure around. Before that, doctors and lawyers had had a monopoly on the best-looking women in black society.

Roscoe Brown, from Washington, D.C., arrived at Walterboro in June.

My father was well known. He was a member of Roosevelt's 'black cabinet,' in charge of health for blacks all over the country. It made me want to work harder to be better than my old man. As a child, on Sundays we'd frequently go to the Washington airport to watch the planes take off and land. My father had a little clout, so finally I said to him, "I want to ride in one of those planes."

He said, "Well, you know, they don't allow blacks in planes down here." But I kept after him and kept after him until one day he decided to try a gambit. He was light-skinned, so he told us to keep our mouths closed and told one of the officers, "I work for the government, and these are children of French West African diplomats, and they'd like to ride in an airplane." That was my first ride in a plane. After that, that's all I wanted to do.

I went to the Smithsonian with my parents after it had just hung Lindbergh's plane, the "Spirit of St. Louis." I could just visualize myself flying it and imagine what this man did in this small airplane. He wrote a book called *We* about the trip, and I got that book and read every page of it about three times. By the time I finished, I almost knew how to fly.

When I graduated from Springfield College in Massachusetts in 1943, I was valedictorian of my class and had earned a lieutenant's commission in the infantry through the civilian military training corps. But the black press had so elevated the Tuskegee experience that every black man wanted to be a Tuskegee Airman. I resigned my infantry commission and started out as an aviation cadet.

We went to Keesler Field, Mississippi for pre-flight training. The base had a black side and a white side, but many of us from the North weren't accustomed to segregation, and we wandered into the white PX and got cussed out. We raised a little hell about it — we were smart asses and gave them a little mouth about being American citizens.

From Keesler we went to Tuskegee. We started with about forty or fifty cadets, and when we graduated, I think our class was down to twenty-four or twenty-five.

I had just graduated with my wings in March 1944, and was on a bus going from Montgomery to Tuskegee. We drove along about ten to fifteen miles before the driver stopped the bus and said, "Lieutenant, the colored must sit in the back."

I said, "Now, I'm going to fight a war for democracy and freedom in a few weeks, and I'm going to sit right here."

He said, "I'm going to have to call the state troopers and take you off."

I said, "Well, you can do what you want to do. I'm sitting here. I really can't fight a war sitting in jail." So I sat there another ten minutes, and finally he just drove the bus away.

One class behind Brown were Henry Peoples, Hannibal Cox, and White. Watson recalled Peoples: "Henry Peoples was a bad guy, a terrible person. He was a strange guy. The first cadets in Tuskegee were clean cut and eager; later on others came in. No matter what you tried to do, playing basketball or anything, Henry Peoples would hurt you."

Hannibal Cox was a Chicagoan whose parents wanted him to be a doctor, but all he wanted to do was fly. "He was one of those white/black people," Watson said. "But he was fervently black: 'Look, I'm not trying to pass as a white person, I'm a black person. Don't tread on me.' He was another one who had one of the most beautiful wives."

Hannibal's best friend at Tuskegee was Hugh J. White. "Hugh was as dark as I was light; he was the pepper of our pepper-and-salt team. We were inseparable."

Cox was "flamboyant and fun-loving," fellow cadet George Iles said. On leave in Atlanta, Iles laughed, Cox hailed a cab and climbed in, followed by White and Iles. The driver balked. "Ah, let 'em in," Hannibal said with a grand wave of his hand. The others piled in, and the driver obediently drove away.

Cox, nicknamed 'White Folks,' related the following:

> During our advanced cadet program, some of us took a bus from Tuskegee to Eglin Air Force Base, Florida. After four hours on the road, we were hungry as heck, so we stopped the bus and said, "Let's get some sandwiches."
>
> I said, "Man, you know we can't go in there."
>
> Hugh said, "Well, White Folks, you're going to get our sandwiches for us. You go in there and play your role; tell them you've got some niggers out here that you've got to feed."

I said, "OK, fellows." I went in and said, "Ma'am, I got some niggers out here, and they're hungry as heck."

The lady said, "Son, I understand the trouble you've got with these boys, and I'll fix them up." So she fixed up nineteen fabulous bags.

I said, "Lady, I thank you, and the niggers out there thank you."

When I got to the door of the bus, Hugh was waiting for me and hauled off and hit me upside the head and knocked me down the steps. As I got up, I said, "Hugh, why'd you hit me?"

He said, "Hannibal, you played the role just right. But you said 'nigger' one time too many."

Cox's classmate was Earl Lane from Cleveland, nicknamed Squirrel by the others. He was happy, fun-loving, popular, "and he was willing to take chances," Iles said.

Iles himself graduated a month later, in May, along with Charles Brantley, Bob Williams, and Bertram Wilson.

A CPT grad, Iles had started out a month behind the others, but was promoted into their class because he had already had CPT. "He was a brain man," Watson said. "A gentleman's gentleman," Sheppard called him. Quiet and studious, Iles was elected class captain.

His roommate, Bobby Williams came from a well-to-do family from Ottumwa, Iowa; Bob, his father and brother all had pilot's licenses and flew their own family plane. Williams volunteered for the Air Corps right after Pearl Harbor but was told, "The Air Corps don't take niggers." So he and his brother hopped in their convertible and drove to California to work as electric arc welders building Liberty ships until Bob finally got the call to Tuskegee. He drove up in his convertible to the envious stares of the other cadets – he was the only cadet in camp with his own car. He was "very sincere, studious, and really wanted to be a soldier," Iles said. "Everything he did, he attacked with the desire to be the best."

Bertram Wilson, was a New York pre-med student and "a very quiet guy," according to Iles, "but recognized by all as an excellent flier."

Wilson's grade school teacher recalled the twelve-year-old attending an assembly to hear President Franklin Roosevelt, but Bert ignored the famous guest. Instead, he spread his arms like a plane and "flew" out of the auditorium.

At Tuskegee, Wilson shrugged at the racial restrictions. "We knew what we were up against. You had to conform, so you conformed. It pisses you off, but it doesn't make you bitter — it doesn't make *me* bitter, anyway." Laughing at some of the "stupid" rules helped get him through. "Some said, 'Heh, we're not going to take this crap.' They were the ones that washed out."

Wilson found the black upperclassmen tougher than the white instructors. They were "really bastards," he recalled, "but they didn't want you to screw up. You hated their guts. But you learned the hard way."

Bert laughed that he had never flown anything more than a broomstick before. Yet he soloed before Williams and liked to rib Bobby about it.

Brantley was Wilson's roommate. "He was always a happy-go-lucky guy, crazy as hell."

Bert said:

> Everything was funny to him. I remember he had athletes' foot, and the doctor gave him some medicine. I had jock itch. He said, "If this stuff works for my feet, it should work for you too." Like a damn fool, I tried it on!
>
> One time he loaned me his parachute because mine was wet. I was flying a Stearman and doing something over the school that I shouldn't have been doing. My engine started messing up, and I said I was going to bail out. I got out on the wing and thought, "Hell, this isn't my parachute." I got back in and nursed the thing back to base.

Three months behind them was Jimmy Fischer, a tall, skinny youngster from Stoughton, Massachusetts, who had been waiting since Pearl Harbor to get into the war.

> I was kind of naive about segregation. There were only four or five black kids in my high school, so we really didn't catch any hell. My father disappeared when I was a baby, and I have no recollection of him. My grandfather had a big farm,

but he got wiped out in the Depression. When I was about
four years old, I got TB and was in a hospital for four or five
years; by the time I got out, I was in the third grade, and the
farm was gone.

I was seventeen on December 7, 1941. As soon as I graduated that June, I went right off, all starry-eyed, to join the
Army Air Force. That's when I first ran into segregation.
Twenty guys went over to the local Army field for an interview, and they called us in alphabetical order, but when they
got to me, they skipped over me. The guy told me, "I can't
recruit you. There aren't any Negroes in the Air Corps."

When the new 99th Squadron was being formed, I sent my
application to Washington and waited and waited but never
heard anything. Finally the draft board sent me to Fort
Devens, where a colonel, a doctor, typed on my record:
"Qualified, aviation cadet." The other officer looked right
at it and stamped "Infantry" on it. And that's where they sent
me. I did a lot of bitching, and eight months later I finally got
into the Air Force. You had to have two years of college to go
in, but if you could pass an exam, they'd send you to Tuskegee Institute for a six-month university program and flight
training.

Meanwhile, Harry Sheppard's kid brother, Herb, was awaiting assignment to Tuskegee:

Harry is six and a half years older; he was my role model.

I went to vocational school; I wanted to be a plumber in
the worst way. I didn't want to be a doctor or lawyer. I said,
"Plumbers are making more than the doctors are."

We had a teacher who preached to us every day: "You
guys ought to get that vinegar out of your blood and do
something for your country." Every minute. He talked us
all into joining up, but he stayed back — he was too old. I
couldn't wait to go in. Really. I enlisted in the Army as soon as
I graduated in June 1942, with the intention of going into the
Air Corps.

I had a good infantry basic — map reading, weapons —
and I had been to Ft. Sill, the Artillery School. I was in ordnance, at Aberdeen Proving Grounds, when they opened the
quota [for ground forces to apply for cadet training]. I didn't
have a college degree, but they were doing it on an exam

basis, and they called me to go to Keesler Field in Mississippi, the pool they were drawing from for Tuskegee. I figured I was going to wind up in Harry's outfit.

In April 1944, we were just set to go to primary and Hap Arnold sent out a telegram that the Air Corps had not lost as many men as they anticipated and thanked everyone. They wiped us out and sent us back to the ground forces.

We were all crying.

I got orders to go to Italy as replacement for the 370th Infantry in the 92nd Division.

Meantime, training at Walterboro proceeded. A black P-47 student with a white instructor collided with a B-24. It wasn't the student's fault, Watson said, "but it brought up the whole racial thing about blacks flying. The next day the whole Group of B-24s flew over Walterboro with their flaps and wheels down, they knew their man had made a big mistake. The next day our squadron passed over their Group."

If training on base was harmonious, conditions off-base were not. Macon was chatting at a bus stop with a white sergeant from Brooklyn, and when the bus pulled up, they sat down together, still talking. A white man behind them asked the sergeant what he was doing sitting with a colored. In reply, the sergeant, a boxer, smashed the man's face, knocking him into the aisle. While women screamed, the man quietly picked himself up, resumed his seat, and the bus drove off without a word from the driver.

Another incident did not turn out so fortunate, Watson said:

A white bus driver slapped a black female on the bus to the base, and a black guy jumped up with a knife and put it to the driver's throat. They arrested the man and tried him that night and sent him to prison for a year and a day, and the goddam post commander let him go.

Another man refused to go to the back of the bus, the white police hit him on the head and blinded him. There was almost a sitdown strike the next couple of days. All the black folks said, "This can't go on, this kind of justice."

Watson himself was in the middle of a racial fight that could have been tragic.

During Christmas holiday 1944, I went to a Chevrolet dealership and asked to have a flat fixed. The black flunky said, "Sure, leave it, come back tomorrow."

I went back every day for about four days, but it was never ready. Finally, I said, "To hell with the damn thing, all you're doing is lying. Give me my damn tire back."

Some little short stumpy dude was standing by, said, "Who are those remarks directed to?"

"I was talking to him, but it could just as easily be you."

He hit me right in the mouth. The President himself isn't going to hit me in the mouth, so I floored him. He got up, and I floored him again − I beat the hell out of him. Then everyone in the shop jumped over the counter and rushed me, swinging at me with a long hose. I knocked one of them backward.

I found some MPs and told them I was having some trouble.

With that, two of them jumped down from their jeep and sent the driver to the base for help. The MPs said, "Here they come now. Lieutenant, you just can't talk back to them. No matter what they say to you, don't answer."

I said, "Look, this is not going to be a situation where one black man, usually in shackles, is shot dead and they said he was trying to escape. You leave your holsters open; when the time comes, I'll get 'em, you won't have to."

The city cops came, and the state cops, and the little guy who had the battered face, and a mob developed. They were calling me all kinds of names. The greatest hatred I ever saw was on the faces of these little scrawny state police. They'd snap their heads back and forth like goddam rattlesnakes.

By this time more MPs from the base had arrived. The MP officer was a redneck with a long-barreled gun, a private weapon, that stuck out of his holster half-way down to his knee. He went to the white folks and asked them what happened. They said this nigger had beaten up the mayor of the town for no reason. Then he came over to me, and I told him what happened. He said, "That ain't what they say."

I said, "You're a mobster like the rest of them. I don't want to talk to you at all."

The deputy base commander, Colonel Lockwood, arrived. He came straight to me and told the MP officer, "I'm in command now. You follow my orders. Watson, let's go see if we can reason with these people. I'll do the talking."

We started over to the dealership with the mob behind us. Everyone started screaming, "Don't let that nigger in here."

Lockwood said, "OK, Watson, stand here, I'll go in and see what I can do." He came back, said, "We can't deal with them. I'm going to give you six or eight police. Get your car and go straight to the base and don't go off until I tell you."

Lockwood said, "Of course you're going to be transferred. Where do you want to go? Do you want to go back overseas with the fighter Group?"

"Not particularly."

So I went to the 477th.

Meantime, in July, Cox, Peoples and their class had received orders to join the 332nd. Cox described it:

I was nineteen years old when sixteen of us arrived by bus in a small town in South Carolina, where we were to board a train to our port of embarkation. We were in uniform, outfitted with field packs and armed with .45 automatics, and walked into a sandwich shop to buy sandwiches and soft drinks. As we walked in, the woman behind the counter screamed, "My God! The niggers are attacking our restaurant." We were dumbfounded.

A sailor jumped up from a booth and marched toward us screaming, "You niggers get the hell out of here!" One of our lieutenants, Henry Peoples, told him to "watch his mouth," that he was talking to officers of the U.S. Army. The sailor responded that we were a bunch of impostors; he had never seen nigger officers. He knew niggers were not pilots, and any nigger that carried a gun in that town was strung up. He said that was going to happen to us that night.

Peoples took up the narrative:

Vincent Mitchell from Mt. Clemens, Michigan, hit the Navy blue. He was the last guy in the world you would expect to do such a thing. He was the quiet, gentle type, besides, he was awkward, he wasn't exactly hung together right. He knocked the Navy clear over the counter. The joker behind the counter sticks his head up and Mt. Clemens laid a right on him like Joe Louis. Right from the shoulder. The Navy had been sunk; he did not rise again.

We paid for our beer and departed, leaving the unconscious big mouth behind on the floor.[3]

Cox:

We decided to get to the train station and regroup. We had to pass the sheriff's office and saw lights coming on and people running in and out — we found out later the sheriff was giving out guns. It was after 9:30 at night, the train station was closed, so we decided to seek the safety of the darkness at the station and wait to see what would happen.

More people arrived, a hell of a lot more, and they stood among the parked cars and screamed epithets at us; the worst of the screamers were women.

"Ol' buddies," Peoples said, "I think we got a problem." He sent two men to take over the control booth above the station.

Cars pulled up, about thirty in all; they circled the station and played their lights on it. They were armed with everything from pitchforks to blunderbusses, to modern high-powered rifles with telescopic sights. One of our men had been left in the station to negotiate with the tobacco-chewing, pot-gutted sheriff. He said, "Tell them niggers to come on out. We have to take them in.[4]

The sheriff gazed up at the signal tower and saw a black pilot smiling back down from behind his weapon. "The lawman," Peoples said, "couldn't get up enough saliva to spit out his chaw."

Cox was the designated negotiator, playing his role as the white man in charge.

Fortunately, a white lieutenant who was apparently on leave approached to talk with us. The lieutenant said the people were ugly, but he'd contain them if we remained hidden.

When the train finally came, as luck would have it, the sleeping car stopped right in front of us and the door opened. As we filed out to board the train, the people formed a line and spit on us and hit us with their gun butts.

As they stepped off the train at Hampton Roads, Peoples said:

> We were greeted by several men in Ivy league suits. One of them said, "Which one of you is Henry Peoples?"
> I said, "Who wants to know?"
> He said, "The FBI."
> And I said, "Oh. I'm Peoples."
> To make a long story short, I have on my file in the Pentagon and at the Federal Bureau of Investigation that I started a *race* riot if you please, in South Carolina!
> They did the fastest processing job on record on us. We were checked in and out in eight hours and were on a ship heading overseas. They placed us in two stinking compartments, nine men in each one. We were locked in, practically standing on each other's backs, and given no food or water. When we were out at sea, about thirty-two hours later, they let us out."

Commented Cox: "That was our send-off to fight for democracy in the world."

Major General Frank O'Driscoll Hunter (*l.*) and Colonel Robert Selway.

11

Red Tails

The P-51

Meanwhile, back in Italy, the 332nd pilots were happily getting acquainted with their new plane, the P-51 Mustang. It has been called "the plane that won the war," and even the Germans agreed.

"If the P-39 was a VW and the P-47 a Buick," Walter Palmer wrote, "the P-51 was the Cadillac of fighters with a Rolls Royce engine."

Woody Crockett called it "a dream airplane. It could climb, turn, and fight at low level and at high altitude." The Mustang carried six 50-mm machine guns, three in each wing. "It was great for strafing. It was fearsome." It was also big enough for a six-foot, 190-pounder to fit comfortably on a seven- or eight-hour mission.

Lou Purnell:

If that plane had been a girl, I'd have married it right on the spot. Damn right! It was like dancing with a good partner. You could almost think left turn, and the damn plane was right with you. Good response on controls, good stability. It was a miracle to get in and fly with all that horsepower at your fingertips. Speed, maneuverability, climb rate, reliability? We had it in the P-51. The cockpit was designed beautifully. Where you'd expect to find something, you'd find it. Anyone who has flown a P-51 will agree with me. And those who haven't, wish they had.

But the Mustang had one important drawback. Like the P-39, it was water-cooled and thus vulnerable to a hit in the engine. Once the plane lost its coolant, as Johnny Briggs said, "you gotta come down."

Newcomer Roscoe Brown had another complaint:

The '51 had tremendous torque. The propeller spun in a counter-clockwise direction, and you countered with a little right rudder and a little right stick and trimmed it — trim tabs are little air foils within the wing that help you keep the plane straight.

But if you were all tensed up, the P-51's torque could get away from you. My good buddy was also my wing man, and was on his first trip in a '51 when the torque pulled him over, and he crashed on the runway. The plane caught on fire, and he never flew a day's combat.

However, the pilots generally loved their new plane.

More replacements arrived. Bobby Williams, George Iles, and Bert Wilson landed in Oran, Algeria after twenty-nine days on a Liberty Ship that left everyone sick and vomiting. Like ants, long lines of trucks took supplies from the ships. As soon as the ship docked, white troops poured off, but a second lieutenant stopped the blacks, because they didn't want "any trouble." Williams, a second lieutenant himself, "gave him a contemptuous look and just walked off," followed by the others.

They ended up in an Officers' Club, but none of the Arab women would dance with them. Commented Iles dryly: "We were told we weren't welcome. Gee, we had come back to Africa and were told we weren't welcome!"

The next day, on a British liner to Naples, a British naval officer began assigning lifeboat commanders. "Are there any generals aboard?" No answer. "Any colonels? Any lieutenant colonels?" A black chaplain stepped forward. The officer just looked at him: "Are there any majors?" he continued.

Trucked across the mountains to Ramatelli on the eastern side of the Boot, they found P-51s lined up waiting for them. None had ever flown one. "You had to learn it on your own from the tech order, sort of an 'owners' manual,' Wilson said.

"We had three days to switch over to the '51," Woody Crockett said. "The fourth day we went out fifty-four strong with the Mustangs. Some guys flew without reading the pilot's handbook." Brown had a total of three hours of transition training, then he was off.

Chris Newman, just out of the hospital and still badly scarred, checked out his P-51: "I took the darned thing up, came down, and took it up a second time, a total of about two hours. The next day I was on the mission."

Reminiscent of 'the Red Baron,' Manfred Von Richtoffen of World War I, they painted their tails bright red. "Rather than camouflaging the planes," Herbert Carter explained, "we wanted the American bombers to know we were escorting them. The red tails would also let the German interceptors know who was escorting those bombers."

The Red Tails also gave themselves a nickname. Some whites derided them as "night fighters," so they began to call themselves 'spooks' and their outfit, 'the *Spookwaffe*,' or Spook Air Force.

The 99th joined the other three squadrons on July 3, creating an unorthodox Group of four squadrons and touching off a rivalry between the 'old hands' of the 99th, most of whom had close to fifty missions or more, and the 'newcomers.' The 99th had been happy flying with the white 86th Fighter Group and resented returning to a segregated Group. As a special concession, it was allowed to keep its former blue-and-white checker pattern on the noses of its '51s.

The Red Tails had two main missions. First, they flew protection for bombers pounding the big German oil refineries at Ploesti, Rumania. Second, they softened up the coast of southern France prior to the Allied invasion of August 15. In between, they often took the bombers into industrial targets in Southern Europe and Germany itself.

The 15th Air Force was formed specifically to conduct daylight bomber raids. Its five fighter Groups had one overriding mission — to protect the bombers — and Davis called his pilots to an assembly to make sure they all understood it.

He had been told by General Eaker: "We don't want aces. I don't care if you never shoot down another airplane." There would be opportunities to go hunting for enemy planes on other missions, Davis told his pilots. But when they were escorting bombers, they were to *stay with the bombers*, no matter what. "Protect them with your life." Any man found leaving the bombers helpless in order to chase enemy fighters would be grounded and court-martialled.

This caused some grumbling. "We were damn unhappy," the erstwhile tiger of Hampton Roads, Charlie Bussey, said, "because the name of the game was shoot down airplanes. This took some of the glamour out of being a fighter pilot, because the movies create this glamour with the white scarves and all that."

But nobody dared disobey. Archer said, "I never considered wandering off, and I'm considered a very independent person. We did not take on Colonel Davis. He could be as nice as possible and then turn around and tear your head off if you did something wrong."

Davis' orders "were brought home very vividly," Crockett said, when a white Group shot down eight or nine enemy fighters but lost seventeen B-17s on the same mission. Each B-17 cost a half million dollars and carried a crew of ten men. "So that wasn't a very good tradeoff." Davis was emphatic that would not happen on any mission the 332nd flew. And it didn't.

What was a typical long-range mission like?

Two or three hours before the mission, the Operations Officer came by and woke everybody, "though he didn't need to," said Bussey — "you were already awake. Chances are you didn't have any sleep the night before, because this was hair-raising stuff."

William Mattison was Operations Officer in the 100th. Crockett recalled: "He was a pretty big guy, and he might turn a young pilot over in his bed if he didn't respond immediately.

The guys said, 'I'm going out to be shot at, I don't want you to come in and wake me like that.' They said to me, 'We want you to do the job.' So Major Mattison got out of that work."

In the 302nd Dudley Watson "would stick his head in the tent and roar the names of the guys who were going on the mission. As usual, Sheppard hung a nickname on him: 'Fearless Fosdick,' "because he was a hammerin' son of a gun."

Grumbling, the pilots climbed out of their sacks and took a sponge bath with a helmet full of cold water — water was a scarce commodity. "Then we rushed into the mess tent," Sheppard said, where "the fiendish cooks could ruin the best food in the world." (Bussey recalled the menu as "powdered eggs and oatmeal.")

Then they piled into a truck or walked down to the flight line for the briefing in a huge converted barn. They took their seats on bomb casings, then a sheet was pulled away from the wall, revealing a tremendous map with a line drawn to the target, deep in the heart of Germany or elsewhere.

"We were briefed by the weather officers — a bunch of liars," Sheppard said, "and then by the intelligence officers, another bunch of liars."

Bussey recalled: "The operations people plotted our mission and told us what to do if we were shot down. For example, in Yugoslavia, there were the Chetniks and the Partisans, the same groups that were fighting each other in Bosnia fifty years later. Sometimes they'd take their pitchforks and kill a pilot." He also told them what time to start engines, what time to begin takeoff, and where and what time to link up with the bombers.

The pilots picked up their parachutes and drove back to their squadrons where they were told who would lead the flight and what planes would be used. Then each man carefully inspected his plane, though the mechanics had already done it once.

Sheppard:

> We'd check the gas tanks personally to make sure they were topped off. The armorers and ordnance people checked the gun belts. At first the P-51 had some trouble when, in tight turns the gravity forces exerted resistance on the

movement of the ammunition belt, although later models corrected the problem. Then we'd wait for the signal to start our engines.

When they taxied to their takeoff positions, everyone on base turned out to wave them good luck. The fuel trucks drove slowly by and topped off the tanks again, because the planes had already used up some gas getting into position. "The pilots' eyes would be right on them to be sure they put the gas cap on tightly," Sheppard said, otherwise gas would vaporize and stream out in flight while the gas needle went down.

Then the pilots sat under the wings of their planes or on the wings watching the slower bombers pass overhead, wave after wave.

Red Jackson:

I had some very vivid impressions. My strongest was the feeling of participating in a gigantic effort. I'd say to myself: "Here I am with seventy-two planes going to join with a whole armada of planes — big bombers, P-38s, P-51s — a gigantic effort coordinated to the second. We are to appear over the B-17s' wings at a certain minute over one little town in Germany. And a similar gigantic effort is taking off out of England." I said, "Gee, I'm a part of something big! I'm a real key part of the effort."

When the bombers had passed, it was time to start engines and catch up with them.

Ed Gleed:

Three or four minutes before we cranked up engines, I'd always get a rumble in my stomach. Anybody who said he didn't is pulling your leg — I'd say even Pruitt did. The only way to get rid of it was to get out and stretch flat on my stomach on the wing until we got the one-minute notice to crank up, climb in, and buckle on the 'chute. Then I never thought about it again. You hope all your calculations are correct and you haven't forgotten anything. Then you're off and gone.

Felix Kirkpatrick:

We had four squadrons, two side-by-side at one end of the runway and two at the other end. The first plane is waved off. No sooner than he takes off, the second airplane lines up and waits for a signal to take off until we get all eighteen off the ground for that squadron. Then the next squadron lines up and does the same thing. When they all clear the runway, someone shoots a flare, a signal for the planes to take off from the other end.

One by one, seventy-two planes — sixteen plus two spares from each squadron — took off. They joined up in slow climbing turns. "We circled the field in two 360s until we were all in position," Kirkpatrick said, "then we'd head off to rendezvous."

By now the pilots were too busy to pay attention to butterflies in their stomachs. "You don't have time for apprehension."

They flew a 'four-finger pattern' pioneered by the Germans — wingman, flight leader, second element leader, and his wingman — four ships to each Flight, four Flights per squadron, four squadrons in the Group. The spares flew as far as the 'bomb line,' that is, enemy territory. If no aircraft had dropped out with problems, the spares returned to base.

Sometimes the bombers went out in a different direction because of weather, and the fighters met them at the appointed place and time. The Group leader navigated for the Group. When there was no visibility, he flew by 'dead reckoning' — taking a compass heading for a calculated number of minutes. "We got pretty good at it," Sheppard said. Everyone else guided on the leader, almost wingtip to wingtip. "Those cats could fly formation!"

Lucky Lester:

Navigation was one of the big problems. I guess the biggest problems were, one, mechanical, two, weather, three, navigation, and four, the enemy. Only after you overcame the first three did you have to worry about the fourth.

Let's say it was overcast, which was not unusual, with the top of the clouds at twenty thousand feet. Each flight took off at a certain time on a climb-out heading, designed to get you above the clouds and to the Rendezvous Point to meet the bombers. The climbs out of Italy were over mountains most of the time, so you didn't have a lot of latitude for error.

And you didn't have any navigational aids. Now they have all this fancy automatic equipment for navigation. Airplanes now can fly themselves; I flew jets later on, so I know it's nothing like flying a propeller airplane. On one jet recently, the crew was knocked out from loss of oxygen, and the airplane just flew on auto pilot until it ran out of gas and fell into the sea.

Back then ground radar had a very limited range to reach out and see in those days, and, of course, you didn't have any radar on board the airplane. You had to maintain radio silence. You couldn't talk to anyone in your flight or on the ground, because that would give away where you were and what direction you were heading.

They used to marshall hundreds of airplanes out of Italy, all going basically the same place. Italy is not a very big place for hundreds of airplanes.

You started out on a correct heading as you entered the clouds, but if the wind was blowing, and you didn't know it, you might be drifting. You might be flying a heading due north but actually be going north-northwest. In the clouds you had no way to check visually.

You had to fly formation, guiding on your leader only, wingtips almost touching, and he in turn maintained position on his leader. It really took a strong heart to sit there, and you had no idea whether you were right-side up, in a turn, or upside down.

If the flight started feeling turbulence in the clouds and the plane started bouncing around, you began to wonder: What is it? Is it rough weather? Is the enemy shooting flak at me and I'm feeling the concussions from the exploding shells? Or is it the prop wash from another sixteen planes crossing through your flight? More than one time there were mid-air collisions. A voice would yell on the radio, "I'm hit, I'm hit!"

That's where discipline was required. You just had to sit there and sweat it out. Boy, it took a strong heart sitting there and saying, "I'll just keep going, keep going, keep going, and hope I'll break out." It added years to your life. Those are the kinds of things you don't hear about in the movies.

"We lost more people in weather than to enemy aircraft," Bobby Williams said. "The P-51 is perhaps the best prop-driven plane you could have − as long as you're over land and level terrain. Then it sounds like a Singer sewing machine. But out at sea, or over the mountains, every little pop scares the pee out of you."

At last they broke through the clouds. "One of the most beautiful things I can recall is seeing seventy-two sleek P-51s climbing up from an overcast," Sheppard said. But where were the bombers? The fighters weren't only worried about being lost but also about being late. "We had a ninety-second window of rendezvous − that wasn't very much. After that we were considered late." And Davis would not tolerate being late.

On strafing missions, where time was not critical, the planes could still miss their targets.

Kirkpatrick recalled one mission:

Navigation was usually by checkpoints on the map. But one time I was leading my squadron, and when we got to the Yugoslav coast, there were mountains and a wall of weather there. I couldn't see the ground so I took my squadron and kept climbing over the top of the clouds. The Group leader was also trying to poke some holes where those clouds were, but he went ahead and aborted his mission and went back. I did some dead reckoning until I thought we must be where the objective was, and I put my planes in echelon [staggered] formation, and we came down through the clouds, and there was the target, a railroad marshalling yard, right below us. We completed our mission and came on back.

Fuel consumption was critical, Lester said:

The P-51 had five tanks of fuel. The two main tanks were in the wings. Then there were two external tanks on the wings, but you had to get rid of those before you could maneuver in combat. Finally there was a tank right behind the pilot, but if you kept that tank full, it threw your center of gravity off and you lost a lot of maneuverability; you stalled at much higher speeds. Our instructions were to take off on that tank, fly it forty-five minutes or so, down to twenty-five to thirty gallons, then switch to your external tanks.

Your point of no return was the point where, if you burned off your excess fuel in the tank behind the pilot and dropped your external tanks, you still had enough fuel to get home straight-line, plus about a fifteen-minute reserve − if you were lucky. Some pilots didn't want to burn off the fuel in the main tank. They figured, "Heck, that's 45 minutes worth of fuel I might need on my way home." But this could cause trouble later on. I religiously believed in getting rid of that gas first.

There was another enemy not mentioned in the movies. They flew at twenty-five thousand feet or higher − about the height of Mount Everest. The cold was numbing. "We knew we were going to freeze our behinds off," Kirkpatrick said. "We didn't have any heat in our airplanes; the bomber crews had heat in theirs. The cold was something we had never considered. Summer or winter, it didn't make any difference − it was the altitude that made the cold."

"And aluminum was cold as hell," Sheppard shivered.

Crockett admitted that the P-39 may have had the poorest performance, but it had the best heater. "The Mustang had no pressurized cockpits, even though we flew at twenty-five thousand feet. Even in the summer months you ran into temperatures below freezing."

They were issued fleece flying gear, which worked well in the bombers but was too cumbersome in the tiny cockpit of the fighters. At first the fighter pilots were issued electric suits like those the bomber crews wore; they could be plugged in like blankets.

"But it overloaded the electrical systems, and we had a lot of communication failures. Rather than that, we didn't plug them in," Woody said.

The bomber crews had more room than we had, and they had time to change if they got hit. We couldn't do that − if you bailed out, you've had it. We had to wear what we could walk home in. So you just bundled up. You wore thermals outside and dress uniform underneath. You had heavy gloves and fur-lined boots that you put your GI shoes in.

"By the time we got down to lower altitudes," Kirkpatrick said, "we were sweating through our leather jackets."

Added to all their other problems was the strain of long hours. "Several missions lasted six and a half hours," Charlie McGee said. "To look back now, I find it hard to believe I sat in that little cockpit that long. The Ploesti oil fields in Rumania were particularly rough missions because it was a very heavily defended area, so it kept you on your toes for a long time."

Kirkpatrick:

> On a long mission we were on the ground for a full half-hour before we took off. In a fighter aircraft you're very confined. We had some pretty big guys — I'm five-foot nine. You can't stretch your legs. Your butts get really tired, but you have no choice. If we want to set down, we can't. The minute we take off, we're over water, and coming back we're over water. We're either over enemy territory or over water.

Each man sat on a bag containing his parachute and life raft. "It didn't help any," Bussey grouched. "When you came back, your ass was raw!"

Sheppard:

> It was torture, because the last thing an aircraft designer puts on an airplane is the cockpit. He has room for the engine, he designs the size of the prop, the ammunition has space allocated for it. The last thing is the cockpit, and that's usually the most uncomfortable place.
>
> You're sitting on the floor with the comfort level of a brick, and most of us had bony behinds. A lot of fellows developed hemorrhoids. The B-17 had inner tubes in the tail wheel, about ten to twelve inches in diameter. We'd blow them up and sit on them. As you went higher, the outside temperature and air pressure went down, which meant pressure in the tube was more, and it expanded, which pushed you up against the safety belt even tighter, which didn't do your piles any good. We had to stab the inner tubes to keep them from inflating under us.

Finally, there was one more hidden agony that the movies don't mention. The men had now been in the air two or three hours and were long over-due for urination.

"We relieved ourselves the last thing we did before we left," Kirkpatrick said. "We also had 'relief tubes' leading out of the plane, but you can't use them when you're tied down in heavy clothing."

Sheppard:

> A flier had to unbuckle the parachute straps between his legs. You had to unzip your flying suit and fish around. By that time, whatever you had down there was frozen up. The relief facilities were a funnel on the left-hand side under the seat. It vented outside to a Venturi tube, which was supposed to suck the fluid violently through the line. But it also froze up at altitudes and caused a lot of mental anxiety. Plus the fact that, if your wing man saw you holding this funnel up, trying to get it to empty, he'd fly ahead of you and put you in his propwash, which meant you got a flying bath. And sometimes, I suspected some of our friends on the ground had reversed it so you got pressure blowing it back from the funnel.
>
> We roll on the floor sometimes when we get together and recall those days. We'll never forget them.

"Now I tell people fifteen minutes is my limit," Kirkpatrick smiled. "But we were young and gung-ho and in A-1 physical condition. We had a mission to do, and we did it, that's all. We didn't expect to be in a soft plush chair to do it."

Then, too, over Yugoslavia they had to cross 'Flak Alley.' "Those goddam German 88s were waiting, and they were deadly," Alexander Jefferson said.

Sheppard:

> At last we'd spot the bombers pulling streamers, and we'd head over there and see if it was our bomber Group. We were careful not to get between the sun and the bombers, because their gunners were keen-sighted people and could tear us up with their .50s. We'd fly a big circle so they could get a good look at us, zigzag across them and give them a good silhouette so they could see our red tails.

If the Red Tails could spot the streamers off the bombers' wings, so could the Germans. "They could see us coming for a hundred miles."

Spanky Roberts:

The fighter outfits met the bombers before the enemy line. 'A' Group would pick them up first. 'B' Group takes off forty-five minutes after 'A' Group, picks the bombers up and relieves 'A' Group. 'C' Group takes off maybe an hour later and picks them up at target and takes them around the target. The fighters have to fly slower than their maximum performance to stay with the bombers, so they use more fuel to do that.

Since we had four squadrons instead of the usual three, they seemed always to put us where they felt the highest concentration of enemy fighters would be. Quite often it would be in one of two locations: The German fighters would try to hit us just before the target, to protect the target, or just as we were coming off the target, when we were likely to be disrupted.

Kirkpatrick:

The enemy aircraft knew we were coming two or three hours before we got there, so they were positioned well above us when we arrived.

I suspected sometimes the white boys were using the bombers as bait to get some kills — you wondered if their bombers had any cover or not. But we were there where the enemy aircraft could see us. When they saw the bombers had good cover, they'd say, "Heh, let's get some stragglers instead."

Lester:

Very seldom did the Germans try to attack the bomber formations we were escorting. Three squadrons had the mission of providing close support for the bombers. The fourth flew what we called a fighter sweep. They were free to do anything they wanted to as long as they kept the bombers in sight. That's when you had a chance to get at the enemy aircraft if any attacked.

Gleed:

Because we were faster than the bombers, we'd fly 'S' patterns back and forth above them, then we'd break off as they approached their Initial Point. The flak from the German 88-mm anti-aircraft guns was so black you could walk on it.

"When you see the flak, it's too late," Kirkpatrick said. "There were big puffs of smoke all around. When they shot at us, we assumed they'd tracked us, so we changed altitude, speed, and direction."

"That shrapnel is ragged," Bill Melton shuddered. "You could damn near shave with it."

The German anti-aircraft was very effective below twenty thousand feet. Although the B-24's ceiling was about twenty thousand, the B-17s climbed to twenty-five thousand to get above the flak if possible. The fighters liked to keep a protective position about five thousand feet above the bombers, which meant that they were pushed up to thirty thousand feet or more.

Sheppard:

I was pretty glad to be up at twenty-five thousand because the bombers would soak up the flak. Every once in a while, a round would get through and cause a lot of excitement among the single-engine guys.

Also, the extra five thousand feet gave us an edge if we had to ward off attack. If you have speed, you can get altitude, and if you have altitude, you can get speed. That P-51 really accelerated when you put its nose down. Man, altitude just disappeared like smoke in the wind.

McGee:

In many cases we went in with the bombers over the target. The ack-ack fire from the German guns was like a black blanket. Our fighters usually flew above the bombers, and we had the ability to do a little 'jinking' around — dodging. But, boy, once the bombers got on the IP to go into the target, regardless of how heavy the flak was, they'd ride right on through to be sure their bombs were on target. You couldn't help but admire the guys who were flying them.

Over Ploesti, Jefferson said, the ack-ack fire looked "like a huge black doughnut suspended in air." Inside the doughnut, the ack-ack "was so thick you could damn near walk on it."

"We didn't want any part of that flak," Gleed said. "The bombers *had* to go in. It was a horrendous sight to see six B-24 Liberators with all that flak starting to come up and — bang — there's only five airplanes left and one big ball of smoke. Or see one plane start lagging back and try to make it on into the target anyway.

"We'd pick them up coming out, some with three engines out, or half a tail shot off."

To Sheppard his most vivid memory of the war was not aerial combat. "It was the sight of bombers being hit by an 88 and the bombs going off — a big red eruption with black smoke going by you. With one detonation we had just lost ten crewmen. Ten families had been left bereft — mothers, wives, children, brothers and sisters. All bereft."

Jefferson: "Planes fell in flames, planes fell not in flames, an occasional one pulled out and crash-landed, sometimes successfully, sometimes they blew up. Men fell in flames, men fell in parachutes, some candle-sticked [when their 'chutes didn't open]. Pieces of men dropped through the hole, pieces of planes." The fighter pilots prayed and wept. "Have you any idea what it's like to vomit in an oxygen mask?"

"After the ack-ack fire," said Melton, "the Germans fired a pink flare as a signal for their fighters to go in, and we'd take the bombers back."

"We didn't worry about the Luftwaffe," Jefferson said. "These bomber guys had seen the inside of hell, and if they could stay airborne, we damned sure were going to take them back. They would jettison everything aboard but the men. Many had wounded aboard and couldn't effectively man their guns. Hell, the holes were so big in those damn planes, sometimes we could see the interior."

After their 'babies' were safely home, the Red Tails could head for home themselves. But the danger wasn't over yet. Often the planes had been separated in dogfights and had to find their way home as best they could.

If a fighter was crippled, the pilot headed over the Adriatic Sea, praying he could make landfall in Italy. "Most of our flying was great distances over water," Bussey said, "and three-fourths of our men couldn't swim. We lost more men in the water than any other way." It's the only thing in life he was bitter about, Charlie said, thinking back to the big Olympic-size swimming pool at Selfridge. "Forty white officers and their wives could use it; we weren't allowed to swim in it." At least, he said, they could have given the fliers swimming lessons in Detroit.

> Sometimes, if you can't swim, you panic. Clemenceau Givings, the captain of our class, bellied into the water. He was fumbling, trying to get that dinghy to inflate, and the airplane sank under him. A damn good man; he should never have died in such a miserable way. It was sinful. No man should have to die because no one took time to put him through swimming lessons.
>
> The survival equipment we had in the old days was crude; it did very little to help people survive. Survival is just as important as accomplishing the mission itself — if you survive, you can fly again and accomplish other missions.
>
> An accomplished swimmer at least had a fighting chance. We lost a lot of guys, and we shouldn't have. It's the only hurt I've brought with me from the Service.

Even if they had escaped damage, the pilots often had to contend with heavy cloud cover. As Williams explained: "You've gotta get back home, you're over the top of the clouds, and you don't know where the hell you are. You've got to get back down to find your base, and you're over the Alps. It was very, very hairy."

Lester:

> I can remember several occasions where we navigated to the point we thought we were over the Adriatic Sea and we started letting down. Sometimes we would let down from, say, twenty thousand feet to five hundred feet before we saw the water. The mountains around Yugoslavia and Italy were ten to twelve thousand feet, so once you got down to twelve thousand feet, you better hope your dead reckoning navigation was correct and you were over water and that your altimeter was set correctly.

They used their compasses and watches and tried to pick out landmarks when possible — a mountain, river, or coastline.

If the weather was closed in, or there were other problems, such as an oil-smeared windshield, the pilots could switch to their emergency radar homing service, 'Big Fence,' and get a heading to fly back to base. "Big Fence was good!" exclaimed Sheppard. "It had been helpful to us a number of times."

Jefferson:

> Many times we flew with the bombers beyond our Point of Departure, where we were supposed to leave them, and sometimes it made us run low on fuel. If you got over your field and suddenly the gas gauge is empty, you joined the caterpillar club [that is, bailed out].
>
> Once Henry Peoples ran out of fuel as he was coming in and was ordered out. He said they were out of their minds, he wasn't about to take to the air; he was allergic to heights. That fool cut off his radio and rode his plane down to a perfect landing.[1]

"Everybody on base would be there for the landing," Kirkpatrick said. If there was a victory or more to celebrate, the pilot went into his victory roll to the cheers of his crewmen, one roll for each enemy shot down. "The Red Cross girls would serve coffee, and we'd have a critique, whatever the intelligence office wanted to know" — where and what kind of enemy fighters and ack-ack they ran into etc. "From there we'd get in our trucks and go back to the base area and try to unwind."

But out on the flight line, one or two ground crews might still be keeping a vigil, searching the skies for a warrior who hadn't returned. Charles Hill said, "You'd see them hanging around his stand, every now and then sneaking a look at the horizon as if to will him back." Sometimes "they stayed there for hours looking in the sky."

On one long-range flight deep in Germany, Hill took off with a bad stomach ache and returned with acute appendicitis. The pain was so intense that he slipped in and out of consciousness as the tower screamed at him, "Drop your wheels! Drop your wheels." Then, "Drop your flaps, man, drop your flaps!...

OK, cut back on the throttle...." Then, apparently on the ground, he heard a hysterical, "Your brakes, baby! Cut your brakes! Cut your motor! Cut it off!" His crew chief was on the wing holding on for dear life as the plane spun on the runway toward a row of parked planes. Hill remembered turning off the switch, and when he came to, his crew chief had pulled him out onto the wing. An ambulance rushed up, and four hours later, he was on the operating table. In about three weeks, he was flying missions again. "If it hadn't been for the tower and the crew chief, I wouldn't be here."

For most pilots the first objective was a good shower and scrub-down, a luxury because water was rationed and uniforms even had to be laundered in 100-octane gasoline. Then they made a rush for the mess hall. "By mid-afternoon we were ravenous," Sheppard said. "Our flight surgeon firmly believed there was tremendous benefit to our eyesight from eating carrots, so carrot sticks were the first thing on the table. I didn't find out until I was fifty that I had to eat fifty tons of carrots to get any benefit."

"The food was piss-poor," Bussey said. "Very little meat. Dehydrated food — I'd never even heard of it." On the whole, he said, between missions, "we lived a very bleak and miserable life."

After supper Sheppard's day wasn't over yet.

> I'd hear what squawks the mechanics had. They were proud of their work and didn't like aircraft down for any nonsense. They were quite peeved if pilots brought the aircraft back early for insufficient reason. I'd fly the airplane. It gave me a chance to do aerobatics and go places I had no business doing or going.
>
> Close to dinner time, we'd get another bite to eat. Then I'd have to go back to the line to check out the mechanics again. They worked outside, no indoor facilities. They swung engines on an A-frame, changed the props, changed the engines. I worked many nights late at night at fuel dumps, pumping gas by hand from 55-gallon drums into 1200-gallon tankers to refuel the airplanes. There were some damn good men, and I considered myself part of them. We had A-1 maintenance.

The bond between the fliers and their crewmen was strong. Bill Melton said:

> It was just like being on a football team, we depended on each other. We had some shitty airplanes at first, but we had some superb, well-trained, bright ground people that kept us flying. No one ever gives enough recognition to those eight or nine people who are immediately behind the pilot. The early enlisted men who went to Tuskegee had to have two years of college. They were the high-tech boys of fifty years ago.
>
> My crew chief came into my tent before he went on leave. He could borrow my money, my gabardines [dress uniform], anything else I had. We got two ounces of Old Hickory whiskey on each mission; when it was his turn to go into the rest camp, I'd give him my whiskey. All rank ceased when he walked through the tent door, because these were our backbone. My life depended on him. We were in fact like brothers.

Meantime, at sundown the pilots repaired to their tents. One way they unwound was cards.

Sheppard:

> We played 'dirty hearts' with about seven guys, two decks of cards, and we played endlessly, night after night after night. The penalty was twenty-six points per hand — thirteen for the queen of spades and one for each heart. The first one who lost 104 points had to drink a whole canteen of water. Some people who got nailed would come back for revenge and have to drink a second canteen of water. We played this thing until after midnight, knowing that we had to go over twenty-five thousand feet early in the morning with all that pressure on the kidneys. Fighter pilots are known for doing dumb things.

"You can always tell a fighter pilot," Kirkpatrick nodded, "but you can't tell him much."

In the morning they did it all over again. Sheppard would be up at dawn to fly the problem plane again, "and if possible I flew it again on the next mission." The early morning flights also gave him a chance to make a weather-check and report on where the holes in the clouds were. "I was the first guy off the ground in the morning and the last one in at night."

Our predecessors in the 12th Air Force had been rotated home after fifty missions. I flew eighty-seven missions with the 12th and thirty-six more with the 15th. That was largely because Tuskegee was now equipping a bomber Group and siphoning off a large percentage of pilots to put into twin-engines, which meant that our replacements were at low ebb. So we shook the dice and went up on the mission, hoping the dice wouldn't turn craps on us.

12

AIR WARS

Roscoe Brown's first mission was the Ploesti oil fields — "a tough mission. I was riding with Johnny Briggs as his wingman, and I told myself, 'Whatever he does, I'm going to do.' Johnny said afterwards, 'I never saw anybody stick so close to me!'"

"The transition from being just a good pilot to being a combat pilot occurs in about four or five missions. If you don't get the feel of it, you'll be scared all the time, and if you're scared, you can't fly."

Brown and Chris Newman became tentmates and good friends. "Brown was aggressive," Newman said. "When he got the opportunity, he jumped on it." ("We were all good pilots," Bert Wilson agreed," but 'Bruno' [Brown] was especially hot.")

Newman:

Some bombers next to us were being attacked, and we were going over to give them a little assistance. The leader said, "We're breaking left now." I didn't know what to expect. We pulled around 180 degrees and saw an enemy 109 on the tail of a B-17, just riddling away. It zipped by.

There were four fighters coming through this bomber formation. We dove down behind them, my canopy popped open, and dust started flying in my face and eyes. We dove from twenty-five thousand to fifteen thousand feet. The enemy kept on going down, but we pulled back up with the bombers and continued our escorting. We would ward them off but not chase them. If Brown had been in my shoes, he would have continued on down. With luck, I would have had a victory, but I never got the opportunity again.

Alex Jefferson received an early shock: "My tentmate was Othel Dickson. After about a week he spun in, doing acrobatics upside down in a Mustang. One of the hard and fast rules was don't do any upside-down flying with over a half-tank of gasoline; it upsets the equilibrium. When they found him he was dead, burned, decapitated, footless and handless, but still sitting in the cockpit as if he were flying."[1]

Meanwhile, B.O. Davis had the unpleasant task of relieving two of the five original Tuskegee Airmen.

One was Charles DeBow, the 301st commander. There was a strong personality conflict between the two men. DeBow was a school teacher from Indiana and "was kind of laid back," Charles Dryden said. "He and Davis didn't quite fit in harness."

"Davis was a very strict disciplinarian," James Wiley said. "DeBow was defiant. I didn't care for DeBow too much either. He wasn't a good pilot — I don't know how he was selected and got through the training. I like people with guts. He didn't have it. B.O. Davis just threw up his hands."

De Bow's replacement was Lee Rayford, back for a second tour after flying with the 99th over Anzio.

The second to be relieved was Mac Ross, the Group Operations Officer. Again, as Clarence Jamison observed, Ross "never clicked very well with Colonel Davis. Maybe Davis had higher expectations for the first class."

Ross was replaced by Alfonso Davis.

When the units were formed, "we all had the same amount of experience," Bill Campbell explained. "You don't know who's going to exhibit leadership traits. Davis had to pick someone as leaders, and some didn't do as well as others. It wouldn't have happened if we had had more experience."

On July 11, depressed at his demotion, Mac Ross was killed while checking out a new P-51. The accident report called it suicide, though Davis refused to accept it, fearing that the Pentagon would seize on it as a sign of bad morale. He told the writer of the report, "You'll be confined to the base for two months, when you'll have plenty of time to think about it." But the report remained unchanged.

The P-51 was fitted with an oxygen tube that automatically increased the oxygen as their altitude increased. But, said Sheppard, sometimes the tube could become blocked, and the pilot didn't realize he wasn't getting enough oxygen.

Lou Purnell described the experience:

> I was flying at about eighteen thousand feet, going out on a top-cover mission. All of a sudden, I felt like this was the best day I had ever lived in my whole life. Everything turned beautiful, I could hear music coming out of nowhere, I wanted to roll back the canopy and climb out on the nose of the plane and direct all 64 pieces of the orchestra. I didn't know it, but I had hypoxia, not enough oxygen. At first it feels as if you've had three martinis, the best feeling in the world.
>
> Then, about five minutes later, it felt as if someone had lowered a great mosquito netting right in front of my eyes. All of a sudden I began to get really sick to my stomach. It was an effort to do the things that should have been second nature. For instance, I saw the squadron leaving, climbing and making a turn. Usually my reaction would have been automatic, but now I had to think: "If I want to catch up with them, I'll have to advance my throttle, a little left rudder, yeah, that gets it." Then I got to the point where I said, "I don't give a damn." I had a feeling as if I was going to sleep. I remember the plane veering off to the right. I was following the plane, it wasn't following me. It was taking me where it wanted to go.

Luckily Lou landed safely. Not everyone did.

Leon Roberts, the last of the original 99th, had volunteered to stay in Italy when the others were rotated home, and had 116 missions to his credit. The same day that Ross died, the Group hit German shipyards in southern France, and Roberts plunged to his death from thirty thousand feet. Friends speculated that he may have blacked out from lack of oxygen.

Meanwhile, Spanky Roberts returned from the States and a replacement, Dick Macon, was assigned to the 99th:

> Spanky Roberts was my idea of an outstanding pilot. In my estimation he was fearless. There must have been many things that scared the hell out of him, but he always chose the most dangerous missions to lead the squadron. I enjoyed flying with him, and he enjoyed flying with me. When he took one of the dangerous missions, he'd say, "Come on, Dick, let's get 'em," and I'd fly on his wing.
>
> He and Bill Campbell were two of the best. They knew so much about flying formation, and they thought I flew formation pretty good, so when they went on missions, Spanky or Bill would say, "I'll take Mac."
>
> Campbell was a big brother type to me, my idol as a pilot. He had a good seventh sense. He could look down, and when he saw gunfire on the ground, he could dodge the bullets. He saved my life a couple times. Campbell would suddenly say, "Break right," and we knew what to do. You look back and, boom, you see flak where you would have gone if you'd stayed straight. (Of course, if the guy on the ground was a pretty poor gunner, you could break into the bullet.)
>
> Ed Toppins, I really liked too. In fact, it was Toppins' airplane that I was flying when I got shot down; we new guys didn't have our own airplanes yet.

Walter Palmer of the 100th recalled one mission to southern France:

> We had an overcast sky over our field, and we were the last flight. I took off, leading the flight, and got to eight thousand feet, above the clouds, and circled around, waiting for my flight to come up. None of them came, and I assumed they couldn't make it through the clouds. But when I took off on a mission, I never came back without completing it, so I flew off and tried to catch the rest of them.
>
> By the time I hit the coast of southern France, I saw a plane coming the opposite way. He waggled his wings, which was always a friendly sign among the Allied aircraft. I waggled my wings back at him, and he started to turn toward me as if he was going to join me, because it's terrible to be out by yourself in enemy territory. He came on in behind me, and I

figured there might be something wrong there, because usually he'd join me from the side. The idea was never to show your guns to the plane in front of you, and sure enough, after a little while I noticed fire coming from his guns.

I whipped around tight and recognized that he was an ME 109, which was similar to the P-51 we were flying. I knew my Mustang could outmaneuver him, so I kept it in a tight turn. When he noticed I was getting position on him, he decided to split-S and head on out. He was going all the way to the ground. I said, "No point going down there and endangering myself with small arms fire. I'll forget about it," so I turned around and headed on back.

It was my first encounter with an enemy plane.

On July 12, the Red Tails were over the French coast again in weather so bad that they were the only fighter Group to get through. They were jumped by twenty-five enemy fighters. Harold Sawyer and Bernie Jefferson, an ex-football player at Northwestern, followed them down. Sawyer peppered one plane until it dove to the ground and crashed.

Three enemy flew across Joseph Elsberry's bow. He told author Robert Rose:

I picked out a Focke Wulf within good shooting range and fired away. A mild explosion occurred amidships and he rolled over and headed straight down.

A second 190 crossed at about a 70-degree angle, and I turned inside him, and he began to smoke and fell into a dive toward the ground. I followed him through a series of split-S maneuvers as he tried to avoid me. We started at 11,000 feet, ending at about 2,000 before I broke off my attack.... Just before reaching the ground, he tried to pull up, but ran out of sky.[2]

That made Elsberry the first Red Tail to claim three victories; however, for some reason that isn't clear, the Air Force has not accepted them. They do appear, however, on the log of the 301st, along with an additional probable for him.

On July 16, the 332nd opened a sensational five-day scoring period. Alfonso Davis and Chubby Green started it off by downing two over Vienna.

The next day the Group got three more over southern France, by Luther 'Quibbling' Smith, Robert 'Dissipatin'' Smith, and Lawrence Wilkins, all of the 302nd.

On the eighteenth, Rayford led sixty-one fighters on an escort mission over Germany, but when they arrived at the rendezvous, they learned that the bombers had not arrived. If the Red Tails waited for them, they would use up precious fuel and might not be able to get home, but if they left, the bombers would have no cover. Rayford decided to wait. In the next few minutes, the Group would bag twelve enemy fighters, their highest total thus far.

Toppins and Charles Bailey of the 99th each got his second; they had scored their first ones six months earlier over Anzio. After six months in a P-40, Top was "thrilled to have a ship that gave me overwhelming mastery."

"Toppins was a very aggressive, almost a daredevil," Howard Baugh said. "He was chasing a German fighter and got the airplane well above the designed speed limit in a dive. He shot the other airplane down, but when he got home, they found he had actually warped the fuselage. They had to junk his airplane."

Wendell Pruitt and his wingman, Lee Archer, of the 302nd were inseparable friends and rivals. "If there was any way we could fly together, we did," Archer said. "I flew 169 missions over there, and Pruitt and I flew close to 100 together. We were the two 'Hip Cats,' because we were both from big cities. We each had a little guy painted under our horizontal stabilizers, a guy with a zoot suit and a funny-looking hat." That day Archer scored his first victory, to match Pruitt's total.

Another member of the 302nd, Roger Romine, also scored his first, along with Hugh Warner. Charles Francis also credits Weldon Groves with one, though this is not confirmed.

The 100th was also busy.

Palmer:

> We were three or four thousand feet above the bombers, and we noticed about twenty-five or thirty planes above us. Not knowing what they were, we called them 'bogeys.' They usually didn't make aggressive moves toward the bombers

while we were nearby. On this day they did! They dived at the bombers, and we, of course, followed in hot pursuit. I got on the tail of one ME-109, and on the second or third burst all of a sudden he burst into flame and heavy thick smoke and headed straight into the ground. I broke it off, because there were others to shoot down so the bombers could safely make their run.

When I pulled back up, I was under another 109, and this time he didn't notice me, because I came up underneath him, which is unusual. As I got close to him, I tested my guns, but only one of my four gun's fired, and then it jammed, but those few rounds were enough to alert the pilot that I was on his tail. I figured, I'll just go chop his tail off, not thinking that I'm going to have to hit the ground too, because my propeller will be bent. Anyhow, I was closing in and sensing my second victory when he turned sharply and headed into the clouds. We were near the Alps, and I said, "Well, he knows his way through the mountains, I don't. I'll let him alone."

When Palmer got home, he did a slow victory roll, landed, and learned that others in the 100th had been busy too.

Palmer's tentmate, Jack Holsclaw, shot down two more enemy.

A third man in the tent, Lucky Lester, flying 'Miss Pelt,' encountered enemy aircraft for the first and only time during the war.

The fourth man in our Flight of four planes drifted off six or seven hundred feet, and suddenly he was attacked by Messerschmidt 109s. As they came down from above us, they saw him out there by himself, and he probably looked like a straggler to them, so they jumped him. Either he couldn't get his external fuel tanks off in time, or, some people theorize, he might not have burned off the fuel behind the pilot's seat, so he wasn't as maneuverable. At any rate, they shot him down. The other three of us made a turn around to head into them.

I dove in behind one plane as he flew level. He started maneuvering a little bit, I started shooting, and the airplane started coming apart on him, smoke poured out of him, and he exploded. I was going so fast, I was sure I would hit some of the debris.

As I dodged pieces of aircraft, I saw this other plane all alone to my right on a heading ninety degrees to mine. I turned onto his tail and came up behind him, going like a bat out of heck. I closed to about two hundred feet and started over-running him and began firing. The engine on the ME-109 was an in-line type, meaning it was liquid-cooled like the P-51. If you hit the coolant, the airplane was through. His aircraft started to smoke and almost stopped. I was going so fast I skidded my airplane to the side, because I thought I was going to run right up his tail. I saw him climb out on the wing and bail out. I can still see him today with his blond hair, standing on the wing, just as plain as then. It was an amazing sight.

Then I saw a third airplane down below me, and I took off after him. I picked him up going pretty fast, because I had a two thousand-foot start on him before he saw me. He started to dive, trying to out-dive my P-51. Well, there's no way he'd be able to do that. When he got to about a thousand feet, he leveled but wasn't having any luck, and I was still peppering him. He was desperate by then, because I'd scored so many hits, so he decided on a Split-S maneuver, that is, roll over and pull the airplane down so he was going back the other way. It's a very basic maneuver — but not at a thousand feet. I wasn't about to follow him through on that. He never made it and went straight into the ground.

All this took place in four or five minutes — six at the outside. On the return flight, it took a little while to realize what had happened. Only then did the danger hit me.

It was the Group's eleventh victory of the day (twelve unofficially) — and Palmer's tent got six of them. "There was some celebrating in the tent that night," he remembered.

The Red Tails paid a price, however. Oscar Hutton died in a freak accident when his plane was hit by a belly tank dropped by another.

On the 20th the Red Tails accounted for four more enemy planes, plus two by Bussey that were not officially confirmed. Bussey:

Bomber Groups stretched out for miles and miles and miles. We would fly by one Group to cover another Group in front of them. Passing them, I saw a flight of about five or six German fighters about one or two miles away in a continuous vertical loop. Every time one got his nose pointed up, a bomber blew up right in front of him. I'd never heard of this maneuver before; it wasn't in our training. But that's where the bombers were most vulnerable, up through the belly. They had a belly gunner, but he's standing on his head.

So we joined the loop; we just nuzzled right into their flight, and every time one of them got his nose up, we blew him out of the sky. I got one of them. It was damned dangerous business. We'd see a propeller come flying by, or we'd see a tail section come flying by, all kinds of crud.

Of course my squadron didn't stop for this but went on ahead to our bombers, and I was left alone. A single airplane in that killing sky was in a hazardous position, so I headed for home. On the way back, somewhere in the Swiss Alps, I saw a German ship and got on him and put a couple of bursts into him. He started to dive, and I followed him, firing every time I was in range until he finally hit the field and blew.

Destroying another airplane in combat is probably the most exhilarating experience a man can have. You're trained so you don't have to do a lot of thinking, everything is pretty automatic. But your heart's as big as your head, and you don't breathe throughout the encounter, and when it's all over, you realize you haven't taken a breath. It's a fantastic experience.

I wish I'd gotten pictures, but gun cameras are just like other cameras, sometimes they're good and sometimes they're not. I got pictures of firing at him, but I didn't get pictures of the final kill.

If Charlie's claims had been officially accepted, he would have had three and a half total.

The 99th's hottest pilot, Ed Toppins, shot down his third.

Joe Elsberry of the 301st registered one which would have been his fourth, depending on whether the first three were counted, and was in pursuit of a fifth when his windshield frosted up. Squinting through the ice, he raced after his foe until he found a mountain looming before him and had to pull up. It was the last shot Elsberry would get at an enemy fighter.

Armour McDaniel, also of the 301st, caught a German plane trying to evade Elsberry. McDaniel went into a seventeen thousand-foot dive, firing as he closed in, until the enemy sliced through a cloud and into the side of the mountain. McDaniel barely missed it himself.

Langdon Johnson of the 100th scored his first victory.

Author Charles Francis described another kill that day, the most controversial in the record of the 332nd. According to Francis, Bussey chased an enemy ship into Archer's path, and the two gave chase, Archer in the lead. Archer hit the ship with a burst, and it crashed into a mountainside.[3]

If confirmed, this would have been Archer's second victory. He later claimed three more, which would make a total of either four or five, depending on whether the July 20 claim is included. If they are all counted, then Archer was the only black ace of the war.

However, Archer's own recollection is not clear, and Francis' account is not confirmed by Bussey. "Hell, no," Charlie said. "Lee flew with a guy who would never have given him a chance. Pruitt was a real hawk and wouldn't allow any room to anyone. Lee was lucky to have a shot at anything."

When asked, Red Jackson, the squadron commander, said:

> The dispute arose after we came back [from Europe]. I didn't even hear about it before we came back. I didn't know he'd claimed five victories. No pilot had claimed five until we came home. Not until the 1980s did he claim one victory that was supposed to be shared by him and someone else."[4]

The following day, July 21, Jimmy Walker, a veteran of eighty missions, was returning from Ploesti.

> I was leading the Yellow Flight of four planes, and on the way home my commander told me to cover a crippled B-24, stay close to him, and keep enemy fighters away. He was losing altitude all the time, and he went over an area we hadn't been briefed on. When flak came up, three of our four airplanes got hit, including mine. My oil line got shot up, and I could see the gauges going down like you'd punched a hole at the bottom; oil was all over the cockpit and windshield. My engine caught fire, so I shut off all the switches and slipped and slid the airplane and dived to get the fire out, which

fortunately I did. But when I tried to start the engine again, it was frozen.

Intelligence told us that the Germans would shoot you in your 'chute, so I glided down to minimum altitude, between a thousand and five hundred feet, rolled it over and dropped out. I was about to land on a house, but I reached up and pulled on the lines of my chute and slipped the air out and landed on the cottage next to the house.

The Germans were aware there was an American in the area. They knew they had shot me down; they had my airplane, but they didn't have me.

Aleksandr Zivkovic was a seventeen-year-old anti-communist guerrilla in charge of gathering intelligence in a huge area of eastern Serbia. He was driving a two-wheel cart, and, in his words:

I saw an American plane coming back from Rumania. I saw it bank on its side, and I saw a 'chute, so I turned back about two miles, looking for where he could be. The country was flat, and I could see for miles and miles around. I saw approximately where he had jumped. I looked in a big forest with big trees and small bushes between the trees. For five

Alekandr Zivkovic (r.), the seventeen-year-old Serbian guerrilla who saved James Walker from capture by the Germans after Walker's plane had been shot down.

minutes I called, "Heh! Hello!" the only English word I knew. No one answered.

.Then I heard something. I turned and saw behind a bush a black man stand up, wearing a khaki military cap. He was the first black man I'd ever seen. My father had told me about them; he had been in World War I, and he had seen French colonial soldiers from Africa. So I had no hesitation. I said, "America? America?" In sign language I told him, "Heh, come," and in Serbo-Croatian I said, "I'm not Communist, I'm not German, I'm in the Serbian Nationalist army." He spoke French, not perfectly, and I had learned some French in school. I said, "Where's your baggage?" and he went back and picked up his 'chute and his baggage, an inflatable raft.

Alex put Jimmy into his cart, covered him with straw, and drove about three miles to his headquarters. "I told my commandant, "Heh, I found an American!"
Walker:

I didn't have time to get nervous until that night. About two o'clock in the morning, all of a sudden I started shaking, thinking about what could have happened.

I was moved to Alex's family, who were part of the underground. One day they took me with a guard to a barbershop with a German soldier in the next chair while my protection sat over in the corner with his automatic rifle in his lap.

Walker was wearing his Air Force uniform so he wouldn't be shot as a spy and still doesn't know why the German didn't report him.

After thirty-nine days, he and several other downed fliers were picked up by the U.S. Air Force in a daring night-time flight. "The Yugoslavs set fire to bushes to form a runway, and the plane blinked its lights in code and lined up and landed with the fires on its right wingtip. We jumped in the airplane, and as soon as we were in, they lit another fire, the pilot pointed the nose of the plane at it, and we took off as the German guns shot at us."

Back in Italy, Jimmy's tentmates had just sent his gear home, and Hungry Peirson had moved into his bunk. When

Walker walked in, Peirson had to pack up. Walker arrived with a beautiful white silk shirt. He explained that the Partisans had kept his parachute — silk was scarce for them — and had made him a shirt in return.

He thought he'd be going home, "which they usually did to pilots who had been shot down. But they were short of pilots, so I was told I would be flying again, which I didn't like at all. I objected until they scheduled a court martial. The next day I was on another mission. I flew 102 while I was over there."

Several other Red Tails were shot down over Yugoslavia. One of them was Henry Peoples.

> I spent two months with Tito and his [Communist] Partisans. I went on a couple of their raids, and they were exciting, to put it mildly. They were fine people, and their women — such women! You talk about Amazons: Those Yugoslavian female Partisans, I swear they could outfight their men. They were strictly f. and f. — fearless and ferocious.
>
> The partisans somehow got hold of a P-38. I had never flown one, but my own bird wasn't going to fly any place, so I took off homeward bound.[5]

Spanky Roberts told of another pilot who went down in Yugoslavia. "Emile Clifton was a hell of a good fighter. He had been a professional magician on the West Coast, and when the Partisans picked him up, he started picking lighted cigarettes out of the air for them, or some such sleight of hand, and eventually got back to us."

The 332nd resumed its scoring on July 25, when Harold Sawyer gained his second victory.

A day later they added four more victories. Toppins got his fourth to tie Elsberry, or so he thought. His squadron-mate, Leonard Jackson downed his third. Romine claimed his second, and Luther Smith, his first, although neither appears on the Air Force's official roll. Chubby Green and Weldon Groves claimed one between them.

The following day, July 27, was another big one with eight more enemy down, all officially confirmed.

The rehabilitated Gleed scored a double.

We had just arrived at our rendezvous point with the bombers and had been S-ing over them fifteen to twenty minutes with some seventy-two aircraft, when someone called, "Bandits high!" They'd sit up there and come into you out of the sun. I was leading the Group, so I said, "Stand by and watch them."

Then somebody called, "Here they come!" Most of the time the Focke Wolf 190s flew like a gaggle, no real formation, just a bunch; the Messerschmidt 109s were in formation when they came in. It was the 109s that hopped us first.

I told my squadron to break left, drop fuel tanks, and pull up into them. They busted through us, and we lost two guys on that initial pass, but I think the bombers got a couple of the 109s. After the 109s had made their pass, the 190s came in behind them. They had a mess of them, just like a flock. Must have been about thirty of them.

I got some holes that day. They were firing 20-millimeter cannon; we had 50-mm machine guns, three in each wing. Two of my guns were shot out, probably on that initial pass.

When you get in those scrambles, your blood pressure goes up a little bit. Most of us were pretty split up. You break down into basic elements of two, and your wingman tries to help you out. You're yo-yoing back and forth, very easy to get mixed up, and the P-51 didn't look a whole lot different from a 109 in battle. It's hell for breakfast.

I was busy trying to keep from getting knocked out, and at the same time I was on the tail of a 109. I hit him, and he exploded; I must have gotten his ammunition. He just trailed smoke and went down. Meanwhile, my wingman knocked another one off my tail.

When we attempted to get back to the bombers, we saw some more 190s, so we struck out after them and got into another running battle. I got one. I had to follow him right on down to the deck [the ground] to get him knocked down. Before it was over, two of my remaining four guns ran out of ammunition.

I'd gotten separated. My wingman went peeling off, facing a guy, and the battle proceeded on. I had two of them on my tail, one guy was peppering me, and part of one wing was gone. I got down on the deck, where there were hills and valleys. They chased me down the stream and up the stream and around church steeples − I went past one steeple by five feet. Every time I would try to come up, they were sitting up there waiting for me. I was heading in their direction, away from home, but I finally maneuvered around into a valley and just flat-out flew on the deck and outran them. I had the throttle to the firewall as far as it would go. I was just going to go as long as I could, then pancake it in or jump out. Fortunately I got there. At the end of the runway, the engine quit. Not a drop of fuel left.

Alfred Gorham of the 301st also scored two, Leonard Jackson of the 99th, one — his third altogether.

Felix Kirkpatrick of the 302nd got one.

I was the Flight leader of four fellows, and when the enemy aircraft made an approach to our bombers, we went over to intercept them. This one aircraft made a quick pass through our bombers and made a dive for the deck, heading for his base as fast as he could get there, and we followed him down. There was no problem in catching him; you dropped the nose, and the plane would drop out of the sky. The problem was not to overrun him, and we caught up with him and shot him down.

But we were so intent on getting the airplane that we didn't realize where we were. We were so close to his base, the next thing we knew, we were in the middle of a lot of flak, so we climbed back up and headed for our own base.

In all, in the twelve-day period, July 16-27, the Red Tails scored thirty-eight confirmed victories and another six unconfirmed. But an even more important record was growing — the Luftwaffe still had not managed to break through the tight security screen and knock one of their 'babies' out of the sky.

In fact, the Red Tails were so effective that kills became harder and harder to achieve. "The Luftwaffe began dodging us like the plague," said Walter 'Moe' Downs of the 301st. "They were jumping all over the Groups in front of us or behind us, but they left us and our birds alone."

Bussey had another theory: the Germans were literally running out of gas.

We had hit Ploesti nine times, and by June we had destroyed it. It was the only German oil source, so they were able to fly damn few missions. To transport oil over a thousand miles by road was bad — the roads were bad, and the guerrillas were giving them hell. The only way to get their oil to Germany was on river boats up the Danube or by train, and we shot up a lot of railroad stock. They finally had to use peroxide as fuel. So they had a tremendous shortage of oil, and we saw relatively few fighters in the air after that. A lot of guys [in other units] shot down twenty or thirty planes, but they did it early in the war; we didn't get there until 1944.

Historian Frank Olynky, who has carefully researched every victory claim in World War II, said the major reason for the abrupt drop in kills was that Germany withdrew its fighter planes from southern Europe to protect the homeland. In addition, Hungary and Rumania, where the Red Tails had scored many of their kills, changed sides in late 1944, thus removing those countries as aerial combat arenas.

Meantime, Carl Johnson of the 100th closed the month with a victory July 30. He added another a week later.

George Rhodes of the 99th scored one August 12.

About that time, B.O. Davis called Gleed in for a talk. As Gleed described it:

> I was always bitching about not making rendezvous with the bombers on the minute as planned. After sixteen missions the Old Man told me to come to headquarters. "What do you think about taking over the Group Operations job? Do you think you could handle it?
>
> I said, "Anyone could handle the job as well as those clowns missing Rendezvous Points."
>
> He said, "I want you to go down right now." So I had the Group Operations job, as well as flying, and started getting compliments on the exactness of the planning. So now I'm back in the good graces of the Old Man; I'm not in the outhouse any more. My effectiveness actually improved.

Purnell was forced to make an emergency landing on the island of Vis off the coast of Yugoslavia.

> I lost control, and I think I dinged a wing. My first thought was to get out and hide, because I didn't know what the situation was, although we had been told that if we were captured,

the Chetniks [anti-Communists] and the Partisans were killing each other, but no matter which faction got you, you were safe. It was the Chetniks, I found out later, who got me. They put me in a hut that evidently had been used by some shepherds, and I was told to stay there. That night I was pretty shaken up and couldn't get to sleep.

Next morning I was awakened by a lot of voices on the other side of the wall. I couldn't imagine what they were. I looked out a high window and saw faces of nothing but women, old men, and children. They had never seen a black, I'm quite sure. I went out, and while we were standing there, one little kid wanted to share the stage with me. He ran his fingers across my arm and turned around and looked at his fingers to see if the black had rubbed off.

I hadn't quite made up my mind how to handle it when I spotted a woman with a baby in her arms, so I held my hands out for the baby. I put my finger out, and the baby grabbed hold. I remember the expression on the mother's face: She offered the kid as though she were handing it to some strange kind of creature — she must have thought this black monster was going to eat her baby. I held it, burped it, and gave it back to her. The baby laughed, and I heard this soft murmur go through the crowd.

They brought up wine and fruit, and I knew I was all right.

13

Ground Wars

In August, General Eaker had a new assignment for the Red Tails — the invasion of southern France.

As the invasion forces gathered off Marseilles, the Red Tails flew in to "soften the beach up." Bill Melton recalled: "We'd hit German coast watching stations, then go after rail traffic, vehicles — anything moving, we'd shoot."

Ground strafing could be more dangerous than a dogfight. Bob Williams called it "the most exciting thing we did. You can see how fast you're going — 350-400 miles an hour — you can see the action, you can see the damage you're doing. You see the locomotive's steam shoot skyward when you hit it, or you shoot up an airfield full of planes and they explode. *That's* exciting — except when you hit an ammunition car and you have to fly through the debris."

On August 12, three days before D-Day in southern France, the Red Tails made a low-level strafing run to knock out radar stations in the big harbor at Marseilles.

Lucky Lester:

We went in under the enemy gunfire, and all three of the other planes either got shot up or shot down, and there I was in the harbor all by myself. I said to myself, "Well, how do you get out of here?" I decided the best way to get out was to get as low to the water as possible and try to get below the gunfire. They were shooting down at me from the hills, but I never did get a hit.

Six others did. Joseph Gordon and Langdon Johnson failed to return. Alexander Jefferson watched Robert O'Neal crash on the coast — he was picked up by the Free French Resistance — and John Daniels was also hit and crashed into the water. Jefferson was hollering, "Not the water, man, don't ditch it!" when he was hit himself: "Oops, Jeffie, boy, you're on fire." He rolled the plane over and dropped out.

My 'chute opened just before I hit the ground, which shows how low we were. When I got to my feet, I was looking into the shooting end of a German soldier's rifle. I said, "OK, OK, just get that damn thing out of my face."

I was escorted to this magnificent home, and this resplendent German officer was having tea on the veranda. He smiled pleasantly and in perfect American English told me to have a seat. I was flabbergasted as I dropped into a chair. He offered me a cigarette and asked me if I knew anything about New York, Chicago, Detroit. When I answered yes, I lived in Detroit, he talked about the Forest Club, the Oakland bus line to the Cozy Corner cabaret. I was being royally entertained with the details of the ghetto areas of my hometown. He said he had lived in Detroit and he actually knew the names of some of the bartenders.

The guard marched Jefferson to the town square, where he met another armed guard coming toward him with Daniels, "looking like a wet rat."

After three days of solitary confinement on bread and water, the interrogation began. An officer gave Jefferson a cigarette, pulled out a book, flipped a page, and said, "Lieutenant, that's you." Jefferson's eyes grew bigger as he recognized the photo of his Tuskegee graduating class. The officer then told him his birth date and birth place, his parents' names, and even his sister's latest marks in school. Alexander himself had not had any news from home, but after the war he found out the officer was right.

Meanwhile, some one hundred miles away, Dick Macon had crashed into the ground.

I was strafing at four hundred miles an hour. The plane crashed into a building and caught fire. Apparently it killed some people, because the building was completely demolished. So was my plane. I don't know how I got out. My 'chute must have opened just about the time I hit the ground.

I 'redded' out. When you black out, the blood rushes to your feet. But if you're upside down, the blood rushes to your head, and you 'red out.' A negative G force popped the blood vessels in my eyes, so I bled out of my eyes instead of my brain.

My plane was demolished, so they reported me dead, but some Power much greater was responsible for my escape.

When I regained consciousness, I didn't know where I was or what I was doing. I tried to get up and hide the parachute and get to someone who was friendly. But my third, fourth, fifth, and sixth vertebrae were broken in my neck; I was paralyzed from the waist down. And my shoulder was broken with a compound fracture so the bone stuck out, and that's what started the pain. I lost consciousness again, and when I regained it, the pain was excruciating.

I saw three Germans standing over me with machine pistols, and fifteen to twenty Frenchmen standing at a distance in a circle. The Germans said, "*Raus mitt ihnen!!* I didn't know what that meant, but I figured it meant "Get the hell up." Of course I couldn't. They helped me up very roughly, put my arms around their shoulders, and took me to a waiting vehicle, which looked something like a VW Beetle. I saw charcoal burning on the back bumper in a big tank like a water tank. Throughout the whole ride it went pop-pop-pop.

They took me to a schoolhouse, which was a field hospital. Intelligence said the Nazis had some of the same fetishes as the Ku Klux Klan and that they would remove the genitals of an African American and push them into his mouth before they killed him. I knew this was going to happen to me, so I tried to fight them off with my left hand. It wasn't much of a fight. They put ether over my face, and I was soon out.

When I came to, my first interest was to see if I was all still there. I'm happy to report I was.

The next day more trouble. The Germans learned a plane the day before had killed a lot of Germans and the pilot had been captured. And that was me. "Let's go get the son-of-a-bitch and bring him over here and kill him in front of our troops."

There was quite a scene when they came and tried to get me. A French boy of about fifteen was in the room to try to help me. He tried to tell them I wasn't capable of getting up, but they didn't pay him any attention. One of the guys kicked him, and the little fellow bounced across the room like a basketball. I passed out.

Next thing I knew I was in a vehicle, blindfolded; they were taking me to a place with walls around it, and I could hear a whole bunch of troops talking. By this time I could tell that they were going to kill me. It wasn't a nightmare for me, it was a welcomed event, because I anticipated much more excruciating pain, and this would put an end to it. I didn't get frightened until months later when I was much better off.

They tried to prop me up against the wall, but my legs kept going limp. I even helped them; I wanted them to hurry up and get it over so I could get out of my pain. Once they got me on my legs, I could hold up my body, and when they leaned me a certain way, I saw I could stay upright leaning against the fence.

I heard an order by a guy, and some soldiers marched in. They were ordered to halt, and another order was given. I could hear the *clack* when they put a round in the chamber. Another order — it must have been "Aim!".

Then the gate opened — an old gate that needed oiling; it was creaking like the gate on the old "Inner Sanctum" radio program. "*Achtung!*" I could hear heels clicking, and shouting. One guy was talking loudly, like talking to underlings, and they said, "Yah, yah, yah" — like they would wipe the saliva off after he left.

He took my blindfold off and took me down to a *hauptmann*, a captain, to interrogate me. He spoke perfect English and had been in the States for ten years — New York and Los Angeles. Sitting in the room were two Gestapo storm troopers, over in the corner, just listening. The captain was very cordial, he even occasionally said, "Sir." He showed me how much he knew already. He had my cadet graduation picture, with a circle around my head and Joe Gordon's head, who was also shot down, and the grades I made. I asked him about William Griffin of the 99th. He found Griffin, a POW: "He has a tennis court and golf course. He's there because he's cooperating. You can have the same things."

When we took off on the mission, they gave us another ID in case we were captured. The Germans had searched me and found my two IDs. One was mine, and the other one was a Moroccan airport worker who was deaf and dumb — how 'bout that? They didn't know whether I was me or the Moroccan.

"Why are you strafing there, when the fight is going on in the north?" he asked. I was thinking name-rank-serial number. "What field did you take off from?" The only thing I could remember was Walterboro. I didn't know how the hell I got here in France. He was really teed off. "Look, I've got a way to get the information if I have to." I looked at the two Gestapo. "OK, here's the last chance you have: What was your code name in combat?" The *hauptmann* said, "Do you know what that is?" These were top secret, because lives were at stake. My code was 'Subsoil 6.' "If I give you the first half, will you give me the second?"

No use fighting; I told him yes.

He said, "Sub."

I said, "Soil."

He said, "That's right." I don't know how the hell he knew that, but he knew it.

They locked me in a stable. By this time I could walk a little bit, but very gingerly, because if my head shook, I would pass out. I had to walk with two people on each side. They helped me get into a trough where they fed the animals, with straw in there to lay on. When I sat up, someone had to help me raise my head up. When I laid down, they had to hold their hands cupped against my neck until I was in a supine position.

That night I heard the lock unlock: *Clank, clank, clank.* I thought, "Hell, here we go again." A guy with a flashlight was speaking German. Then I heard other voices. They found me in the trough.

When the light shone on me, I heard, "It's a *spook!*"

It was Jefferson and Daniels, but they didn't recognize me, that's how terrible I looked.

The prisoners went to sleep, with Macon shaking uncontrollably.

Back home his wife had refused to give up hope. "My sister-in-law had Ouija boards and got the vibes and said, yes, I was dead and buried in France. My mother had given up. But my wife knew I wasn't dead, that I had miraculously survived. It was her strong will not to accept that I was dead."

Next morning they were put on a train. "Do you know what it was carrying?" Jefferson asked. "Those goddam German 88s [anti-aircraft guns], going east to be set up for another go at us." While Jefferson cursed, not a single Allied airplane tried to hit the train.

Macon:

The trip to the POW camp, *Stalag Luft-3*, took several days. We had no transport. We had three guards, and they'd commandeer any transportation that passed and make them take us as far as they were going – wagons, pickup trucks, even a train for a short distance. Then we'd start walking again.

We passed through a little country town in France. There was a German enlisted men's club by the side of the road and Germans going in and out with beer in their hands. Our guards wanted to go in and get a beer, so they told us to sit on the curb, and the three of us sat down while German troops passed by, talking.

Along comes a Frenchman, his lady, and a little girl, riding on bicycles. The man stopped and came back. He had taken out some francs and stuck them in Daniels shirt – the guy was giving us money in case we escaped. Just then some Germans came and snatched it out of his hand, and there was a big commotion. Germans were running from everywhere. They grabbed the man, his daughter, and his wife, and along came a truck, bringing a cloud of dust with it. It came to a halt and they just threw those three people in there. The last time we saw them, they were yelling and screaming, and the truck disappeared in another cloud of dust. We knew they must have been executed for helping the enemy.

Further up the road, there was a club with some women, and our guards made some passes at them. They commandeered a house to spend the night and said, "We want to chain you to the bed so we can go out and have a party."

I said, "No, no, no — Geneva convention. *Officers*." They looked so sad, I said to the others, "Look, this may be the best deal we can make. If we give them a break here, they may give us one later."

The others said, "Oh, hell, OK, they can tie us up." The guards had their party, and after that every time they went to a farmhouse, they came back with six bottles of wine, three for them and three for us. They even came to attention when they talked to us. We got along very well with them.

Once they went to a farmhouse about five hundred yards away and left us on top of a wagon filled with hay. We saw some B-25s fly over and bomb the next city. One of the planes got hit, and we saw five 'chutes, so we knew they all got out. The Germans put a cordon around where they had bailed out. Some soldiers with guns, thinking we were from the B-25, told us to get down from the wagon. They were about to shoot us when our guards came running across the field yelling, "They're our prisoners!" and they finally stopped aiming their guns at us.

We went through some mountains, walking at that time. I don't know what happened to my jacket, and I was freezing, so Jeff took his jacket off and let me wear it. If he hadn't done that, I don't know whether I would have survived or not.

To Jefferson,

The most frightening part of the war was when I saw the Hitler Youth. When they saw us, they started their tirade — "Yah, yah, yah," — saluting and heel clicking. It reminded me of the Klu Klux Klan. That's the only time I really became frightened. Being shot down? No big deal. Bailing out? No big deal. Flying combat, flying through flak. No big deal. It was the terror of seeing how children's minds can be so warped.

They finally reached *Stalag Luft-3*, mid-way between Berlin and Warsaw.
Jefferson:

The camp commander was named Galadowich, from Budapest. He was dressed immaculately in jacket and leather boots and said, "Men, you are prisoners. For you, the war, she is over." I think he had in the back of his head that when the war was over he wanted to live in America, because he kept asking us about things in the U.S. All the prisoners and he got to be good friends. But he couldn't understand a joke. All the things they did in the TV show, 'Hogans' Heroes,' we did as prisoners.

The old-timers got to pick their roommates. One "cracker with the deepest southern drawl," pointed to Jefferson: "Ah thank ah'll take this 'un." Jeff's new roommates represented every state of the Confederacy and had chosen him because they knew he couldn't be a German spy. "They could trust a black man, but they were afraid of a strange white face." They "treated me as one of them. Each man performed a duty, we combined our rations, cooked our meals together, and shared equally." Jeff helped them dig escape tunnels, but there was no hope of escaping himself – he would have a hard time passing as a German civilian. *Stalag 3* was his home for the next nine months.

On the 23rd Luke Weathers of the 302nd and his wingman, William Hill, claimed a victory between them. Again, like several others, it is in dispute and is not found on the official record; however, Weathers was adamant that the plane did go down.

The next day, August 24, Johnny Briggs, Charlie McGee, and William Thomas each scored victories, and this time there was no dispute.

Briggs described his action.

We were coming back from a mission up in Germany, at about sixteen thousand feet, and a 109 pounced on us from above. My wingman, George Taylor, said, "Bogey, six o'clock." The 109 had pulled up in a climb, and when I saw the swastika under his wing, I dropped my tanks. After you drop your external fuel, you have to select an internal fuel source, turn on your guns, your gunsight, throttle, and proper controls.

The 109 didn't stop climbing until twenty-three thousand feet. I was down behind him, and I don't think he could see me at first. Then he leveled off and made a turn to see if anyone was back there, a slow turn to the left. I said, "No, you don't," and I shot — *Brrrt*. He started a slow turn to the right. *Brrrt* — I let him have it again. Bullets bounced off him. He slowed up, and I thought he was deliberately pulling power so I'd zoom by him and he'd be on *my* tail. I said, "Oh, no you don't." I pulled up beside him and above him, and he went into a spiral, going down, and I saw his 'chute open. He was probably saying, "Well, you got me today, but I'll be back tomorrow.

McGee described his victory in his usual laconic way.

The bombers were hitting an airfield, with a lot of fires around and buildings burning. The combat lasted about as long as snapping your fingers — you see them, they see you, and you get mixed up. I stayed on the tail of one all the way down to the ground and was able to get a burst in on him before he crashed.

On August 27 and 30 the Red Tails wiped out twenty-two enemy planes on the ground and possibly eighty more that couldn't be confirmed because of the smoke. They destroyed eighty-three more on September 2, yet not a single enemy plane rose to challenge the destruction.

On September 22, Chris Newman was returning from Munich over the Adriatic Sea when he had another of his now familiar close calls in his plane, 'Goodwiggle.'

I got hit by flak up around twenty thousand feet, and my engine started sputtering. I started smoking and burning, and my escort screamed, "You better get out of there, it's going to blow!" To go down in the sea was the last thing I wanted to do. We had lost nine men in the Adriatic, and none of them were recovered, so I was trying to make it back to Italy. I could see the coast, and if I could just make the beach, I could belly land easily, no problem. I was doing everything I could to keep the airplane going, but I didn't have any power and was coming down pretty fast. All I could see was fire, and I radioed, "I've got to leave." Yep, no doubt.

I pulled my oxygen mask and radio headset loose from where they snap into the airplane, because you don't want anything loose entangling you. Then I pulled the lever to jettison the canopy, rolled the plane over on its side, popped the stick forward, and the airplane ducked down and left me in the air, it just dropped out from under me. That was the system the Germans used. I tried it, and it worked fine.

I was tumbling out of control. Then I remembered in training we were taught to snap to attention, and when I straightened out, the tumbling stopped. I said, "It worked!"

Next I pulled the ripcord and waited for the 'chute to open, thinking, "How long does it take?" until I saw the oxygen mask in my hand and realized that I had pulled the oxygen tube instead, so I grabbed the ripcord and pulled again. The 'chute opened with a bang. It was quite a jolt. Luckily, I had altitude, so I could freefall for a while and recover from mistakes.

The 'chute has a survival kit with a one-man dinghy, dye, and other survival items. It's attached to your belt when you get in the plane, so that in the water you won't lose it. It had ripped open, so the dinghy was hanging beneath my feet by an umbilical cord, you might call it. That meant there was more room in the harness than normal. The chest strap normally goes across your chest to hold you in, but it was above my head. If I had been thrown forward, I would have tumbled out. I had seen a movie where a guy fell out of his chute, and I was thinking about that, so I grabbed the strap and pulled myself back in.

Before I hit the water, I unfastened my leg straps and just hung by the chest buckle. As soon as my feet hit the water, I turned loose the chute harness. The wind pulled the harness over my shoulder and pulled me back to the surface. I pulled the CO_2 tube and inflated my dinghy. I felt completely exhausted, just worn out. I guess I was just tense and thankful.

It took a minute or so to get my dinghy inflated, and my escort was circling where the plane went down, and was getting farther and farther away from where I was. It's easy to lose a man in the water, from the air he looks like the head of a pin. I started to wave my scarf at him, and it was bloody. I was bleeding from a gash on my neck, and I didn't even know it. A big fishing boat, splashing water, just chugged right on by me. I think I threw up once or twice, rocking around in that little dinghy.

Then a P-38 came along and saw the dye I had put in the water. He came down, buzzed me, and put in a May Day [call for emergency help]. He circled until a Spitfire came out and it circled for about an hour. I was in the sea about six hours when a twin-engine British bomber dropped a great big eight-man life raft. I got into it and an Air/Sea rescue boat, like a PT boat, picked me up.

When I got back, it was possible I could have been rotated back to the States. They must have thought I was losing my nerve, because they didn't put me back on the schedule for missions. Alfonso Simmons, had gone down in Yugoslavia, and the guerrillas picked him up and brought him out, so the two of us walked around for two weeks, then we told them we'd get back on flying status. He was subsequently lost in combat. I continued flying for the rest of the war.

Combat was taking its toll on Howard Baugh.

I had flown more combat than normal, 125 missions in the P-40, then ten in the P-51 — all the way over to southern France, across Italy, across the Mediterranean Sea, strafing radar just before the invasion. But it never made the papers; the only invasion that made the papers was Normandy. Then we made a few runs over to Ploesti and southern Germany.

It worked on your mind. You know you've got to get up at five o'clock and fly a single-engine plane over water six or seven hours, encountering enemy aircraft. The mind can only take so much of that, so I went to see the flight surgeon and told him I was tired. He called it combat fatigue.

This one mission turned out to be my last one. We had been on a long flight, and everyone was anxious to get on the ground. We were supposed to stagger, one on the left side of the runway, the next one behind it on the right, alternating right and left. Spanky Roberts told me an airplane behind me almost landed on top of me, just barely missed me, and I didn't even know it. When I parked the airplane, he was there in his jeep and told me to turn in my gear: "You're not going to fly any more."

"Who's going to tell Colonel Davis?"

"I am. Right now. As long as I'm commander of the 99th, you're not flying any more combat."

Baugh called Roberts his favorite commander, even ahead of B.O. Davis. "He had a compassion for his people, and he looked out for me."

On October 12, the 302nd was the low squadron flying an escort mission into Germany. For the first time in almost three months, the Luftwaffe scrambled to repel them, and suddenly enemy fighters were buzzing as thick as they had been back in July.

The squadron had just crossed Lake Balaton, Hungary, Lee Archer told Charles Francis, when Lee spied a group of enemy aircraft at two o'clock on the tree tops, just taking off. He called out, "Bandits," and Pruitt immediately rolled his plane, 'Alice,' over and dived at a Heinkel bomber with Archer close behind in 'Ina, the Macon Belle.' The Heinkel began pouring smoke, and Archer finished him off — "he disintegrated in the air" — though Lee refused to claim credit for Pruitt's kill.

Twelve enemy fighters then took to the air, and Chubby Green knocked out one of them.

At that point Pruitt saw a flight of enemy planes heading toward them. He flew directly at them, guns blazing. Then Archer said, "we made a tight turn and fell in behind three enemy aircraft." Archer gave one of them a short burst and tore off its wings.

Pruitt sent a second one down in flames.

He was pursuing the third, when a 109 came from the side and slid in behind him. "I pulled up behind him," said Archer, "and gave a few short bursts, and the plane exploded, throwing the pilot out."

Meanwhile, Pruitt's guns had jammed, and Archer saw him furiously trying to unlock them. "Move over," Lee said, "and let a man shoot." Pruitt pulled away, and Archer eased into his position and fired two long bursts. The enemy appeared to be trying to land, and "I opened up at ground level with a long volley, and he crashed onto the runway. Then "the German ground crew opened up with all their guns. Lights were blinking at me from all directions. For a few seconds I had to dodge flak and small arms fire that burst all around my ship. But I was lucky and managed to wiggle out."

Not entirely. Archer's propeller had been hit, and Pruitt pulled in beside his friend and stayed with him over the Alps to the emergency field on the Yugoslav island of Vis.[1]

Luther Smith, Milton Brooks, and Roger Romine also received credit for one victory each.

The score for the day: Nine more enemy planes.

For the next five months, they would get only two more.

"At Ploesti I almost bought it," Moe Downs said. He was strafing an airfield when he banked his plane onto its side, and "as I looked down the wing, I looked right into a German gun." Luckily he "clobbered it" before it could clobber him.

In October, the British were preparing to invade Greece, and the 99th was sent in on a low-level attack against Nazi airfields in Athens. Nineteen year-old Hannibal Cox remembered one day well; it was his first day in combat.

> It was a real hotbed. The fields were circled by ground fire. Guys were going down – we lost four out of my squadron that day. That's where I picked up my nickname, 'Killer.'
>
> We were supposed to make one sweep across, hit as much as we could, and get out of there. But there were a lot of aircraft left on the ground, so I pulled up and went in again in spite of the fire and shot up some more. I was the only one. I picked up a few hits, but by the grace of God, nothing vital.
>
> Later, when the gun films were shown at our base, my film showed pass, pass, and pass, aircraft after aircraft blowing up. The guys said, "That man is a killer!"

On October 4, the 99th hit another airfield. The commanding officer, Erwin Lawrence, the last of the original 99th, was flying his last mission before going home; one report said he volunteered when another pilot was scratched. "We came in right over the trees," Shelby Westbrook recalled. "The Germans had strung cables in certain areas and I believe Lawrence ran into a cable." He crashed and died.

"It was an unneeded mission," said Bill Campbell, who commanded the flight. "When we got down low enough to see them, most of the planes were already damaged. We lost two or three on that mission, and it really was a mission that intelligence screwed up on."

Most of the planes destroyed were on the ground, but Westbrook, flying his seventh mission, recalled: "Thomas and I caught two Junker-52s in a landing pattern. They were slow, lumbering aircraft, and an easy target."

Charles Francis wrote that three more planes were shot down in the air, by George Gray and George Rhodes, plus one shared by Milton Hayes and Henry Perry. However, Campbell did not recall anyone claiming a victory in the post-flight briefing. The Germans had removed most of their fighters to protect Germany itself, he said. None of the victories was recognized by the Air Force and, in fact, do not appear on the records of the 99th in the National Archives.[2]

All the pilots, except Westbrook, died before they could be interviewed for this book. Westbrook just shrugged: "The Air Force hasn't recognized a lot of the aircraft that we destroyed."

A frequent target was enemy trains. Each pilot had a map with an overlay marking the target off into squadron sectors, and each squadron hit everything in its sector.

"If it was moving," said Williams, "we'd blast it." On one mission to knock out a locomotive and cars, "the Germans had an ingenious trap. On the far side of the tracks there was a wooded area, where they had anti-aircraft guns – intelligence hadn't told us that. Suddenly that forest looked like a New York Christmas tree. It was like flying through rain drops all around me, great round circles with orange in the center. How I got through without being hit, I'll never know."

Near Munich, Wendell Hockaday flew into the train he was strafing. His wing clipped the train, but he managed to fly the plane to the Alps, where he was forced to bail out. He was never seen again.

Bert Wilson recalled one four-man flight. "I was the only one who got back, because when I pushed the button to drop my tip tanks [on the wings], one just hung. The other three planes went across the field to strafe. I don't think any of them made it. It's target fixation. You get so intent on the target, you get lower and closer until you hit it yourself."

Roscoe Brown:

We used to have film sessions Tuesday nights after the missions. They'd have your trailer on the screen, and if you made claims that you couldn't substantiate, you got a big boo, and it sort of pushed you to do more than you really needed to do. So when I was flying ground support, on each mission I fell lower and lower and lower, because I wanted to get good pictures,

One day I was strafing an ammunition train in Austria, doing about 350 miles an hour. I had some guys behind me, and there was a lot of ack ack, so I dropped even lower than I normally dropped until I was below the level of the train. In fact, I got so low that just as I went over it − boom! I must have hit it with my left wing just as the train exploded.

The plane almost went into the ground, but fortunately, I was able to grab the stick with two hands and wrench it to the right and added a right rudder. That's one of those split-second things − if you don't do it, at that speed you're dead. I pulled it up and looked over. One wing was half off and was turning upside down.

Gradually I pulled it up to ten to twelve thousand feet and flew it on home. At the base there was a question whether I was going to bail out. I called in to the tower and said I was coming in to land, get the emergency equipment ready. When I got close to the ground, I cut the engine and pulled back on the stick, held it hard right, and it settled right in, a three-point landing.

Bob Williams:

Brown was flamboyant, he really took chances. When we'd come in off a mission, everyone tried to make the tightest turns and real steep approaches and buzz the field − it was show-off time. Brown would always get down lower than anybody else, just barely touching the ground. One day he didn't quite make it.

He flipped the plane over and ended up with 100-octane gasoline pouring out all over him. Richard Caesar, our engineering officer in the 100th, dug him out from under that plane. He had to dig in the ground from below so Brown could get out of the hole he'd dug.

"Gasoline was flowing everywhere," Caesar remembered. "Brown was inside with his seatbelt on in this little cockpit. I had to go under the plane and maneuver his legs up to unhook his seatbelt and finally got his head coming out and dragged him out. By the time I got him out, the sucker [the plane] blew up." Caesar shrugs that he wasn't a hero. "I did it without thinking."

Three months after Hannibal Cox arrived, he took over as a Flight Leader in the 99th.

> I was leading one Flight up to Lake Balaton, Hungary, and we destroyed everything in the airdrome, pass after pass, ripping everything to pieces. It was impossible for the enemy planes to get off the ground. One plane was taxiing to a take-off position, and my number-three man clobbered him before he got into position. I hit a revetment that had aircraft in it and pilots attempting to get in the aircraft. The .50-caliber shells just lit up when they hit the enemy. We bored in on one aircraft, destroyed it, and came in on another. The 15th Air Force just refused to believe that four ships could do that much damage.

Spanky Roberts:

> On one mission we shot up and destroyed an estimated one hundred fifty German aircraft. Because of problems we had had in proving we had done the things we had, after the second pass, I backed off, and as the other crews were going in, I took a long-range shot so you could see the aircraft burning. They sent out a recon pilot to assess the damage and made the mistake of not telling him not to find anything. The poor fellow did what he was told and reported the damage we had done. After the war an officer in the Pentagon found my films to prove it.

Strafing made the war personal. Melton recalled, "The durnedest thing that ever happened to me was in a place called Narbonne, near the French-Spanish border. I hit a hay stack that caught fire. Two Germans came running out and disintegrated in front of these .50-caliber machine guns of mine. I never will forget it."

Purnell:

On a mission to Yugoslavia we spotted a lot of German lorries filled with troops. We peeled off and came down, strafing them, thinking only of those swastikas on top of the trucks. The guys inside jumped out, headed into ditches, set up their machine guns, and started firing at us. We flew right into the fire with our guns going.

When I got back to the airfield, as after every strafing mission, I checked the plane for bullet holes. Hanging over the edge of the scoop on the intake under the P-51 was a strange object. On closer inspection, it looked like a black-brownish glob, wet in some places. I took a stick and poked at it, and it fell off the scoop. It was fleshy, and then it came to me: It was part of a man. I must have gotten a portion of his chest or his behind. It also hit me that his family had raised him, just as my family had raised me. Then you begin to think of the futility of war, that wars have been going on for ages and ages, and they never settle anything. And you wonder why we do it. You wonder why we do it.

14

Christmas

That winter Europe was hit by the worst storms in a century. From October 13, through March 23, the Red Tails scored only two victories in five months.

However, day after day their most important record was steadily building. The men of the 332nd climbed into their Mustangs and droned through the clouds to shepherd the bombers safely to their targets and back. Their reputation was building too: Not one friendly bomber had been lost to enemy fighter planes while they were flying cover.

When Spanky Roberts was named assistant Group commander, Alfonzo Davis took over the 99th. Within days, at the end of October, he failed to return from a mission over the Alps. "He sailed off and went down and away," one pilot said. Davis' replacement, Bill Campbell, speculated that he may have fallen victim to oxygen deprivation.

Frederick Funderberg was lost in a storm and never found.

Lawrence Dixon, the guitarist, went down in the Alps. His engine quit, Woody Crockett said, and he started down, then tried to return to the formation to complete the mission but went down again. This time he didn't return. "He must have walked away from his plane and then went back to it for warmth. We heard he was found frozen to death in the cockpit."

One day, Ed Gleed remembered:

It was raining like holy be-jesus. You could hardly see the other end of the runway, and clouds were thick overhead — we didn't have any way of knowing how thick. The fighters would have to break out over the clouds and then join up with their leaders.

The Old Man was flying the mission; I was in Group operations. It was near the time of take-off, and I called back to General [Dean] Strother's 14th Fighter Wing headquarters to find out if the bombers had taken off. I got some jughead major down there who wouldn't give me the information. I said, "I want to talk to your boss. Is General Strother around?"

"Yeah, he's here."

"We'd like very much to know whether the bomber Group has actually taken off on time, because the weather is stinking here, and I don't want to jeopardize our men any more than we have to."

Strother said, "You get that outfit off on time!"

I sent a jeep down to the other end of the runway to tell Colonel Davis. He said, "You call him back and ask him directly if the bomber outfit has taken off."

So I did: "I've got Colonel Davis at the end of the runway. He wants to know positively, because he can't see the operations office from there."

"You tell Ben Davis to get those airplanes off the ground and make that rendezvous!"

So I sent the jeep back down with the message. We initiated take-off three minutes late, but we got them off. He didn't know how deep the crud was, but they took off on blind faith and got up there. Ben Davis swung away and attempted to calculate mentally how to get to the rendezvous with the bombers. The join-up was at fifteen thousand feet. It would have been completely in the clouds to do it, but somehow our planes got up and joined up and started out. I don't think even I could have flown it, and I was pretty good.

The bombers never did take off. We were informed three minutes after we lost radio contact with our planes. Strother also called back and wanted to know did we get those airplanes off. I said, "General, I haven't seen any flashes [of colliding planes]." I banged the phone down.

We lost one man trying to get back home through that stuff.

A few days later Strother came down to our base and proceeded to give us a third-grade lecture about how to respond to authority: "The most vitally important thing is to make rendezvous." He particularly jumped on my tail for challenging his operations people and demanding to know whether the bombers got off. He never has apologized for the fact that the bombers didn't take off that day. That remained a bad taste in my mouth forever.

It was shortly afterwards that we had a visit from a reporter from the black New York *Amsterdam News.* They had been raising hell editorially about why the 332nd hadn't been put in for a Presidential Unit Citation, compared to what some of the other units had done. This guy had gone to 14th Headquarters, and General Strother told him to his face: "Ben Davis is OK, but those other guys he's got flying for him are nothing," and he wasn't about to recommend us. The reporter came back and spread the word. You can imagine what a blow that was. That was a big dip in our morale there.

As it turned out, the request for the Citation was made by 15th Air Force Headquarters, General [Nathan] Twining's office, not Strother's 14th Fighter Wing. After the war, I think Strother made lieutenant general. Twining became Chief of the Air Force.

The weather grew worse. "One cold, cold morning [November 16] it had snowed," Gleed said. "On a cold morning the darned engine on the P-51 was subject to detonate, that is, prespark." Crockett, "an old auto mechanic out of Fort Sill," speculates that after a few days layoff, water got into the engine and made it "spit and sputter on takeoff." For that reason pilots liked to warm their planes up thirty minutes before takeoff.

Gleed:

The only other way to correct it is to ease up on the throttle so you aren't going full-bore. That's a hard thing to tell a guy trying to get a P-51 off with loaded wing tanks. We had a single runway of inter-locking pierced plank, and we had so many airplanes, with four squadrons instead of the usual three, that in order to get off in a minimum of time and to save fuel, we'd take off at five-second intervals. That's what we shot for. We came close.

Just as we started to take off, an Italian proceeded to drive a herd of sheep across the far end of the runway. The first two aircraft got off, but we could definitely hear the detonations. Roger Romine in my former 302nd, was the third man to take off. He barreled on down the runway, realized he wasn't going to get off the ground, and there was nothing else he could do — he plowed into the sheep and went off the end of the runway into the mud. By this time the next man was already rolling down the runway behind him. He saw the mess, chopped throttle, and rolled off on the side, where Romine was mired down in the mud and slush and snow.

Romine never got out of his aircraft; why, I don't know. I started to stop the takeoffs then gritted my teeth and decided to keep going; I figured they could clear the two planes and the rest of the sheep. About the sixteenth aircraft after that we had another guy cut his throttle, and he went straight into Romine's plane down there. Immediately on impact Roger's airplane blew.

Crockett was at the other end of the runway, having just sent off the last plane of his 100th squadron:

> I had fired the flare gun to let them know my last airplane was off, and the other squadrons started taking off in the opposite direction. That's when William Hill's plane smashed into Romaine's. There were two airplanes, and every one was fully combat-ready, all guns armed and full of .50-caliber ammunition, and each carried a full load of fuel, two 75-gallon tanks under the wing. That made a pretty good fire. There was a big ball of fire, ammunition was exploding, and I threw my flare gun away and ran out there wearing my British combat boots.
>
> William Hill was trying to get out of the second airplane onto the wing. He didn't have his goggles down and got burned around the eyes, but I pulled him to safety.

Crockett was awarded the Soldier's Medal for non-combat heroism.

Gleed:

> Now I'm looking at these two balls of flame, and I've still got twelve aircraft left to take off. Damn it, I sent them up. When I think of it, that may have been one of my worst mistakes, although I don't know what else I could have done. It was a matter of timing and making rendezvous when you're supposed to, and war was war.
>
> Fortunately the rest of them got off, they didn't miss the rendezvous, and they also got in a scrap. But I had one damn good pilot gone and two severely injured. Those are hard ones to forget.

Rookie Bertram Wilson, who had just arrived, was on his first mission that day and watched the tragedy from the flightline.

> I was the third or fourth guy to take off, and I had to fly into all the smoke. I flipped my oxygen tank to 100% so I wouldn't breathe the smoke in my cockpit, but you get nervous trying to remember to do everything, and I forgot to turn it off, so I was using it even when I didn't need it. Over twenty thousand feet, that's when you need it, and that's when I didn't have any.
>
> Over the target, at thirty-five thousand feet, I looked down and I didn't have any oxygen left, so I had to come down to where I could breathe. We were on radio silence over the target, but I broke silence and told my leader I was going down.

On the way home, Luke Weathers of Romine's 302nd told Charles Francis he was escorting a crippled bomber home when two bogeys were sighted at two o'clock high. Weathers flew into them. After a short burst from his guns, one enemy fell into a dive. At the same time Luke saw little red balls flying past his canopy — the whole German 'wolf pack' was closing in. "It looked like they had me," so he dived and shook off all but one enemy. "I chopped my throttle and cut my flaps. The fellow overshot me and left me on his tail.... A long burst and a few short bursts sent him tumbling to the ground."[1]

Back on the ground, all the pilots assembled for a debriefing. Davis looked them over. "Who was the asshole who broke radio silence and said he didn't have any oxygen?" he barked.

"Everybody looked around," Wilson said sheepishly. "I looked around too. I certainly wasn't going to say it was me."

On his next mission, Wilson's engine "started acting up, and Crockett had to follow me down." Bert got his name in the paper, but Woody was the hero of the story.

However, Wilson said, "it didn't take long to get to be a veteran. After ten or twelve missions you were made a flight leader because of attrition. Older guys were going home, and you had to be the leader for the younger ones."

Spanky Roberts:

> I remember one seek-and-destroy mission when all Europe was covered with clouds. After we got airborne, the order came down canceling the mission, but we were already gone. A Major Gray had come down from headquarters to fly with us, and I let him fly number-two spot on my wing.
>
> I found a hole, went down, penetrated, found the target, brought the group down, and proceeded to wreak havoc on German trucks on an open plain just south of the Alps. They weren't expecting us, with the cloud cover what it was, and it was great hunting — I hate that term, but that's what it was.
>
> To get back home with that cloud situation, we had to form up in a formation which we did quite well, a squadron of planes in a line abreast going down the east coast of Italy. I went down on the deck, not more than fifty to seventy-five feet off the water. I had to get down that low to find out where we were. The only way was by sight. The major on my right was a few feet lower than me and so on, so the sixteenth man was just skimming the water.
>
> Everybody had to fly perfectly and stay in position for the whole hour or two it took to get home. I think that major went back and advised all the people in headquarters that he knew where the best fliers in the theater were.

Rest and rehabilitation was a problem issue. As Gleed said, "Capri was the rest camp for everyone except the 332nd. Our guys needed R&R as badly as everyone else. We could have gone to Capri, they had the facilities, but instead we had to scrounge around and find a place just for us. We were finally given a villa right on the Bay of Naples, and this became the rest camp for the 'Black Air Force' pilots."

Actually, they were very happy with it. "It was on a precipice," Sheppard said, "you could overlook the sea and could see Pompeii and Vesuvius. But it took too long to reach camp by truck across the mountains, so the 332nd found a twin-engine plane to take them there. Gleed was chosen to fly it.

> First time I'd ever touched a twin-engine. I got one of the finest crew chiefs we had, Sergeant Bobby Damsby of the 99th. He didn't have a flight manual, but he took this airplane and checked it out. In two days he said, "It's ready to fly."
>
> I said, "You going with me?" He got in that darn thing on his stomach behind me where the radio used to be, his forehead right behind my head. I said, "Well, if he's going to ride with me, he must believe it's flyable, and he must believe I can fly it." The engines sounded good to me, so I said, "Let's go." I poured the coal to it, and we were flying.
>
> We contrived a way to fit people in the bomb bay. Later they gave us a B-25 with enough space to carry fifteen guys, just jammed in.

* * *

Meanwhile, another dramatic experiment was going on on the west coast of Italy. The all-black 92nd 'Buffalo' Division had arrived in August and was about to receive its test by combat.

The Division was assigned the extreme left flank of the Allied line, facing a rugged mountain barrier, and went on the offensive in October. Replacement troops also began arriving, including Herb Sheppard, Harry's younger brother. Shep decided to "drop in" on their bivouac. "It cost me a hundred dollars and a three-month restriction," he said ruefully.

> E.J. Williams had just had an engine change, and I had to put four hours of slow time on it to break the engine in gently. I had started out early in the morning, and I had put in a couple hours when this P-38 came down and "bounced me,"

trying to get a ratrace or a dogfight started. When I didn't respond, because I didn't want to overtax the engine, he pulled up on my wing, and we just flew formation.

He just took off and went along a dry river bed through the Apennine Mountains, right through the spine of Italy, and ended up at Casserta on the western side of Italy. As we dropped down the slopes, here was the Fifth Army Replacement Depot and hundreds of tents.

My brother had just landed. They were all sitting on boxes in an open area, evidently having a lecture; the oldtimers were breaking the newcomers in, and these two crazy airplanes come over at head-level and buzzed that cantonment area up and down the company streets, just raked them back and forth. As we pulled up after the first pass, those guys were heading for the weeds!

Herb Sheppard:

I was very afraid for him. The tents were only fifteen feet high at the ridge pole, and he was fifteen feet off the ground. He cut our communication wire, and it looked like he was going to clobber the town, with the mountain right ahead of him. I tried to wave him off, but he came back four or five times. Scared the daylights out of me. I was no good for weeks after that.

I saw the commanding officer writing his number on a pad, so I went AWOL and went to the 332nd rest camp and told them to tell my brother he's in trouble.

Harry:

The booms on a P-38 are rather narrow, so the other plane's numbers were not as conspicuous as the numbers on my big flat-sided P-51. So they sent a report: "Find this man." It went all the way up to 15th Air Force and came back down to the squadron. I was worried sick.

When the report came in to Spanky Roberts, he said, "That's E.J. Williams' plane."

So I went to Roberts: "It was me."

He said, "Well, were you lost?"

I said, "Nah."

He said, "Well, was it cloudy or anything?"

"No. Clear day. Could see forever."

He said, "You're not making this any easier."

I said, "What I want you to do is give me company punishment [in lieu of a court martial]." The Old Man was back in the States, and if he saw this report, with the signatures that were on it, I could see myself down there, stomping around attacking on foot.

So he said, "OK, a one hundred dollar fine and three-month restriction to the base."

I said, "Heh, wait a minute, don't overdo this damn thing." I wasn't making too much, and I was sending my money home. I just had a new son.

He said, "No, that's it."

So nothing ever happened to me except I lost the money that I would have sent home for Christmas.

The 92nd Division was soon the center of one of the great controversies of World War II. General Mark Clark would brand it the worst division in Europe. The 92nd and the 332nd faced similar tests, but the differences between them were huge. For one thing, the top officer corps of the 92nd was all white. For another, its enlisted men were a far cut below the elite men and officers of the 332nd.

The commanding general, Ned Almond, was particularly controversial,[2] and training at Fort Huachuca, on the blazing hot Arizona desert, had been beset by morale problems.

Herb Sheppard offered a candid summary of the Division's men and their record:

> I can't say anything great about Almond, and our assistant division commander was worse; he was a mean guy. The field grade officers were white, and many of the company-grade officers were white. Finally they began to move blacks up into captain's positions.
>
> A lot of the NCOs had come from the Army Specialized Training Program and had pretty high IQs. But usually seasoned troops show the new guys all the things to watch out for; we didn't get any assistance.
>
> For most of the enlisted men, we had a pretty high illiteracy rate; that was one of the major problems. Most of these fellows were from the deep South and had no schooling. The

guys trained on mortars weren't mathematicians, but when they were trained, they were accurate.

They didn't have many trained infantry replacements. A lot of them came from stockades; the Army threw them right overseas as replacements. They said they needed more bodies, but you needed someone who was trained. They used anti-aircraft troops, quartermaster troops, truck drivers. That was another morale buster. When I think of all the guys who didn't have that basic infantry, I appreciated that I did. You can show a guy how to field strip an M-1 rifle, but squad tactics, or coordinating with other units, you need a team that's been trained together. To get an anti-aircraft outfit and throw them into the line immediately, it was pretty rough.

The Division went into combat on the left flank of the Allied line, on the west coast of Italy. They faced a wall of rugged mountains where the Germans were dug in on the Gothic Line and quickly got a reputation for "bugging out" and failing to take their objectives.

We did take an awful lot of criticism, and we never got credit for doing things that were positive. Many good guys were wiped out and never got any credit.

You'll find one or two in any division that might, after an artillery barrage, get nervous and fade out. But the way they tell it, whole units would just take off. Although it's true that some people didn't hold up their end of it, it wasn't an overall truth.

We weren't the only ones who lost ground when the Germans were looking down your throat from the high observation posts. Every division takes ground one day, loses it, and goes back the next day. [In our case] they elaborated on it.

It looked at times that they were trying to get us wiped out. Most commanders would send a company to take an objective; we'd send a squad or a platoon. They were whittling down our squads. The Germans would send a whole mass of people [on an attack]. If we hit them, you can bet that within an hour they would always counterattack. But instead of catching the enemy with their heads down and sending another patrol, [our commanders] would just whittle us down. They were trying to do us in instead of using us the way everyone else was using their troops.

We lost a lot of good guys.

Colonel Phelan, our regimental CO, got killed.

Captain Bundy, heavy weapons company was up on a little cliff. He told his men to stand by, and he just went in there and attacked it himself. They really blew him away.

Lieutenant John Fox called for artillery fire on his own position, saying there were more Germans than there were of us. He turned the tide, but didn't get much recognition for it.[3] Morale sank to nothing. When they made all the remarks about the division, I was ashamed to say I was a part of it, until after I saw other divisions lose ground too. Mark Clark sent the 34th and 36th divisions across the Rapido River, and they were drowned — they caught hell. It wasn't until years later that the Army acknowledged those mistakes.

One of the 92nd black regimental commanders, Colonel Howard Donovan Queen, charged that Clark himself had made the division a scapegoat for his own frustration that the Italian campaign was not winning him the glory that other generals were receiving in France. Clark "placed all the blame on the junior officers and enlisted personnel. The statement is unfair and untrue... Whatever shortcomings the 92nd had rested entirely on the shoulders of Major General Almond. His entire staff was incompetent, excepting Brigadier General Coburn, the artillery commander."[4]

Toward the end of the war, the best men in the 92nd were formed into one regiment and augmented by the famous Nisei 'Go for Broke' 442nd Regimental Combat Team. Herb Sheppard called it one of the best divisions in Europe.

But the 92nd is remembered for its troubles in the first few months. The parallels with the green and untested 99th in Africa are apparent. Colonel Momyer wanted to scuttle the 99th, as General Clark later did the 92nd. Without the leadership of B.O. Davis and the determination of his officers and men, the 99th might have been remembered by history as is the Black Buffalo Division. The comparison makes the accomplishments of the Tuskegee Airmen that much brighter.

* * *

Meantime, day after day the Red Tails were adding to their luster. Day by day their reputation grew. If the relief Fighter Group was late arriving, the Red Tails stayed with their 'babies.' It made the bombers feel they had an additional life insurance policy. "Coming home," Charles McGee said, "there were German fighters who did nothing but wait and look for a guy who maybe had one engine hit and couldn't quite keep up with his formation. We were attentive to that, and if we saw stragglers coming home, we'd send a flight down to stay with them as far as our fuel permitted. It was just something we felt was part of our mission."

Walter Palmer: "If we saw a disabled bomber, we would dispatch two planes to see that it got back to safety. It was for that reason that we earned the name, 'Red-Tailed Angels.'"

"It ran our fuel down," Spanky Roberts said. "On some long runs, we had pilots extended to the point they had to land at the first and closest field and couldn't make it home."

The reputation of the Red Tails was growing. However, other squadrons were getting more victories. The 15th Air Force had three other P-51 Groups and three P-38 Groups. The 31st Fighter Group had what they called a 'Black Flight.' According to Lieutenant Bob Goebel, it consisted of four extra planes who "could range far out to either side of the bomber stream, free-lancing" in search of enemy fighters. They would also "loiter in the target area after most of the attacking force had left for home."[5]

One can imagine the Vesuvian wrath of B.O. Davis if any man in the 332nd had even thought of trying such a tactic.

Gleed:

> Some of the other fighter outfits went out looking for enemy aircraft, didn't hang around to pick up any cripples getting home. But we'd see if we could protect them on the way back. Our guys would get up so close to the bombers we could wave at one another.
>
> Often times the bombers asked if there was any way they could request the Red Tails to escort them. We had made a name as the guys who wouldn't leave them. The record was building day after day: No bombers lost to enemy fighters. As

compared to when we first got there, the attitude toward us had changed; it was almost a welcome reception of our guys.

It was primarily because Ben Davis was our leader, there's no question about it.

"The B-24 and '17 guys used to request that we escort them," said Crockett. "When they saw the Red Tails, they got their coffee."

The men had been away from home for more than nine months, which meant their wives had all had babies at the same time. Walter Palmer had already lost several close friends — Clemenceau Givings, Robert Tresville, and Joe D. Lewis — and after 158 combat missions, the record for the 332nd, and over 400 combat hours, he began to worry that he could be next. Turning down a promotion to captain, he decided to go home and see his new daughter.

As Christmas approached, the weather grew even worse, and the Germans launched their big counter-attack at the Bulge. Most black ground troops were employed driving supply trucks on the 'Red Ball Express' or in other rear-echelon tasks. But as the Germans smashed forward, Eisenhower, over the protests of his chief of staff and Third Army commander George S. Patton, called for rear area volunteers "of all races" to join the infantry and fight "shoulder to shoulder" with whites. Some forty-five thousand blacks responded. One black quartermaster battalion picked up infantry weapons and captured forty-nine German prisoners. African-American artillerymen fought beside the beleaguered 101st Airborne at Bastogne. Segregation was dropped until the German drive was stopped.

In late December, according to Gleed:

> We ran into snow so bad that half the bombers aborted before they got to the target because the targets were also closed in. So we, in turn, turned around and came back, and I think we got all our guys but two or three back to the field.
>
> One bomber outfit, not one of the ones we had gone out to meet, did get to their target but got the holy be-Jesus shot out of them. They found their way back through the crud somehow and came in to our field — four B-24s, a couple shot

up too much to take off again, one guy pretty badly hurt. In all, they had some fifty-five white crewmen, both officers and enlisted men.

We got extra cots and spread them out among the enlisted men and put several more bunks in the officers' tents. The mess hall started cranking out extra chow.

This one captain wouldn't allow his men to leave the aircraft. He himself came out to our operations office, which was an old farmhouse where we had phone contact with 15th Air Force Headquarters, and for over an hour he tried to convince them that they didn't know what they were talking about, that he could get back to his home base. When they finally told him he would *not* take off, he went back and told his guys they would stay in the aircraft overnight and eat C-rations [Army canned food].

One of his sergeants went up to the enlisted mess and found everyone else sitting in tents with pot stoves in oil drums and actually comfortable. The sergeant flat-out defied his commander and stayed there.

I went out and tried to convince the guy that he and the rest of his men were going to freeze to death and to at least come into our operations building, where we had stoves upstairs and down.

At last, about three a.m., he reluctantly said OK, his men could come in. He himself accepted one of our cots, but he didn't sleep in our office, where we were sitting, waiting for possible orders for the next day's mission. And he brought his own C-rations from the plane.

We never got another mission off for six days. About the third day this captain finally came around and found out that the color wasn't going to rub off. We weren't monsters. I'll be damned if before he left there he wasn't converted!

Davis reported that by New Year's "our bomber friends were still weathered in with us and took communion with us at the Sunday service."

Lou Purnell added a detail to the story.

When we weren't flying, we had "other duties as assigned." My duty was to censor the mail of the enlisted men. I came across a V-mail letter, and I couldn't believe it. It said:

"Dearest,
"The most sentimental time of the year is approaching. It makes my heart bleed to know I'll not be with you at Christmas. May God speed the end of this war. It's bad enough I'm not on my home base. I'm stranded at a nigger base, eat nigger food, and sleep in a nigger bed."

I said, "My God! They're the very guys we're protecting!"
It was from a Sergeant Schwartz. My mother was part German, and I knew a few words of German. Translated into English, the man's name was 'Sergeant Black.' I decided to find out who Sergeant Schwartz was. So I got an orderly and a guest book and went to different tents and asked all the visitors to sign the book until I found Sergeant Schwartz.
The next day our runway was cleared, and they all jumped in trucks and were driven to their ships. When they were assembled in front of their planes, I rode up and said to him, "Why, Sergeant Schwartz, you're not leaving anything behind, are you?"
He looked surprised that I knew his name. He said, "No."
I said, "The word is 'No, Sir.'"
That just boiled him. I said, "After all, it wasn't so bad sleeping in nigger beds and eating nigger food, especially when we protect you in flight. I'll see you up there."
I walked away. I knew he wouldn't shake hands with me. I never turned to see the expression on the guy's face.

Colonel Davis told his command: "Your achievements have been recognized. You are known by an untold number of bomber crews as those whose appearance means certain protection. The bomber crews have told others, and your good reputation has preceded you in many parts where you might think you are unknown."
Henry Peoples told of going on pass to Bari, Italy. "Being typical upright young Americans, the first place we hit was a bar. Sitting at the bar were a couple of bomber pilots and navigators. One of them noticed us and said, "Pardon me, but are you guys with the Red Tails?" We answered yes, and before we knew it, we were surrounded and being kissed. If it was possible, I was beet red."[6]
McGee reported a similar tale:

Some bomber pilots were glad to get together with us and reminisce about getting through a scrap safely. We were both professionals, and they said, "Let's go in here and have a beer." But there were others who wanted to continue the segregation in Europe that existed in America, and they tried to put us out of eating or drinking establishments because we "weren't supposed to be there." Our friends just said, "Well, either they stay, or we tear this place up."

Scenes like this happened more and more frequently. Oddly, said Henry Borland, another Red Tail, "I never had a bomber guy stop me to shake my hand or buy me a drink who didn't have a southern drawl.... They were damned glad to see our black faces up in that 'wild blue yonder.'"[7]

Melvin McGuire, a bomber crewman, in his book, *Bloody Skies*, told of another mission when his crew was limping home, carrying seventy-five bullet holes, with one engine out and their fuel almost gone. They were about to bail out and had radioed one last distress call when a strange voice came over their frequency: "This is Gallant. We're right off your starboard wing, the landing strip that's right under you. You're welcome to come in here. I can see you."

The pilot didn't wait but went straight in and sputtered to a stop on his last drop of fuel at the end of the runway bordered by red-tailed P-51s. Trucks raced up with fire extinguishers, and the crew was driven to headquarters, where they finally yielded to hysterical laughter. There were not enough chairs for everyone, so McGuire sat on the desk, laughing, when "suddenly this black major walked in, looked at me, and said, 'Get your ass off my desk, will you?'" (The major is not identified, but it sounds like something Ed Gleed or Spanky Roberts would have said.)

He turned out to be "a fine man," however, and asked when they had last eaten. They told him 0230 that morning, more than twelve hours earlier. He said, "I figured that, so I stopped by the kitchen, and the cooks are going to fix up a snack for you."

McGuire wrote:

> That day I ate the finest meal I had in Europe. They didn't serve us standard fare. They had dipped into their goodie bag

for treats they were saving for special occasions and served us pork chops, all we could eat. They wanted to make sure we didn't leave hungry.

While we were eating, the terrible screeching and banging and hollering and noises of props beating on the landing strip assaulted our ears. A P-38 was crash landing, a solid mass of bullet holes.... It came skidding in, stood on its nose, and plopped back down.

Ten minutes later the pilot arrived, his head swathed with bloody bandages, saying, "They told me we're having meat!" and helped himself to a plate of pork chops too.

Most squadrons stockpiled some good things or materials for special occasions, but these guys were sharing them with us.... We knew we were eating somebody else's pork chops, and we ate enough for fifteen to twenty men.... That meal was just another example of the excellent outfit they were. The relationship between the Tuskegee Airmen and the bombers in the 15th Air Force couldn't have been closer. They were one of the premier groups in Europe. I can't say enough good about the Tuskegee Airmen....

When you were six hundred miles from home, those red tails looked mighty nice. I never heard any racial slurs from bomber crews directed towards the Red Tails. Lord, we loved them.[8]

15

VICTORY IN EUROPE

That winter the Germans threw the first military jets, the ME-262, into the air to try to stop the Allied drive. Chuck Yeager of the England-based Eighth Air Force had shot one down in November. However, General Adolf Galland, the chief of the German fighter command, wrote that "from American flight reports one can see that the ME-262 broke again and again with ease through the American fighter screen and shot down one bomber after the other from the tightly closed formations despite an inferiority of a hundred-to-one."[1]

The Fifteenth Air Force also spotted some jets, and George Iles "got into a few frays" with them.

> It was a mismatch in numerous ways but not in others. They were extremely fast, but to engage in a fight, they had to slow down, and we were more maneuverable. The dogfights didn't last very long, we were moving so fast. The ME-262 pilots would play with us. They could come from behind, then zoom up right in front of you. All of a sudden, for a brief second you had his full silhouette right in your gunsight. If I'd been fast enough and had the reflexes, I might have had a hit.

On February 25, Iles was shot down:

I got hit by the 'flak train,' as we called it. Flames were licking past the cockpit and got sucked in, and I started to bail out. I even turned the plane upside down so I'd fall out, but then I turned it back upright and decided to ride it down myself. I did everything according to the book, except I forgot about the air scoop on the underside of the P-51; it acted like a shovel and dug into the dirt and plowed a big line across the field. I would have slid in much better without it.

We had classified gun sights, so I shot mine up so it wouldn't fall into the hands of the Germans. I don't know to this day whether the plane burned completely or not. I got away from it as fast as I could.

At first no one was around, so I started to hike toward the Swiss Alps, which I could see in the distance. I stopped a fellow on a bicycle coming down the road, trying to find out where I was, but he didn't speak English, and I could only speak a few words of German. In half an hour I became a guest of the Germans. Two trucks converged from two directions, and an element of the Home Guard picked me up. They treated my injuries, and I was taken to a jail in the little town of Tiefenreid, near Munich.

I was fortunate to be grabbed by the military. One of our pilots in the 332nd, Lincoln Hudson, was beaten severely by civilians before the German military got to him. The civilians had been bombed and shot, their homes had been burned, and they were more angry than the military, who thought of war as a job.

The next day I was put in a boxcar with a couple of guards for the long ride to the interrogation center at Frankfurt. The guards treated me very well and shared their food with me. At Frankfurt we went out of the station to catch a streetcar to go across town to the prison camp. As we stood there, a mob gathered around. I was roughed up by the civilians, and if it hadn't been for the guards, I would have been beaten, I'm sure. (Incidentally, the streetcar conductor refused to let us on until the guards paid three fares, one for me. It tells something about the German mentality.)

The Germans tried all the old tricks to get information out of us, such as planting English-speaking Germans in the group to try to elicit information. They didn't have any English-speaking blacks they could fly in, but they had obviously made a study of our Group. We were required to tell only our name, rank, and serial number, so the interrogator said, "OK, then I'll tell *you* a few things," and took out a book with "332nd" on the cover. He opened the book and began to read. He had a list of all the classes that had graduated from Tuskegee, with names of all the pilots and a lot of personal data, the radio call signs of the units, and even the code for the day of the flight I went down on. So they obviously had someone feeding them information from our camp.

If you talk to other black prisoners of war, we all mention the same thing: We had been segregated all along in the Air Force. Prison camp was our first experience in the military of being non-segregated. The Germans treated us just like any other American pilot. It was ironic: You had to get shot down to be treated as an equal.

One German, who spoke excellent English and had lived many years in Chicago before the war, said, "I know how they treat you people, especially in the South." He often wondered "why you fellows choose to fly and fight, and perhaps die, for a country that treats our German prisoners better than it treats you."

That was sort of thought-provoking.

I was the only black at the interrogation center at that time, and the other Americans were kind of stand-offish to me. There were no overtures of friendliness. My best friends were not Americans but British. Everywhere it was the American soldier who carried prejudice with him. Not until you got in life and death situations was all of that torn away.

A couple weeks later George's old classmate and buddy from the 99th, Harold Brown, walked in. Iles continued:

Prison camp was not like 'Hogan's Heroes' on TV or the movie 'Stalag 17.' There was no time for escape schemes — survival was uppermost in our minds. No food was coming in, and the Germans had even begun to take the prisoners' Red Cross parcels. In all fairness, though, the Germans themselves didn't have enough food. So our whole day was centered around eating, getting ready to eat, or trying to find scraps of wood to make a fire if you did get something to eat.

Black bread and soup was a staple. We'd get barley soup, but the barley had weevils in it. The weevils would float to the top, but you drank it anyway — well, some drank it. Some didn't have the stomach, but if they didn't, some of the old-timers would take it until the newcomers got to the point where they'd eat anything.

Some people, who were supposed to be officers and leaders, sank to a very low level, while some of the enlisted men emerged as real leaders. That kind of experience brings out the real person.

Meanwhile, a scandal hit the 302nd when the technical supply officer, who had washed out as a pilot, was caught selling parachute silk on the black market to support his girl friend; he stuffed the packs with newspapers instead. Luckily it was discovered before any deaths resulted, and he was given twenty years in federal prison.

With spring, good flying weather returned, the air war intensified, and Hitler's once-vaunted Luftwaffe became increasingly powerless to defend its homeland.

With prospects of victory growing, on March 6, the 302nd was deactivated. It had written a unique record: They shot down twenty-seven confirmed enemy craft and lost four pilots themselves, and none of them in aerial combat. Chubby Taylor and Roger Romine perished in accidents; Walter Westmoreland and Emory Robbins were lost and presumed downed by groundfire.

Meanwhile, in the face of the Allied advance, the Germans decided to move their prisoners to Moosburg in southern Germany, near Dachau. The temperature plunged to 15-20 degrees below zero.

Iles recalled:

> I guess it was seventy or eighty miles, and it took us sixteen days walking. The clothes we wore were the ones we had arrived with. Some men who bailed out lost their shoes. With the shock of the parachute opening, the shoes just flew off — so they had to wear make-shift shoes.
>
> On one occasion, our column was strafed by four American P-47s. Everybody just ran — blindly ran — guards included, and seven or eight prisoners got killed. But as the planes came down low, they recognized that they'd made a mistake,

and the fourth one didn't fire or drop his bombs. After that, every day a couple of P-51s hovered over our line of march, to prevent it from happening again.

Dick Macon:

On the 'Atrocity March' we were going through the mountains, it was freezing rain. I was completely exhausted when we got to a little town with a wall around it; they had closed the gates and wouldn't let us in. The guards couldn't find any place for us to sleep, so we slept out on the highway in that rain. I almost froze that night.

Just about dawn two guys got me up and started walking me around, and we started walking toward a light. One guy, his parents were born in Germany, knocked on a door. A lady came to the door, and he told her I was his comrade and I was freezing. At first she was a little hesitant — I guess we'd have been the same way — but she let us in.

She told us about her son on the western front, in the Battle of the Bulge. She said they had been overrun and she hadn't heard from him in two or three weeks. She didn't know whether he was well or not. She hoped wherever her son was, if someone saw him, they would be kind to him, too.

Eventually, they arrived at Moosburg. "We were all in the same camp there," Jefferson said. "A lot of Russians and Poles were across the wire — the Germans treated them horribly. Conditions weren't too much better for us either. Lavatories were open pits, the place was full of lice, and we didn't have enough food, so it's a damn good thing the war ended."

Iles:

Once you're down to the bare bones of survival, prejudice seems to fade away. One guy from Macon, Georgia and I just hit it off during the march. In Moosburg, he was in the bunk on top of mine, and we would talk far into the night. He asked me if I was going back to the States. He said that, just seeing how I was treated overseas, he thought it was better to stay there than go back.

We were pretty good friends by then, and he said, "Well, I'd like you to come visit me when you get back. I know things aren't very good in Georgia, but if you ever come that way, I want you to come to my house, you're welcome, and we'll talk about old times." He was sincere, but I didn't take him up on it, I didn't want to impose on him, because it would have put him under pressure from his fellow Georgians. I don't remember his name, and I never saw him again, but it took quite a bit for him to make that offer.

Meantime the Red Tails were preparing for their biggest mission of the war — a sixteen hundred-mile round trip to Berlin on March 24. Berlin had been in the sphere of the England-based 8th Air Force; this would be the first time the Italy-based 15th would attempt it. To do it, the P-51s would need additional fuel tanks, which had arrived the day before.

Ellsworth Jackson, a crew chief, recalled: "We took them out of the crates and started to put them on the planes on the bomb racks. But when we went to look inside the boxes to get the fittings, they didn't fit. The box said 'For P-47s,' but we had P-51s. These weren't the right types for us."

They immediately informed Colonel Davis, who told them, "Well, the planes have to fly in the morning. They *have* to make that mission."

"So," said Jackson, "we went around on the field and picked up spare parts and fitted those tanks with the scraps. And they flew the next day."

The new German jets rose to challenge the flight. Roscoe Brown was flying his new bubble-canopy P-51-D, with Lucky Lester's old #7 on the side, and 'Bunnie' painted on the nose in honor of his infant daughter. He recalled the day:

> The B-17s were about twenty-four to twenty-five thousand feet, and we were a couple of thousand feet above them. We flew in flights of four planes, eight planes on one side, eight planes on the other side. We would sort of weave across each other, spread out all over the sky.
>
> I was squadron leader, but I decided, since I thought it was going to be an easy mission, to break in a new leader and let one of my flight leaders lead the squadron, while I flew 'Tail-End Charlie' to watch him.
>
> We were supposed to take the bombers to the IP, where they turn to go to the target and we would be relieved by the 31st Fighter Group, a white Group. When they were delayed,

we were told, "Stick with the bombers over the target." So we just kept right on with them over the target.

All of a sudden I saw these little jets. I had seen them three or four times before, when we were escorting P-38s on photo reconnaissance missions. The jets had been maybe five thousand feet above us, sometimes as close as fifteen hundred, trying to scare us; they flew around but never made a pass.

So, immediately, I knew what they were, and maybe I knew a little bit faster than anybody else. I said, "Nine o'clock," which means they were coming in from the left, just about the level of us, maybe a little bit below us. "Drop tanks and follow me."

I made a reverse peel and came down, and everybody came down behind me. I came down under the bombers and came back up to the left of them. I wanted to see where the jets were so I could pull in and take aim, because if I'd pulled straight in, they would have either zoomed back at me or would have flown away.

I've tried to think how we were able to get the jets. For one thing, in spite of their great speed, they had to throttle back somewhat to hit the '17s, and before they could accelerate, we were able to get them.

Second, I don't think they saw the reverse peel. When they flew by me, I don't think this one guy saw me.

Third, our planes had new electronic gun sights. With the old sights, you had to count your "rings of lead," like a quarterback leading a pass receiver. But with the new sight, you put the sight around the wings of the enemy plane as they do now, and that automatically gave you your lead.

I went *brrrt, brrrt* and got him right in the middle. He ejected, and I got a beautiful picture with his parachute and everything. Great show.

Charles Brantley and Earl 'Squirrel' Lane also each bagged a jet.

A couple of the jets got away and shot down two men in the 301st. But we got three that day. The 31st picked up a couple too, but they did it after we did. By the time they got there, the jets were already screaming around.

I must have made some really sharp maneuvers, because afterward I looked around for somebody else, and they were all gone. I looked around for any other planes to shoot down, and I saw one a thousand feet above me with a German cross. I said, "Oh boy, there's another one. This must be a Messerschmidt. Let me go get him."

Then I said, "Damn, that's a P-51." It was a captured P-51, and I was dying to shoot him down over Berlin! I could shoot him down, I knew that, because I had a better plane, a newer plane. But I'd burn up my damn gas. So all of a sudden, I just broke off and let him go and flew back by myself about three or four hundred miles. When I landed, the engine was still going, but I must have had two drops of gas left. It pooped out on the runway.

Someone had seen me get the jet, and everyone already knew what had happened. The crew chiefs were out there jumping up and down. They refueled me, and I went back up and had a great time "tearing up the field," doing victory rolls. The tents were in squadron areas, and I found my own area, dropped down to about the level of the tents, and came down one company street, pulled back up, turned upside down, did a roll, and came back down going the other way. I did that for about ten minutes. At the farm house we used for headquarters, they had these telephone lines, and I came in under the wires and pulled up and did another roll and landed.

That was my highlight. Nobody in the 15th Air Force had ever done it before, shooting down a jet.

On the same flight Cox had half his wing shot off but made it back safely, completing his sixty-fifth mission.

On March 31, the Red Tails downed thirteen more enemy planes. Brown and Lane each got one, to go with their jets.

Lane's flight of four was just below the clouds at four thousand feet, when he called, "Bogeys, eleven o'clock." There were ten to twelve German fighters below them, and Lane dropped his tanks and dove. Bobby Williams, in his plane, 'Duchess Arlene,' was in the flight. "The ideal tactic was to yo-yo — hit and take off — because we were outnumbered," he said. But his wing tanks wouldn't fall at first. "The element of surprise was lost for me," but he dove into the fight anyway. "I was going down, no matter what. I got on the tail of one plane and gave him a few short bursts. He fell off and tumbled to the ground. I had to get out of there.

> As I was pulling out, a German fighter was on my tail, so I made a steep turn, and just as I turned, another enemy plane shot across my nose. I fired and fired and fired until he went into a steep dive and crashed. A steady stream of tracers was coming out of my guns, which indicated I was practically out of ammunition. I poured the coal to my engine, but it started to cough and buffet, because it was too much power. Oil from my cowling was running across my windshield, and I thought I'd been hit. I told the guys, "Fellows, it looks like I'm going to have to walk home."
> Lane asked, "Did you push your prop pitch forward [to absorb the extra power]?" So I did, and the power surge was just immense. That beautiful little P-51 took off like a banshee, and I accelerated out of the area. I looked back and saw another German plane with his wings lit up with fire coming out of his guns, but I disappeared into the clouds and joined up with our other two planes and came on home.

Rual Bell was another 100th pilot. "He was a short fellow," Williams remembered. "Every morning he'd walk into the mess hall and announce himself: 'One heaven, one hell, one rule — Rual Bell.'" That day Bell also scored one victory.

Hugh White of the 99th and Carl Carey of the 301st were also victorious.

Bert Wilson found himself in a low-level dogfight. "I got on the ME 109, and we were in a very steep bank, so steep that when I started shooting, the centrifugal force wouldn't permit my guns to feed. When you're really sucking it in, it pulls the ammunition belts out of the magazines in the wings. Only one of my guns was shooting. It sounded like a BB gun — pop, pop, pop, pop. I got him anyway."

Eventually Wilson's other guns resumed firing, and he got a second enemy, plus a "half-victory." "Somebody else claimed it too; I don't know who. It all happened in about three minutes. It's pretty hard to recall it accurately. It was all a blur, and after fifty years you're going to embellish it."

Bill Campbell, now commanding the 99th, described his victory in his usual soft-spoken way:

We had released the bombers to another Group, and coming back we had permission to shoot anything moving north of the Alps, so we dropped down, hunting something to shoot at. We attacked, and I think we shot down seven enemy aircraft, but we lost two of our own. Actually, we outnumbered them. They weren't looking for a fight, we had to chase them and catch them. I got behind one, fired, and hit him, and he crashed.

In April, the Red Tails flew fifty-four missions, a record for them. On April 1, the day before Easter, they scored thirteen victories. Harry Stewart of Long Island scored a triple.

That same day Jimmy Fischer had a close call:

We got into a little scrap up in Germany, three to four hundred miles away. On our way home, we were free to hunt for trouble, so the 301st broke away from the rest of the Group and flew straight down the Danube River. When we got to Linz, we ran into a lot of flak, and the only thing to do was break away from it. We were looking for enemy barges; instead we saw enemy planes coming our way.

The Jerries attacked us from the rear, and I tried to release my wing tanks, but they were stuck, and by the time I finally released them, the fight had started. I wheeled around and plowed through the enemy, and by luck, I didn't get hit. I picked out one of them, and the fight was on. Then, just when it got hot and heavy, we were bounced by another formation of 109s, who had come up to join the fight.

It seemed as if every Mustang up there had three enemy aircraft on him. I could see an enemy smoking, and looking down I saw one of our planes crash into the ground. I fired and hit two Jerries, but they just wouldn't go down, and I was pouring it onto a third when I spotted one of our P-51s above me with smoke streaming out and an FW-190 right behind him, firing with all his guns. I broke off my attack and pulled up behind the Focke-Wulf and gave him several bursts and succeeded in driving him off.

He made a dive for the ground, and I was right on his tail, but he went down to the deck and lit out across the airdrome, where they threw up everything but the kitchen sink at me. I could feel the hits on my aircraft, but I had finally caught up with the Jerry, and I didn't intend to turn him loose until I had knocked him down. I could see my bullets going into his aircraft until he finally hit the ground and exploded.

The ground fire cut my rudder cable and just missed hitting my heel. If you know anything about flying, that's the end, so I got up a little speed and got the hell out of there. I ducked over a hillside and was checking my gasoline when I happened to look up to see tracer bullets sailing past my canopy.

I finally outdistanced the Jerries and looked around at my tail, and the darn thing was almost in shreds. I was about fifteen miles from Vienna, so I called my leader and said I was going to head for Russian territory and turned south to try to get to Yugoslavia.

Both my rudder cables were gone, but my trim tabs were still working, so, making very gentle turns and climbing very slowly, I began to start back toward friendly territory, begging my aircraft to please make it just a little longer.

I happened to fly over a small freight yard and a little factory town, and the enemy opened up with their 88 gun. Suddenly the plane lurched, and I looked out at my left wing, and there was a huge hole right through my wingtank. Losing all that precious gasoline I almost felt like crying.

Well, I still had about sixty gallons left, so I decided to try it just a little longer. I flew over the lowest part of the Alps that I could find and shortly broke out over the coast. I can't tell you how happy I was. I began calling for help on all the channels, but nobody answered. Then finally I got a response from a friendly field. A British emergency station picked me up and steered me to Zagreb and an emergency field on an island off the coast of Yugoslavia. They gave me a heading, which I flew for a few minutes, and finally the best-looking friendly field I have ever seen came into sight. I don't know to this day what I did to deserve such luck.

But just as the field was in sight, my ship ran completely out of gas, so I knew it was time to give up the ghost. I unbuckled my safety belt and jumped.

They told us to roll the plane over and drop out, but I can tell you it isn't an easy deal. I crawled over the side and fell out, but when I came out, I hit the tail surface, and it banged up my leg pretty good and threw me into a somersault. I pulled my 'chute cord, and when I opened my eyes, there I was hanging upside down, with my leg tangled up in the shroud lines, floating down to earth with silk over my head. I began kicking until I finally shook myself free. Then I whacked into some heavy branches in a wooded area.

I had landed in an orchard of some kind and was immediately surrounded by a large crowd of unfriendly-looking Yugoslavians. They must have thought I was a German or something, because they had big sticks and clubs. After I finally convinced them that I was an American, they all hugged and kissed me.

Soon a Cub plane flew overhead, and evidently it was directing some motor transport to the place, because a jeep soon rolled into sight. My luck had finally changed. I was taken back to the airdrome and arrived just in time to catch a C-47, which happened to be going my way, and I got home in time for dinner.

I still don't know how it all happened. It was the worst April Fool's day and the best Easter Sunday I ever experienced.

"And that," Jim says, "is how I got my Purple Heart."

Meanwhile, Hugh White was shot down near Italy's Po Valley. His friend, Cox, recalled:

A couple of us wanted to go back up there, find some way to land on the beach, and get him out. There was room for two to ride in a P-51, and we thought we could make a break for it, but Bill Campbell, our squadron commander, got mad at us and ordered us back. In retrospect, I realize the idea was foolish as hell and never would have worked.

Hugh got out OK without us. As he told the story later, the Germans captured him, uncaptured him, and finally *they* became *his* prisoner.

The dashing Pruitt had already gone back to the States, where his hometown of St. Louis welcomed him as a hero. The city named a housing development after him, Pruitt-Igoe, in a big ceremony attended by Senator Stuart Symington.

Then Pruitt returned to Tuskegee to train new students, but he chafed with boredom and begged Davis to take him back in the 332nd. He was about to return to Europe when Bernard Knighten's wife drove him to the airfield on a Sunday afternoon, April 20. He was flying with a student doing a low-altitude slow roll and smashed into the ground, killing both men.

One theory is that the student froze on controls. Another is that the AT-6 trainer did not feed gasoline while upside down and that Pruitt tried the maneuver too close to the ground. "He was showing off," Knighten says.

Back in Moosburg, Macon recalled:

> One day, just before Patton's Army moved in on our camp, we saw American planes strafing some marshalling yards. One came close enough so we could see his red tail, and we knew it was one of our boys. We saw one get hit, saw the smoke coming out of the exhaust, and pretty soon the smoke got so thick the pilot bailed out. We saw his 'chute open and the plane crash.
>
> About an hour and a half later we saw them bring Clarence Driver into the camp. He was from Los Angeles, one class ahead of me in Tuskegee. We called him Red, because his skin was red, and he had a few pimples. He wasn't hurt, but his clothes were almost burned off him. In ordinary circumstances, Red cursed like a sailor. Under these circumstances, he had all kinds of epithets about getting himself shot down.

The next Saturday, April 26, the Allies shot down the last enemy planes in Europe. The Red Tails of the 301st destroyed four of them, two by Tom Jefferson and one by each by Jimmy Lanham and Richard Simmons.

In his POW camp, Iles recalled how the war ended for him:

> On the 28th, to our great astonishment, an American jeep had pulled in under a white flag, and that night the U.S. tanks threw shells over the camp into the town all night. The next morning we saw in the distance an American flag going up. It was an indescribable feeling that few other people have experienced.

Dick Macon said: "The duel between the big guns had ceased," Macon said. "We were hiding so as not to be hit by a bullet at this late date, and we saw two American Sherman tanks in the distance." Before long, General George S. Patton, wearing his pearl-handled pistols, strode into the camp in the center of a swarm of MPs.

The American soldiers grabbed Galadowich, three on either side, marching in cadence. One of the prisoners said, "Heh, Galadowich! Where the hell are you going?"

Galadowich stopped and did an about-face and said, "For me, the war, she is over." They did another about-face and took him out of the camp.

The most exciting thing that happened was to see the GIs go over to the flagpole and lower the Swastika and smash it into the ground and step on it. Then they pulled out Old Glory and hooked it onto the same pole and raised it to the top. I looked around at all the tattered prisoners in all their tattered clothes, looking like they're not worthy of a salute, all standing at attention, saluting that flag as it went up, in complete silence.

16

Homecoming

Macon and Iles flew back to France in some old 'Gooney Bird' with the cargo doors open, Macon recalled. "It made more noise than it made speed and was the only time I ever got sick to my stomach in a plane. I had just married my college sweetheart before I left the States, so I opted to go home. Jefferson opted to stay in France, so he went to the Riviera and had fun."

Iles:

> We got a bath and uniforms with rank insignia. Once they got back in uniform, some of the officers who had withered under pressure looked down on the enlisted men, who had done such a yeoman job, and treated them as their inferiors. That came across as a lesson learned for me: Blacks always say you don't judge a person by the trappings of authority, but by what he is inside.

Ed Gleed was a major when the fighting stopped.

I'd finally gotten over to our rest camp myself. The second day I was there, I was loaded just about to the gunwales and was getting ready to have the next blast when a phone call came. It said a captain from 15th Air Force headquarters with a piggy-back [two-seater] P-51 was sitting at the airport with instructions that I report to my unit with him. As drunk as I was, I said, "You got to be kidding, the war's over; I've waited so long, I'm flat not going." And I proceeded to get drunk again.

Early the next morning, about eight, somebody was shaking me, saying, "By orders of General Twining, 15th Air Force, you *will* proceed back with me to your unit!"

He said if they had to bring me orders, they would, along with a few MPs.

When I walked into the Old Man's tent, surprisingly, he wasn't mad. He said, "Gleed, how'd you like to be in New York Sunday?"

"How do I get there?"

He said, "We've got a C-47 airplane due tomorrow." Beautiful. I didn't ask any further questions. Later I found out he wanted me to go back with him to form a cadre of the 477th Bomber Group and take them to the Pacific, but he didn't tell me this. I got pissed off: But then I said, "OK, anything to get back to the States."

Actually, the 477th was in virtual mutiny, its morale shot, its training at a standstill. Once more the issue was whether or not blacks and whites could use the same Officers' Club. Commented Gleed dryly: "Based on the good record of the 99th and 332nd, I think the fracas was absolutely asinine."

It was nonetheless real.

The 477th and its commander, the 332nd's old nemesis, Colonel Robert Selway, had been sent from Selfridge Field to Godman Field, Kentucky.

"Selway was a terrible leader," James Wiley said:

He was my commanding officer, and I never did see him, just like I never saw Kimble, and I saw Momyer only one time, when I flew his wing. Selway never even assembled us to give us a welcome or anything. He didn't demand attention and respect, and his staff didn't demand respect. We could take off and fly whenever we wanted to. We never did march as a unit.

Under B.O. Davis we had parades every Saturday. You got all dolled up, it made you feel good. That's the way to keep an organization together, make them work.

In April, the 477th was to be moved again, to a larger field in Freeman, Indiana. When the Pentagon told Colonel Selway that he could not legally segregate Army facilities, he was waiting for them with another tactic.

Two of the 477th pilots were Chappie James and Bill Terry, the instructors who had been considered too big for fighter training.

Terry:

They were going to move us to Freeman Field, Indiana. We sent a cadre up there, and they found out we couldn't go to the Officers' Club, the tennis court, the swimming pool, the theater. All blacks were called 'trainees,' even those with a hundred and twenty combat missions. They took the enlisted men's club and made it Officers' Club #2, like an Uncle Tom's Cabin.

The President had issued an executive order that there would be no segregation at any recreational facility on any military air base. We knew that. I guess they thought we couldn't read or write.

The very day we arrived, we said we're going to test Army Regulation 210, paragraphs A and B. Were we going to be declared first-class citizens and officers and gentlemen in the United States Air Force?

Clarence Jamison, an instructor in the 477th, recalled the events that led to the 'mutiny.'

Some of the white officers had never been in combat, but they were designated 'instructors,' and we black instructors were designated 'students.'

Selway called a formation and said, "I want everyone to sign this statement," saying we had read and understood his order. It was a setup for a court martial for disobeying an order. You understand that this was wartime and you're talking mutiny, where the penalty is death, so they had a terrible sword hanging over our heads.

By rank I was the first one in line. I said, "I've read it, but I don't understand it," so I deleted that part and signed it. Some of the other fellows behind me did the same thing.

The lieutenants were more rebellious — some were very rambunctious — and said, "Hell, I'm not signing a damn thing." I think Coleman Young was a second lieutenant. He was kind of wild anyway, a real young rebel. Young was a good soldier, he just didn't take any stuff.

They decided to integrate the Club. Terry:

I was sitting at a table, screening the guys to be sure they had first-class uniforms, that their uniforms were on straight, so there would be no objection to them, except that they were colored.

You know the old Army saying, "Eyes bright, ass holes tight, fingernails clean." And we sent them down to the Club two at a time. If you see forty scrappy young Negroes together, people think it's either a riot or a football game.

Someone had snitched to the Man — we called him an Uncle Tom. By the time the guys got there he had the MPs outside, a couple of lieutenants and a major. They took the names and said, "You're under arrest, go back to quarters."

We had sent about sixty when it was my turn. The guy at the Club told me, "You can't come in here." They say I pushed him out of the way and forced my way in. A major there told me I was under arrest.

Spann Watson had just arrived:

I rented an apartment, and my pretty, new wife had me putting up curtains when someone knocked on the door. They said, "Spann, we're going to the Officers' Club tonight. I know you're going with us." Three or four people had already gotten arrested, but I had a pretty good reputation, I wouldn't take any bullshit from the white folks.

They were trying to make us sign a statement that we wouldn't go in certain buildings. I called Hook Jones, a captain, and said, "Don't sign that statement. Go to the club and go in there."

I was surprised and appalled. He gave me holy hell! "Who are you to tell me what to do?"

I said, "I thought we were all for the same cause, trying to change the situation. If you're not, I am, so forget it!"

Then I told Chappie James what they were doing. "Don't let them force you to sign any paper."

He said, "I got you, Spann. I'm with you. I'll get the order out." That's the difference between the two men. Some people try to knock Chappie James and say he didn't participate, but goddam, I know first-hand he did.

I said, "Let's go see if we can get some more of the guys." I went to see some of the brothers, knocked on their doors.

Some of them said, "Look, I'm making more money now than I ever made in my life, and you guys are fouling it up. No, I'm not going."

Bill Ellis and I went and were arrested.

In all, a hundred and one were arrested. James and Jamison were not among them. It is not clear if James signed the statement or tried to enter the Club. As for Jamison, he said later, "I had gotten a lot of publicity selling war bonds and so forth, so it would have been poor public relations to arrest me. But the 'mutiny' shut down the whole operation. We played bridge or volleyball and wrote to our contacts in the civilian world."

Selway finally closed the Club altogether.

"There was anarchy on the base," said Wiley:

There just wasn't any control. Colonel Selway would walk around, and nobody saluted. No black guys would salute white guys. They had the rank, but there was no respect for them. It was chaos. Selway was supposed to be the commander, but he didn't command.

I couldn't understand how a colonel could allow his command to deteriorate so badly. What colonel would have permitted the arrest of a hundred and one of his officers? He should have guarded against that, but he just wanted to settle a score.

Had he been our commander in Europe, I don't see how in the world we could have succeeded. Or suppose we had had a commander like Momyer. We wouldn't have made it, and that would have been the end of aviation for the American colored man.

B.O. Davis was a good commander. We all looked up to him. Without B.O. Davis, we wouldn't have made the progress we made. If it hadn't been for his tenacity to get the best from his troops, we wouldn't have succeeded.

Good troops are well-led.

Meantime, the hundred and one were unceremoniously lined up and taken to Godman Field by C-47s with a whole bunch of MPs on board. They were put in a corner BOQ [Bachelor Officer Quarters], with big lights on the building and cordoned off with MPs walking around, almost like a circus.

Watson:

For the next several weeks we helped direct 'the Freeman Field Movement.' We were organized and had more telephone calls going out than they had coming in. Coleman Young was running the show, and we were sending out news bulletins. My wife would drive by in my beautiful convertible that I had gotten in the fight over. We'd throw notes and news releases to her, and she would drop them in the mail box.

One of the 'guardhouse lawyers' was Bump Coleman, who later became Secretary of Transportation under President Gerald Ford. Coleman contacted Thurgood Marshall [later a U.S. Supreme Court Justice]. Watson contacted Judge William Hastie, who had been Secretary of War Stimson's assistant for civil rights.

He wanted a copy of the reprimand, so we agreed we'd meet in the Howard University library at nine p.m. that same day. I didn't arrive until ten, after the library was closed, but he was still sitting in the library lobby waiting for me. He wrote the rebuttal, and the Air Force didn't have a leg to stand on.

They saw we weren't going to give in, so they put us on trains, and after much movement sent us back to Godman Field near Fort Knox with a reprimand.

They were marched between rows of heavily armed soldiers to C-47 transport planes and flown back to Godman. As an added insult, Watson said, "There were some German prisoners of war sweeping up the service station at Fort Knox, and they'd go to the Brown Hotel in Louisville on passes. We couldn't even go *near* the Brown Hotel."

Terry: "Little did I know they had already worked something out in headquarters. They were going to give these hundred and one guys reprimands but court martial three of us" — Marsden Thompson and Shirley Clinton, the first two to enter the Club, plus Terry, who was accused of pushing a major.

I was one of the three lucky ones. I was charged with mutiny, treason, and incitement to riot.

Lieutenant Bill Parker's mother was chief housekeeper in the White House, a personal friend of Eleanor Roosevelt. He flew to the White House and talked to his momma, she would talk to Eleanor, Eleanor would talk to Franklin, and he would say, "Let my people be free." But Eleanor was in Hyde Park, New York and Franklin was down in Warm Springs, Georgia for rest and relaxation. The joke at that time was, he said, "The Germans gave us hell in Europe, the Japanese are giving us hell in the Far East, and now the colored people are giving me hell at home."

I was put in jail on April 5. Roosevelt died April 8. The new President was Harry Truman, whom we didn't know.

First, he was from the South.

Second, I knew he had been sponsored by Boss Pendergast, who was anti-us — everyone in the South was, and maybe half in the North too. We didn't know what Truman was going to do.

I spent three months by myself. Nobody could speak to me. I had to knock on the door and ask the corporal of the guard to get the officer of the guard to take me to the bathroom. On the hour, every hour, they asked who you were. It was a pain in the ass. After a month and a half, I said, 'Hell, I gotta get some exercise.' Ten o'clock at night, three nights a week, they'd take me to the gym and I'd shoot baskets.

People like A. Phillip Randolph of the Brotherhood of Pullman Porters, Senator Robert LaFollette of Wisconsin, and Judge Hastie brought political pressure. So did the black newspapers. Congressman Vito Marcantonio [a Socialist Congressman from New York] sent legal help. My mother was from Goldfield, Nevada, and one of her classmates was the Senator from Nevada; he said, "Why didn't you call me earlier?" Senator Hiram Johnson of California was in on the deal. The one who really helped most was Helen Gahagan Douglas, the Congresswoman from Los Angeles.[1]

That was the situation when Davis arrived in June, accompanied by General Ira Eaker, now acting commanding general of the Air Force, replacing Hap Arnold. Watson recalled: "Eaker got all the blacks on one side of the auditorium and all the whites on the other and said, 'Here are your new officers [indicating Davis and his staff]. And these people' — the entire white complement at the base — 'are fired.'"

Eaker added: "It was upon my recommendation and insistence that Colonel Davis is to take command, because of the excellent work I saw him do overseas."

Davis was also named commander of Freeman Field. "And that," said Watson, "was how the first black officer became commander of a U.S. Air Force base."

Most of the white civilians walked off their jobs, so Davis sent for black WACs to replace them. When the civilians returned to their jobs, they were told, "Too late."

"We got rid of all the white personnel," Gleed said. "I became base Operations Officer, and we started training in earnest."

(l. to r.) General B.O. Davis, Sr., Truman Gibson, General Ira Eaker, and Colonel B.O. Davis, Jr. at Godman Field, Kentucky when General Eaker turned command of the 477th Group over to Colonel Davis, relieving Colonel Robert Selway.

Unfortunately, however, with wars raging in Europe and the Pacific, and General MacArthur desperately in need of trained pilots, the training of the 477th had virtually come to an standstill for a year. MacArthur said he would take "anyone who will fight," but the 477th never dropped a bomb in combat. Before it could leave the States, Japan had surrendered. General Hunter and Selway had taken an entire Fighter-Bomber Group out of the war more effectively than the German and Japanese military forces could have.

Earlier, Howard Baugh had an experience that underscored how tragically unnecessary the whole episode had been. When his tour in Europe was over,

> I went to Lubbock, Texas to instrument instructor school with Charlie Hall, Ed Toppins, and Bill Melton. We got to the main gate, and the MP told us to get out and take our luggage out, without an explanation. We wondered what we were running into. A staff car came out and the driver took us right to base headquarters; the base commander, Colonel Estes, wanted to see us. We reported to him, and he said, "I want to welcome you to the base. This base is open for your use." He said he was a classmate of Colonel Davis and gave us his office phone and home phone. "If you have any trouble at all, call me up, day or night." Everyone had been briefed and warned that we were to be treated like everyone else, and we were. We didn't have a bit of trouble.

Bob Deiz had a similar experience. "They figured I was a fighter pilot, so they sent me to Louisiana, which was a fighter field, as a supervisor and I got along well. It was strange, this prejudice we ran into; some places it was awful and some places there wasn't any at all. Then someone realized, this black pilot doesn't belong here, so I was sent to Tuskegee as an instructor in twin engines.

After three months a court martial board convened to try Terry and his fellow 'mutineers.'

Terry:

> I didn't see my lawyer until the day I was court-martialled. A buddy of mine was Thurgood Marshall of the NAACP. My

brother and mother got in touch with Thurgood, and he got in
touch with Ted Berry, a fraternity brother of mine and a damn
good lawyer. Ted was later the first black mayor of Cincinnati
and number-two man in the Peace Corps under Sargent
Schriver.

We had four hours to prepare. That's all.

Our defense was: The order given was illegal. All colored
people can't be 'trainees' — how the hell are you going to
'train' a doctor?

Wiley, one of the members of the court, recalled:

It was strictly a black board; I don't know why Hunter set
it up that way, he should have made a mixed thing of it. But it
turned out better in retrospect. There was no pressure at all,
especially from the command that left with Selway. They all
came in to testify and saluted the flag, and George Knox [the
senior member of the court] reminded them they had to salute
the court, which they reluctantly did.

We found only one man guilty, Terry. He admitted he had
pushed the major, and he was a second lieutenant, so we had
to find him guilty. We fined him fifty dollars. At General
Hunter's First Air Force headquarters, they raised it to a
hundred and fifty dollars.

And with that the Godman Field 'mutiny' was officially over.

Meanwhile, when the rest of the Red Tails arrived home
from Europe, they discovered that some things had not
changed.

Roscoe Brown, the last commander of the 100th, remembered walking down the gangplank in Boston, 'cradle of liberty,'
to be greeted by a sergeant calling, "Black folks to the left, white
folks to the right."

Bill Melton:

We came back to an ungrateful country, just like the
Vietnam veterans did.

I was married to a very light-skinned young woman who
appeared to be Caucasian. Charles Hall, Willie Fuller, myself,
and our wives went to the bus station in Tuskegee to go to
Montgomery to do some Christmas shopping, and when the

bus driver used some nasty language, I saw red and went after him. Willie grabbed me and knocked the hell out of me. He said, "Don't you know you can get killed?" But I just forgot where I was.

Another time when I went into the train station to buy a ticket for my wife, I was wearing the uniform of my country with my decorations and wings. There was no one at the colored ticket window, so I went over to the white side. A little twelve year-old kid was very insulting. A kid! This kind of treatment left scars. Those scars will never disappear.

Spann Watson couldn't get a motel room, even in Pennsylvania. The owner flipped off the 'vacancy' sign when Spann arrived, and flipped it back on when he left. "That was so routine."

Happily, Walter Palmer had a better reception.

My wife and I spent ten wonderful days in Atlantic City on R&R. We immediately went to a black hotel. We knew we wouldn't be welcome in a white hotel. But we told the manager we were expecting a call from the US Army. Sure enough, we got this notification to report to the Ritz-Carleton on the board walk: There was a room for us. The black hotel manager said, "If you can get a room in the Ritz-Carleton Hotel, I'm not even going to charge you for last night's rent." He was so proud to see one of our kind getting a room in one of the swankiest hotels.

While we were there, we met many of the bomber crews we had escorted. They were always asking, "Were you members of the Red Tails?" Naturally I answered in the affirmative. They'd say, "Oh, there was a time when my buddy was hit, and some Red Tails escorted him back to safety. Come on, have a drink on me."

A few of us black officers and our wives went out bowling one night with a bunch of white officers. We waited an unusually long time until finally the alleys were clearing up. "How come we can't bowl?" one of the white officers asked.

The manager said, "The pin boys won't set up the pins for a mixed group like you."

So the officer said, "Let's ask the pin boys then."

They said, "We don't care, we get paid for setting up pins; we don't care who knocks them down."

So we spent an enjoyable evening bowling. As I've written in my book, *Flying With Eagles*, the manager must have figured, "What's this world coming to when blacks can walk around with wings on and overseas ribbons and socialize with white officers and their wives?"

However, the civilian airlines gave the Red Tails a different reception. Like many others, Brown applied as a pilot, but a secretary at Eastern "threw my application in the waste basket and said, 'We don't hire Negroes here.'" Brown went to work as a social welfare investigator at eighteen hundred dollars a year, "which was a cultural shock," before teaching physiology and anatomy at New York University, one of the first blacks to join the faculty there. He later became dean of Bronx Community College.

"The aviation industry wasn't ready to absorb us," Harry Sheppard said. "It absorbed a lot of mechanics — they were unseen faces. But I think the airlines had to service all kinds of communities, and they were afraid that if people were to see a black face on a pilot up there, they would lose business."

Bernard Knighten:

I had only three hundred hours of multi-engine flying time, all in twin-engine bombers. There were thousands of white pilots with thousands of hours in the same type of airplanes the airlines were using. Why would they hire me and train me?

I went back to the railroads as a waiter until the fall of 1946, when I used my GI Bill and entered law school. To make ends meet, I was editing and publishing a magazine and waiting tables at night in Brooklyn.

Charles Bussey bought two surplus training planes and went into business for himself, towing signs and dropping political leaflets. It took a year to pay for the planes, and he decided to go back into Service.

Jimmy Fischer:

It was harder getting into civilian aviation than getting into the military. I put in an application, but I was an old man when they finally hired blacks, in the 1970s, I believe.

A fellow who had five or six drive-in theaters in Brockton gave me a job towing a sign, advertising the theaters. Then I was crop dusting gypsy moths up in Maine, blueberries in New Hampshire, and spraying mosquitoes around Brockton. But the DDT killed everything else too, so they cut that out.

Dick Macon went back to Alabama and, against all advice, joined the Alabama National Guard until officials used his wartime injuries as an excuse to put him out. So he and Chief Anderson bought a couple of planes and started a flying school. They dropped leaflets over African-American neighborhoods "to tell them the air belonged to all of us." They offered Sunday rides for five dollars, and business was so good they bought three more planes.

> Traffic was bogged down with people. Bull Connor [Connor became notorious in the 1960s for using police dogs and fire hoses on Civil Rights demonstrators.] was police chief at that time. He had to provide police for us, and he didn't like that too much, but he didn't try to close the school.
>
> I had one run-in with Bull Connor. We were on our base leg, about to land, and Bull Connor's twin-engine airplane was taxiing to take off. The landing airplane has priority, so the tower asked him to hold position, and we came in and landed. The next day he made an announcement on the radio: "They held up my airplane so some nigger could land. If they ever do that again, I'll close the airport."

Many Tuskegee Airmen decided to stay in the Air Force.

Palmer and Lee Archer left New York for Tuskegee in a snowstorm. Palmer was sleeping in the back seat of the car when it went off the road in Virginia. Archer suffered a broken leg. Palmer had a fractured skull and lost a lot of blood while they lay in the rain for some time until a civilian ambulance arrived; then they lay on the roadside some more until a military ambulance was dispatched. The closest military hospital, McGuire Army General near Richmond, did not admit blacks, so the ambulance proceeded to an Air Force hospital. However, on the way, the driver decided that Palmer was close to death and rushed him to Army General because "if I didn't

survive, the record of my admittance could be expunged."
Archer was taken to the Air Force hospital.

When he came to three days later, Palmer learned that the
nerve in one eye had been severed and could never be repaired.
"I could never fly military aircraft again." He could stay in the
Air Force, "but without being able to fly again, my heart would
break every time I heard a plane taking off." After five months
in the hospital, he voluntarily retired on a lieutenant's pension.

Palmer tried stock car racing with his brother, but when his
brother was killed, Walter decided to give it up and bought a
service station in Indianapolis.

Ed Toppins married the widow of Sidney Brooks. Topp
himself was killed in a plane crash, leaving his wife a Tuskegee
widow for the second time.

Harry Sheppard became a B-25 instructor at Tuskegee, then
was called to France during the Berlin Airlift of 1948.

Watson helped reorganize the 99th as a part of the composite 477th Fighter-Bomber Group. "We had some of the most
experienced fighter pilots in the business, and I was one of
them. When I got through, the squadron was second to no
one's."

Among its members was one of the martyrs in the fight for
the right to fly combat — Yancey Williams, the man whose
lawsuit had paved the way for all those who followed. Watson
said, "They had put him in the infantry and wouldn't let him out
until the war was almost over. That's the price he had to pay for
being the complainant against Hap Arnold. Williams made his
way through combat flight training, and they were going to put
him in B-25s. I got him into the 99th, so he finally got where he
wanted to go. He went to Germany as an engineer officer and
test pilot and was killed in 1953 in an F-86.

In 1948, history was made. President Harry Truman faced a
seemingly impossible uphill fight in the election. The South had
walked out of the party, he needed every vote he could get, and
that summer he issued a fateful order: "It is hereby declared to
be the policy of the President that there shall be equality of
treatment and opportunity for all persons in the armed services
without regard to race, color, religion, or national origin. This
policy shall be put into effect as rapidly as possible...."

The Red Tails are convinced they had played a crucial role in the decision.

Spanky Roberts:

> Stu Symington, then Secretary of the Air Force, made the final decision to go with integration. One of the reasons was his meeting with Wendell Pruitt. Symington was from Missouri, and Pruitt from St. Louis. They met when St. Louis was honoring Pruitt, and Pruitt said to him, 'Give my people a chance.'

There was strong opposition, however, as B.O. Davis points out: "The Army Chief of Staff, Omar Bradley, told Truman bluntly that the Army was not going to have anything to do with social reform. And it didn't do a thing about that executive order."

"But in spite of themselves," Gleed said, "the top brass of the Air Force were less bound and determined to keep the segregated ways. Everything didn't flow rapidly; there were still diehard officers. Hap Arnold may have been one of them."

Roberts:

> There were still officers who insisted that "this is a hell of a mistake.... They're no damn good.... They won't.... They can't....' I was told that only when Davis was flying as lead did [black] missions succeed. So someone simply went down the missions when Davis wasn't there and recorded what happened. Missions succeeded under every leadership. Everyone who led missions led them successfully.

"When the war ended," Bill Campbell said, "I think we were the equal of any squadron doing the same thing."

In May 1949, the Air Force conducted its first continental gunnery meet among every fighter Group in the United States, sort of the first 'top gun' competition. The 332nd under Campbell sent three pilots: Alva Temple, James Harvey, and Harry Stewart, formerly of the 301st and 302nd in Italy. The overall team winner for piston aircraft was the 332nd, with Temple second in the individual. The 332nd was disbanded about a month later.

Years later, about 1993, Stewart recalled, Campbell was looking at an issue of *Air Force* magazine and saw a list of winners, but the 1949 winners were marked "unknown." He sent a letter to the magazine: "Heh, look at your own archives there," because it had been published correctly in the 1949 issue.

In 1996, the magazine made a change but still got it wrong. It mentioned only the individual top gun but again left out the winning Group. Presumably the record will be set straight eventually.

Meanwhile, Roberts said:

> During the war, white officers moved up by moving laterally, from one unit to another, wherever a higher vacancy existed. Black officers couldn't do that. When it came to flying, we had as much experience as anyone, but in staff work we were quite short. So when we were integrated, we were one step behind, maybe two. But the Tuskegee Airmen were the cream of the crop, and they didn't stay behind long. It took a lot of hard work, but we did catch up. But what if we had started out in an integrated setting?

The light-skinned Cox recalled his first integrated assignment. "I reported to O'Hare Field, Chicago to Captain Sam Elias in a military fashion: 'Captain Hannibal Cox reporting, here are my orders, sir.'"

"He said, 'Damn, we were expecting a nigger officer.'"

"I said, 'Captain, if that's what you were expecting, I think that's what you got.' He and I went on to become very good friends."

Joseph Elsberry, who had downed four planes in a week, three in one day, stayed in the Air Force with tragic results, according to Charlie Bussey: "He had emotional trouble. He wasn't treated as well as he thought he should have been under integration. He became hostile against whites and was rather vociferous about it. He started to drink and drank himself to death."

Deiz was one of the first lieutenants to go to the Army Command and General Staff School at Fort Leavenworth.

Watson graduated from the Air Force C&GS at Maxwell Field, Alabama: "When I went to Maxwell Field, no damn black officer could go to the barber shop. I broke that down, but it took a lot of courage to have a white woman shaving my neck with a razor."

Ironically, Watson said, integration actually made the future of black officers bleak. "Here I was a first lieutenant. There weren't many black captains and almost no majors; the white Air Force was full of them. No matter how much experience you had, if I went to a white unit, with my rank all I could qualify for was a wingman." Only about thirty-five to forty black pilots stayed in the Service, and most of them were shunted into non-flying roles. "I went to communications, others to weather school, and Bill Campbell, the greatest flight leader we had, went to comptroller school."

Next the Air Force announced plans to cut ten thousand reservists, and most black officers were reservists. Watson warned that the combination of integration and force reduction would virtually mean the end of black officers in the Air Force.

He headed a study committee, along with Charlie Dryden and George Iles, which urged keeping the 332nd as a pool of experienced black veterans. White lieutenants would be brought to the 332nd for training, while black lieutenants went to white units as wingmen. Spann was "argumentative, a take-charge guy, very outspoken," Iles smiled. "He told you what he thought all the time,"

"Did they give us hell!" Watson whistled. Black leaders charged that he wanted to continue segregation, and the few regular officers told him, "Don't screw up my career. You're right, but, damn, don't get me mixed up in it."

Chauncey Spencer, by then personnel officer at Lockbourne Field, Ohio, the 332nd's new home, also urged blacks to request transfers to white units in order to spread their talent more broadly; however, he wrote, they balked, fearing competition in an integrated setting.

Watson saw his prediction come true. By 1949, no African Americans were being admitted to the new Air Force Academy, "and everyone I knew had been either grounded or separated. That just about destroyed us.

"The only thing that saved us was the Korean war."

17

KOREA AND VIETNAM

When the North Koreans invaded the South in June 1950, many of the Red Tails strapped themselves back into the cockpit and put in a second combat tour.

Charlie Bussey was the first ex-Red Tail into Korea, and he did it on the ground. When the Air Force became an independent service, Bussey was a reservist in the still segregated Army as a combat engineer. His unit was immediately rushed to Korea from Japan with the 24th Infantry regiment of the 25th Division, the direct descendant of the old Indian-fighting Buffalo Soldiers.

When he arrived, the news was desperate as the North Koreans bowled over the South Korean defenders. The 24th Division, the first to arrive, was also hit hard and their commander, Major General William Dean, captured. That very same day Bussey, a company commander, jumped in a jeep for what he thought would be a routine trip to one of his platoons, which was supporting the infantry.

Mail is important to all soldiers, so when we received our first mail, I took it to my platoon. Just my driver and I — I had no idea the country was as hostile as it was, or I wouldn't have been out there by myself.

When we arrived at a village called Yechon, there was a big firefight going on in the village. I climbed a hill, and below me was a series of rice paddies which ran the length of a small valley. I saw a column of about two to three hundred men three-quarters of a mile away, coming out of a defilade arroyo, dressed in white like Korean farmers. I could have driven away, but if they cut the road, there would be no getting out for our troops.

I pressed into service three enlisted men. I put two men on a .30-caliber water-cooled machine gun. I had an air-cooled .50-caliber, and I got one man to feed me ammunition. I let the column move in close enough so they wouldn't be able to back out, and put a burst over their heads. They immediately took cover, someone blew a whistle, and things started happening! They started to move toward my hill.

I was scared shitless, absolutely shitless! I had no business facing that many people, whether out of stupidity, drunkenness, or for any other reason. I kept thinking, "God damn it! Why didn't you mind your own business!" I didn't think I was going to get out of that thing. But now that I was engaged, I didn't have any alternative. There was no place to run to and nothing to do except fight. Air combat was sort of a game. Ground combat is not a game — it is dead serious action on the killing floor.

I had a tremendous advantage by virtue of being up on a hill, and I had fairly good cover, while they were down in a rice paddy with almost no protection. But they had a mortar behind them, and it put several bursts on us. I got hit early with a fragment in my wrist and another in my cheek. They bled a little, but a small wound was not important at that time.

The mortar also killed one of my kids on the .30 and wounded the other. My big gun got hot and stopped firing. That's when I was in real trouble. I didn't think the .30 could do the job, but there was no other way, so I went down and manned the .30 and kept the fire up.

It's very difficult to estimate time in a firefight. It must have been seven to ten minutes, but it seemed very prolonged, because things were happening so fast.

I shot them up pretty effectively and continued to fire until they were all still. I took troops down, and we found a few of the enemy still alive but badly maimed. Since we were probably 50 miles from the nearest doctor, we helped them on their way as an act of mercy. We made a body count — 258 bodies. It was a grisly business.

"Thou shalt not kill." That troubled me at the time. It's still not a thing I have fully resolved.

The 25th Division commander, General Keane, came up to our bivouac and passed out some ribbons and told me the Division was going to recommend me for the Congressional Medal of Honor. He said as soon as the paperwork was in, he'd forward it.

That was the first U.S. victory of the war. MacArthur's headquarters hailed it, and U.S. papers headlined it on page one, although Bussey's role was completely ignored.

Bussey's feat is a subject of controversy, and by 1996 the Army still refused to recognize it. There were few eye-witnesses, although several gave affidavits supporting Charlie's claim. However, three of them died before Army investigators could reach them. The most compelling piece of evidence is a photo of a mass grave, which a 24th Infantry sergeant identified as the grave he photographed at Yechon two days later. [In 1918, Sergeant Alvin York became America's most decorated soldier and received the Congressional Medal of Honor for single-handedly killing twenty-five enemy soldiers and capturing a hundred and thirty-one. At Bastogne, in 1944, José Lopez was credited with killing one hundred enemy with his machine gun and received a Medal of Honor. In 1945, Audie Murphy won a CMH for killing "about fifty" enemy in one fight.]

Ten days later Bussey and his men were sleeping in a schoolhouse:

> Right at midnight artillery began coming in. I started yelling and getting the troops out of the building, through the yard, and out the back gate. When the last man was out, just as I went through the gate, a round blew up the mines and threw a twelve-foot mud and rock wall over on top of me.
>
> It was my tomb.
>
> There was three or four feet of rubble on top of me. My head was under it, but I could breathe. I was in a sitting position, but my head was bent over, and rocks were pinching me.

I exhausted myself trying to get out, but the weight of the rubble was too much. I had to sit there completely penned in all day. It was the most devastating experience of my life.

I was cold. I was hungry. Never in my life have I been so thirsty. An insect crawled into my inner ear; it felt as big as a turtle, but I was powerless to scratch. My eyes and nose were filled with dust. I was hours overdue for urination. I ached in every fiber. I lost consciousness.

When I came to, my sphincter had failed. One thigh, hand, and arm were wet, and it felt as if ten thousand ants were crawling over them. I recited the 91st Psalm, and the 23rd: "The Lord is my shepherd." I had a lot of religious — and blasphemous — thoughts. "Why *me*, Lord?" And a towering voice chilled me: "Why *not* you? Why not you?"

At about 4:30 in the afternoon, the sun warmed the rubble, and I began to hear artillery in the distance and even small arms fire. Finally, I could hear very faint speech and felt that people were close by me. I yelled. A voice said, "Heh, it sounds like one of the mothafuckas is under that stuff there" — that's when I knew they weren't North Koreans. "Take that rubble off, and I'll shoot him." They dug down to my helmet, and I heard someone yell, "Heh, this is a captain!"

They pulled me out and stretched me on the ground. Few men have ever come back from their tombs, but by five or six o'clock I was ready to go again. There was work to be done. My faith was restored, and I had a reunion with God.

But for fifteen or twenty years, any time I was on my back, almost asleep, I felt millions of oriental soldiers double-timing over my grave, until I'd wake up in the middle of the night screaming.

A week later one of Bussey's squads was cut off twenty miles behind enemy lines. They were out of food and water, and several men were badly wounded. His CO warned him against going to the rescue, but he took a platoon anyway, marched out, and brought the men safely back.

*   *   *

Meanwhile the Air Force put out an emergency call for P-51 pilots. It found out that the Japan-based jet fighters had only

Captain Charles Bussey dedicates the "Le Tellier" bridge at Pyongtaek on Oct. 3, 1950. The bridge was named for 1st Lt. Carroll Le Tellier, the designer and construction supervisor.

enough fuel to stay over their Korean targets for a few minutes, but the old workhorse P-51 could stay aloft for hours.

Charles McGee was stationed in the Philippines when the war broke out:

> On the 19th of August 1950, I was riding a P-51 down the runway of Johnson Air Base, Japan. When we landed in Korea, the engineers were still laying a thousand feet of steel planking on our runway. The next day we were flying combat.
>
> On one mission supporting the 24th Division, I attacked gun emplacements on a hillside. I was on my dive, firing, with shells going by me just as fast as I was pouring the .50-caliber rounds out on them. About two-thirds of the way down, I took a hit in the left wing and had to break away. It was at least a 20-mm hole, much larger than a half dollar. I'm glad it was out there on the wing and not in the cockpit.

Charles Dryden also was called to Korea, flying fifty combat missions in addition to the thirty he had flown with the 99th.

George Gray of the old 99th had "a very distinctive voice, Melvin Jackson remembered. "When he was speaking over the radio, you knew exactly who was talking."

Dryden heard a familiar voice on the net. "George Gray!" he yelled. "Is that you?"

"Yes!" the voice replied. "Is that you, Charlie Dryden?"

Dryden:

> I was a 'mosquito pilot' in a tactical air control squadron, flying fifty missions in thirty-three days in light T-6 trainers. We were the link between the ground controller and the tactical air control headquarters. We were the eyes of the Tactical Control Center.
>
> One day on patrol I was able to detect a lot of North Korean caches of weapons and had fighters blast them to hell and gone. There was so much notoriety about it, a news reporter, Ben Price, came to my outfit and asked to ride in my back seat and see the hulks that were damaged.
>
> We had some more action that afternoon. At one point troops on the ground reported getting fire from a hill and what could I do about it? I started making diving passes at the hill. "What are you doing that for?" Price said.

"Trying to get them to shoot at me to see their muzzle flashes," I said.

He said, "What! You're crazy!"

I said, "We do that every day."

Bussey remembered stopping his jeep at an intersection in Masan when someone called his name. He looked up to see George Gray. Charlie followed him to his hootch for a big reunion with eight or nine Tuskegee Airmen — Red Jackson, Peepsight Smith, Evil N. Smith and others. "We laughed and talked and had a good time. Every damn one of them got shot down. Most of them died — the Koreans were tremendous gunners."

Peepsight was the first to go. "I saw him in Tokyo," Dryden said. "A month later I heard he was dead." Gray also failed to return from a strafing mission.

They had all been rushed into the fight. Bernard Knighten, a reserve officer working as an aircraft controller at La Guardia Airport, received orders on Friday night to report for active duty the next morning. Saturday night he was on a plane, "next stop, Tokyo."

He was sitting in a base movie theater when the lights went on, MPs took up posts at the doors, and a lieutenant colonel began barking out names: "Get your bags and be at the flight line. You have one hour to be there."

Knighten found himself flying co-pilot on a C-46 transport plane in an all-weather night takeoff with a full load of passengers. "I had never been near a C-46 before in my life, and the pilot had never flown on instruments before. Providence was with us. We made it to Korea."

His job was to fly the orders for the next day's missions to the fighter bases, flying every other night, almost always under bad-weather instrument conditions. When he arrived back home, he was given "a hearty breakfast, a shot of Scotch, and a day off" before doing it again until the flight surgeon took him off the run for exhaustion. "Meanwhile," he said, "you really learned to fly."

Knighten flew paratroopers in the Inchon landing, when General MacArthur hit the North Koreans in a surprise attack on their flank. The troops were to be dropped on the command, "NOW." As they approached the beach, with the troopers hooked up and waiting, the Army commander warned, "Don't drop now." At the magic word, everyone was out the doors and into the ocean while Knighten futilely shouted, "No, No." Luckily, he said, the Navy fished most of them out of the water.

His next mission was to pick up wounded Communist troops. "The weather was rainy and miserable, and I was told by the Army captain, if we had any trouble, 'Just throw those guys out the door.' Of course I wouldn't do that." They arrived at Pusan out of fuel and found the airfield closed. While they prepared to ditch at sea, they finally found a small island, Cheju-do in the nick of time. "We were glad to get down alive."

Red Jackson was also rushed into combat:

> I got home off leave on a Saturday morning and was told, "They've got your orders already cut, you're leaving tomorrow." The record for a ship going across the Pacific was eleven days. We did it in eight. They sent us up to K-8 airfield on the east coast of Korea and told us to get a few hours of brush-up training and sent us into combat.
>
> A Major Dean Hess was training South Korean pilots in the P-51 and wanted some volunteers. I should have known better. You know what they say in the Army: "Keep your head up, your other part down, and never volunteer." But I volunteered. I trained them until we started pushing the North Koreans back.
>
> Korea wasn't a very exhilarating war. In Europe there was more of a spirit to get the war done: We were going to fight that war and fight it to the end. But in Korea we weren't too sure what was going to happen.

Shortly after the landing, Jackson's unit moved up by land to be the first outfit in Pyongyang, the North Korean capital:

> We flew missions up to the Chinese border, flying all up and down the roads, attacking everything we could.
>
> The North Korean troops pushed civilians in front of them. We learned that to our great sorrow: If we let the refugees go behind our lines, they'd hit us in the back. They

shot one mechanic in the back out on the runway one morning. So we said, "Don't let any more refugees come down that road." They had women and children among them, but we had to turn them back. We used to see bodies floating in the river, didn't know who killed them. You didn't know who was who.

I was given a mission with one of the Korean pilots of strafing the sampan boats coming across a river. I said, "Shoot a few bursts in front of them."

"They're not turning back."

"OK, destroy them."

My wingman didn't want to do that. When they got to the shore, we could see soldiers from the first boat dashing into the bulrushes as fast as they could go to get hidden and become guerrillas. We said, "We're not going to let any more go," and went back and shot up the other five boats. We knew there were women and children aboard. That bothered me very much. It was a vicious, cruel war.

Then, all hell broke loose: The Chinese started coming down.

That same night Knighten was given another emergency mission. "The only cargo aboard was an ice cream machine for some general at the farthest northern air base our troops controlled." When they arrived, the retreat had begun. "The only people left were some firemen who had trucks loaded with napalm to burn everything so the Chinese couldn't take it" — planes, plus tents and warehouse filled with clothing and ammunition. The Chinese were virtually across the road, but "all of us ran over and got all the fur-lined jackets and high-top boots we could carry. They loaded as many GI's as they could carry and "left in a hurry. I don't know what happened to the general's ice cream machine."

On "another awful trip," Knighten flew a load of ammunition to marines trapped in a valley on the east coast. "When we arrived, there was no airfield," only a tiny, primitive airstrip, already littered with wrecked planes that had run off the end. The pilot, "an old crop duster," switched off his engine, stomped on the brakes and stopped just in time. "Dead marines were stacked like cordwood along the runway." The crew unloaded their cargo, turned around, gave the plane full throttle, and barely cleared one of the wrecked planes. "Needless to say, operations to that field were discontinued almost immediately."

Returning from another flight to the North, Knighten "lived through another of the many crashes in my flying career." On landing, the plane suddenly veered to the right into an embankment, shearing off both engines. "I sat there, trying to figure out what happened." He learned later that the flight engineer, a fresh reservist, had raised the landing-gear handle before landing. "When I looked up, the general was outside, yelling at me, 'Get out, get out!' I jumped out the window and sank ankle-deep into gasoline" from a ruptured tank. "My luck held out one more time, but one spark and it would have been the end of the whole crew."

Jackson was in the thick of the action:

> The Korean pilots had stopped flying and Colonel Hess and I were going up to attack the Chinese facing the Second Division. The Americans were in full retreat, the Chinese were chasing them, and we were trying to kill as many of them as we could.
>
> We were doing very close ground attack when I heard the plane get hit. Black smoke from the engine cowling covered my windshield with smoke and oil, and I couldn't see. The P-51 has portholes on each side, and fire was coming out of them. I cut the gas off to keep it from feeding the fire, turned around and tried to get back to where the Americans were — there were no 'lines' then — and got ready to bail out. The enemy were still very close, and Colonel Hess says, "Don't jump yet, you're almost there."
>
> There were a lot of hills and valleys and I was losing altitude fast. Colonel Hess said, "You're there now, it's safe to jump out." I yanked my cord, and the canopy flew off, but I could see trees beside me, and I knew I didn't have enough altitude to bail out, so I straightened my plane out. Unfortunately I had ripped my seatbelt open and had no time to fasten it again.
>
> I said, "I'm going to land on this road." I looked out the side of the windshield, and there in front of me were cars, bikes, jeeps, everything, a stream of vehicles bumper-to-bumper, running as fast as they could. I was going to land on *that*?

So I peeled off to the first little hill I saw, and my wing hit one of the pines and jerked me around. I remember the shock from hitting, then blacked out. An ambulance crew came over and pulled me out before the plane burned me up. Colonel Hess returned and told the people that Captain Jackson had been killed — burned up. They packed my belongings and sent the word home that I was dead.

A field artillery crew noticed my plane had Korean markings, so when one of my squadron mates' plane conked out, an ambulance rescued him, and said, "What kind of plane you got there? We just rescued a pilot with a marking like that."

Red Jackson wasn't dead!

Two days later I woke up in Japan.

The left side of his head was badly injured, and he almost lost his eyesight. He would never be able to fly again. "I got out of the Air Force then, decided I'd had enough. I was tired of war, tired of killing people."

Hannibal Cox also flew P-51s in Korea and saw action with ground troops following the Chinese attack. "I was forward air controller, directing air strikes. We were encircled and fought our way back."

Color was insignificant, he said. "Those of us with combat experience were relied upon. However, it was different in Japan during R&R; in a social situation we were back to the old ways. There were some in the unit who were hard core and some who were not."

Meantime, three different battalion commanders sat on Bussey's Medal of Honor.

Months went by, and finally, the last commander, John Corley, a white man, told me, "Well, I thought I should downgrade this thing" to a Silver Star, the Army's third highest medal. He changed '258' enemy killed to 'numerous' enemy. He was a drinking 'friend' of mine, so I asked him why.

He said, "I belong to a group who believe it's our responsibility to keep Negroes in their place, and the most effective way is to deny them leadership. Then there's never any threat to anyone. If the medal was posthumous, no problem. Or if you were an inarticulate enlisted man, I would have no objection. But being who you are, you'd be out encouraging Negroes to do the things you do." Without leadership, Negroes were harmless, he said, but with leaders they could be a threat of some kind. "Our country can't afford this, and that's my considered opinion."

We were at the Yalu River in the process of fighting the Chinese. That's when I found that whites can run as fast as blacks. Winter came on viciously, and I didn't have time to worry about medals. I never did anything about it.[2]

Other African Americans did receive Medals of Honor. Private First Class William Thompson of Bussey's 24th Infantry was awarded one in August 1950, for slowing an enemy advance with machine gun fire. Although badly wounded, he refused orders to withdraw. The following summer, twenty-one-year-old Cornelius Charlton, also of the 24th, received the Medal for leading troops up a steep hill through a rain of grenades to attack the Chinese. Although wounded in the chest, he led three charges and was finally killed while firing on the enemy from the top of the hill. However, not until Captain Wiley Pitts was honored posthumously in Vietnam did an African-American officer receive the highest award.

Woody Crockett flew an F-80 Shooting Star.

I reported in May 1952, to the Eighth Fighter-Bomber Wing, about eight minutes due south of the Demilitarized Zone as the base flight safety officer. I wasn't supposed to fly combat, but since you had to give the pilots a briefing on safety every one or two weeks, I told my Wing commander there was no way I could gain the respect of these young guys if I didn't fly myself. I flew forty-five missions just to gain their respect and do my job. I think we ended up with the lowest accident rate of any flying tactical unit in Korea at that time.

I was hit twice in Europe, around Naples, and once in Korea over Pyongyang on a dive-bombing mission. It must have caught me going down in the dive, because it stuck in the top side of the wing.

Woody won a second Soldier's Medal.

I was in my jeep, midway on the nine hundred-foot runway when I saw an F-86 taking off with full power and his nose wheels still on the ground. I knew he was going to crash if he didn't abort, because he couldn't pick the nose up at that speed. So I just turned my jeep around and followed him to the end of the runway. He ran out of runway, ran three hundred more feet over a railroad track, and dropped off into a rice paddy three hundred feet below.

I drove up to the railroad tracks and went down and tried to pull him out as the aircraft began to burn. I'd pull him up to the top of the cockpit, but he had on this heavy suit and boots, and he'd slump back. I didn't want to stay there and get killed in an explosion, but I couldn't leave him in there to die either. I waved at the crash crew at the top of the hill and finally got someone to come down, and we pulled him away.

Crockett almost won a third:

A British pilot came to pick up his aircraft, which had had a wing replaced. He went up for a test hop and lost his engine on the final approach and crashed into a dump just off the runway. His left wing broke off, and he had a two-inch hole in the fuel line from the wing tanks. We could see the gas pouring out, and if it hit a hot surface, the whole plane could explode. He was inside there, apparently injured, and couldn't get out. The canopy was closed, it was operated electronically, and we couldn't figure out how to open it. We were worried about creating a spark, at the same time trying to keep anybody from walking over there with a cigarette. We finally opened it and got him out, but it had been close to becoming a catastrophe.

On another occasion, Crockett received a famous visitor:

Ted Williams was returning from a mission flying Panther jets out of Pohang and we were the closest air base to the front line. He made a left turn overhead and came in for a landing when we heard an explosion over the field. A piece of the plane dropped off, and you could see the flames coming out of his airplane. They tried to get him to bail out, but he crash-landed wheels up and skidded on his belly exactly 6,200 feet, heading for the kids in the ambulance. They had to roll up their windows, and he stopped just short of them.

When he got out, he looked at the bullet holes in his plane and said, "They were *shooting* at me."

I said, "You're darn *right* they are.

I had to do a lot of paper work on that.

I had lunch with him. His birthday is one day different from mine. I was born August 31, 1918, and he was born August 30.

The next day he was on another mission and landed at our field again. I said, "Ted, are you back to give me more business?"

He said, "No, Major, I'm only short of fuel today."

In the election, Eisenhower made a pledge to go to Korea and end the war, and Crockett recalled, "They got everybody airborne again, just like when Roosevelt visited Italy. So I flew protection for President Roosevelt and for President-elect Eisenhower. Not too many guys get that chance."

After Korea, McGee returned to the Philippines as commanding officer of the 44th Fighter-bomber Squadron, flying jets. One of his second lieutenants was Frank Borman, who later commanded the first space flight around the moon. Borman credited McGee with saving his flying career.

> He was a good, tough squadron commander, as good as I've had in the Air Force, and an important model for me in my Air Force career. I was permanently grounded because of a broken ear drum, and the doctors kept insisting that if I flew again, I'd break the ear drum again. Major McGee was kind enough to give me a ride unbeknownst to the doctors, and my ear's been fine ever since. He took a chance on me, and I'll always be grateful.

"I rated Borman as Outstanding," McGee said. "Fifth Air Force came back, saying, 'Outstanding is reserved for officers who are ready to take higher level commands.' I sent it back unchanged, and this time it didn't come back.

Charles Hill was in the reserves and volunteered for active duty in Korea. Instead of orders, he got a special delivery letter from the War Department charging him with being a Communist! Hill's sister was a member of a leftist university student group. His father, a Detroit Baptist minister, was active in civil rights, and when Paul Robeson was denied a hall to sing in in Detroit, he sang in the Reverend Hill's church. ("Fifty percent of the people came to hear Paul," Hill said, "and fifty percent were government people who wanted to see who were there.") Hill's investigation reached the newspapers, and he began receiving hate letters through the mail and hate calls on the phone until he had to disconnect his phone service. In the end he received an apology from the Secretary of the Air Force, and all charges were dropped. Still, "I was never called up for Korea, even though experienced fighter pilots were needed."

Chauncey Spencer was also accused of being a Communist. A month after receiving the Air Force's highest civilian award, the accusation arrived in the mail. Neighbors threw garbage on his lawn, he was suspended without pay for nine months, and he was not permitted to have a lawyer speak in his defense. Spencer believed his ordeal was the result of refusing to drag his feet on integration. In the end, his superiors, including Secretary of the Air Force William Talbot, stood up for him, and he was exonerated. Talbot was later fired by President Eisenhower.

Meantime Lucky Lester was flying jets in Europe along the East-West border, playing "peek-a-boo" with Communist MiGs.

In 1951, when General Eisenhower decided to come home and run for President, they had a ceremony in Paris to honor the change in command, and our unit was to do a fly-by in F-84s. About fifteen minutes after takeoff, I heard this loud bang and saw my fire-warning light come on right away. I called to my wing man: "What's going on?"

He said, "The Air Force star has burned up on the side of your plane."

I said, "Well, I've got deep problems here. *Auf weidersehen.*"

They have an ejection seat with a shell, which blows you out of the airplane. I was doing about 450 miles per hour at about 800 feet altitude. In those days the thought was that you should slow the airplane up before you ejected, but obviously, if the star had burned off, the controls were going to go next, and I didn't have time to slow it up. So I pushed the ejection button and started looping through the air doing somersaults, still in my seat. The minute the controls burned off, the airplane turned straight down to the ground, and I saw it hit with a big explosion.

Before I could open the parachute, I had to get rid of the seat. So I loosened the seat belts and kicked the seat away, and when I saw it clear, I pulled the rip-cord, and the parachute opened. All this sounds like it took a long time, but it was probably the space of eight to ten seconds — fifteen at the very most. The funny thing: I wasn't losing much altitude, because of the speed I was traveling.

I landed in a soft, newly plowed field, didn't even sprain an ankle. The SOP [Standard Operating Procedure] was to get to the nearest telephone and let them know where and how you were. The nearest phone was in a pub. The other three pilots, who had been circling, came flying down the middle of Main Street, very low and very noisy, glad that I was OK. That was their salute. Later I learned that they radioed back to headquarters that I was going into a beer hall to have a beer!

After that the Air Force decided that maybe it wasn't a good idea to slow up before ejecting. Before this, they had encountered a lot of trouble with pilots hitting the airplane. Pilots had been decapitated, had their legs cut off, and things like that. But when nothing happened to me, they decided to try some tests. The results were, you clear the airplane a lot better the faster you go because of the physics involved. I like to believe my ejection started them thinking that faster is better.

That was one of the luckiest things that ever happened to Lucky Lester.

Vietnam brought a third combat tour for three Red Tails — Cox, McGee, and Charles Cooper. In addition, Knighten was a ground-air controller north of Danang.

Clarence 'Red' Driver flew a transport plane out of Cambodia, though several Red Tails insist that he was actually a CIA agent. His plane was sabotaged — by whom it is not known — and exploded in the air, killing him.

Cox was a full colonel, a staff officer and also flying some F-100 ground-support missions: "Race was not an issue, either operationally or socially. We had good people, and we had a good Wing. We were completely integrated in every respect."

McGee flew an RF-4 reconnaissance plane:

Many times we had nothing to fire back at the enemy, and in that case, we used speed, at night particularly. You could see the enemy tracers, but they were usually behind you. You could look back and see them, so you knew there was a lot of other lead out there too, but as long as they were behind you, you were safe.

I was on a daylight mission on the trail the Communists were using through Laos into Vietnam — of course they claimed they weren't doing it, but they were. I was just dropping down to go to my target, when I took a high-caliber hit, fortunately again out in the left wing. But the loss of fuel meant I wasn't able to get back to my base, and I didn't know whether I had enough hydraulic fluid left to use the brakes. I was able to get to a friendly base at Danang on the coast and get the aircraft landed safely. That was my first tailhook landing experience.

I few 143 combat missions in Europe, 100 in Korea, and 176 in Southeast Asia; that's just over 400 total missions and 1100 combat hours. There aren't many men who have flown combat in three wars.

18

Final Triumph

In later life many of the Tuskegee Airmen left large footprints. Some went into research. James Wiley was one.

After integration in 1949, I chose Wright Field, heading up a group of German scientists working on supersonic flight. We didn't know yet about going from trans-sonic to supersonic and back, and we had to do a lot of experiments in the wind tunnel by looking at air flow over a model. I was able to get the contractors and put them all together, and it worked.

Then I became assistant manager of a pilotless aircraft with an atom bomb on its nose, the predecessor of ballistic weapons, and a single-pilot orbiting aircraft, the X-20, the predecessor of the space shuttle.

I had fifty-five people working for me in my division, the space division. We were assigned to Boeing in Seattle to develop a lunar orbiter to take pictures of the moon in preparation for the lunar landings.

Bob Deiz also went into research: "I was more proud of what I did after I got out of fighters and into flying experimental planes and electronics. I was at Cambridge Research Center in electronic research. Then I worked at North American Aviation in their weapons analysis group.

Deiz indulged his old love, music. Harry Sheppard remembered when they had served together at M.I.T.: "I used to sneak off and go down to a Boston nightclub, the 'High Hat.' One night I went down there and got a seat right down front, and who sneaks in wearing dark glasses with a bass fiddle but Bob Deiz, saying 'Shhhh.'"

After retiring, Deiz played with the Columbus, Ohio Orchestral Society.

> My biggest problem was I was playing big instruments, the bass strings or the bass horn. I had to carry them up, set them up, go back, get something else, carry them back down afterward. The damn piccolo player just put it in his pocket while I was still making my second trip. It just got to be too big a chore.

Robert Williams also went into show business. He attended UCLA, studied business and theater arts, and got a role in the movie "Pork Chop Hill," with Gregory Peck. He also appeared with Rock Hudson and Dick Van Dyke.

> I was in the Phil Silvers TV Show — not "Sergeant Bilko" but the one before that, set in a factory. Silvers was a kick in the head, a very funny guy, but he was hard to work with. He ad-libbed a lot, and you never knew what the cue was. If you jumped in on his line, he'd give you a bad time; if you didn't come in on time, he'd give you a bad time.

Bob had one of the first black radio talk shows, which premiered during the Los Angeles Watts Riots of 1967. It won an award from the NAACP.

For over forty years, 1952-96, he tried to sell his script for a TV drama on the Red Tails. After years of rejections, he finally saw it produced on HBO-TV with Lawrence Fishburne starring as Williams.

Bert Wilson agreed that "it's a hell of a story," but he laughed that "Williams got me killed off in his script."

A play about the Red Tails was produced in the 1980s, though Sheppard for one didn't like it. "They had us depicted as bubble-brained, hard-drinking, and foul-mouthed. That never happened. Why dilute the truth with a bunch of baloney?"

Percy Sutton, an intelligence officer with the 332nd, attended law school, bought the Apollo Theater in Harlem, entered politics, and went on to become Manhattan borough president and a millionaire.

Bernard Knighten retired from the Air Force in 1967, then worked for the FAA for twenty years. By that time, he cracked, "I was too old for the rail lines, the airlines and even the sidelines."

He moved to Las Vegas and was, of all things, "trying to be a standup comedian. I'm on stage every Friday and Saturday at Debbie Reynolds' Hotel, the Celebrity Room. When she takes a break, she puts me on: Mother-in-law jokes, ugly wife jokes. My wife sits in the audience and boos me. We have a party."

Lucky Lester earned a degree from Stanford in international relations, then worked in President Kennedy's Pentagon in the office of Defense Secretary Robert McNamara and the 'Whiz Kids.' "They were a bunch of bright kids, all right, just out of Harvard Business School. I was the 'Old Man.' I guess they needed a wiser, experienced head around to keep them on the right track."

Ed Gleed spent several years in India as an advisor on strategic air defenses on the China border. He retired in 1970 and went back to law school at the age of fifty-seven. "I didn't want to practice, I just wanted to see if I could do it. Those were three of the roughest years of my life." At graduation he was surprised to find that he was "married to a grandmother." He died in 1987.

Despite problems, Spann Watson fondly looked back on his military career. "I don't say all black people are good and all white people are bad. I spent twenty-four years in the military and served all over the world, and I had some of the best leaders, black and white, I'd ever want to serve with."

Jimmy Walker moved to California, where he was active in his church. In 1992, he suddenly got a phone call from Aleksandr Zivkovic, the seventeen year-old boy who had found him in the Serbian woods almost fifty years before. After the Communists had taken over his country, Zivkovic spent many weeks in prison watching mass killings of civilians through his bars. He went to college and, in 1967, immigrated to America, working in Syracuse and Chicago as an air conditioning maintenance expert.

Alex never stopped looking for Jim. At a big air show in Oshkosh, Wisconsin in 1993, he ran into Bill Campbell, who told him, "Walker? Sure, I know him. He lives near me." That Christmas Jimmy and Alex were reunited in Chicago and spent the whole day talking.

Charles Dryden earned a Master's Degree in public law and government at Columbia. He retired in 1961 and worked for thirteen years for Lockheed in Atlanta.

Willie Fuller spent twenty-eight years as a Boy Scout official in Miami. He died in 1995. Among those attending his funeral was Clarence Jamison who traveled from Connecticut to Miami although he had been on kidney dialysis for three years.

Hannibal Cox became a vice-president of Eastern Air Lines; he died in 1988.

Archer was a vice-president of General Foods.

His close friend, Roscoe Brown, became a Distinguished Professor for Urban Educational Policy in New York.

Bill Melton inherited a foundation his mother had set up to help elderly people:

> The state of California was discharging mentally retarded adults, and they asked me if I would take them. I still have a small fifteen-bed facility with very intensive health care and rehabilitation. I helped found one of the largest adult day centers in California. In fact, it was the first one, 'Willing Workers.' The people entrusted to us have been with their parents all their lives. Our whole purpose is normalizing society's attitude to them and their attitude to themselves through education, music, field trips, speakers' bureaus, and elected officers.
>
> I discovered myself when I got into this work; I discovered my real potential by helping these persons of developing needs.

Melvin Jackson thought about going into the ministry:

> I wanted to do something to help people, so I enrolled in the University of Connecticut School of Social Work and got a job as director of social services for the Hartford Council of Churches. Then my school called me back to teach for two years. Next I got a job at Harvard as director of a research project.
>
> When Kennedy's anti-poverty program was started, that was very exciting. I worked in that program in Washington for four years before coming to Harrisburg, Pennsylvania to take charge of the anti-poverty program here. Then it was on to New York and Washington to counsel Vietnam vets.

Jackson also headed the Harrisburg Housing Authority until he retired and is now a Meals on Wheels volunteer.

Spanky Roberts retired as a colonel in 1968 and worked as a banker in Sacramento for thirteen years.

> I'm a 'peopler.' I help senior citizens who have nobody to manage their finances and handle their estates. I'm on the board of directors of Meals a la Cart, delivering meals to those who need them, mostly senior citizens, but for everybody who needs good nutrition. Our organization is open to everybody, payment on a sliding scale. I'm on the board of the metropolitan education council, bringing school and industry together for high school grads. I'm with the Computer Learning Center, a system of continuation schools for everyone from ex-offenders to youngsters who are not making it in regular schools or need help in certain subjects. I've had two hips replaced, so I helped form 'Hipsters,' a support organization for people who need operations.
>
> None of this is for pay. Oh, I do get reimbursed. I get lots of love letters, often in shaky hand-writing.

Wilson:

> When I came back from Vietnam, my doctor said they were starting a new program in Connecticut, called Perception House, for kids on drugs and wondered if I'd be part of it. I said, "Well, why not?"
>
> It's expanded from five of us to at least fifty or sixty employees now. I'm a volunteer on the board of directors. We

have an Alternative Incarceration Program; instead of going to jail, they are in-patients in one of our facilities. We also treat battered women and sex abusers, so it's a pretty big program.

Jimmy Fischer suffered a stroke in 1983. "Blew hell out of my memory, and when I tried to go back to work too fast, I had a seizure. But I was able to get a little retirement from the Veterans' Administration. The Purple Heart opened the door for me."

Charlie McGee became manager of the Kansas City airport and served several terms as president of the Tuskegee Airmen Association.

Lester lamented that few people knew about the Red Tails and what they had done.

In 1975, our daughter Wanda went to the University of Pennsylvania and took a course in ethnic studies. The professor made the casual observation that there were no black officers in the U.S. Army at the time of World War II. Wanda raised her hand and told him, "I beg to differ with you, but my father was in World War II, was a pilot, and was an officer; in fact, he was a captain."

The professor more or less told her, "This is very nice, and he meant well telling you this, but in effect, he lied to you" — not quite those words, but that's the gist of what he said.

She was humiliated, so she called me that night and said, "Send me some of the things from your scrap book." I sent her clippings and pictures, and she gave them to him.

He looked at them and said, "I didn't know this." But he never apologized or admitted that he was wrong and never saw fit to correct it to the class.

Lester died of cancer in 1986.

Gradually the story is becoming known. Roberts:

As my wife says, about every five years the media discovers the Red Tails. I'm on radio, TV, in newspapers, and people find out where I am. I was on a radio talk show in Sacramento, and I don't know how many calls there were, saying, "Heh, you saved my tail," or, "My father told me about you Red Tail guys; he was a gunner" – or pilot or bombardier – "on a B-17 or B-24."

They call to say thank you and that they still remembered.

Woody Crockett worked on the development of the F-86 fighter. In 1951, he was radiological safety officer for an atomic bomb test in the Pacific and visited 'shot island' the day after the blast. Twice he broke Mach-2, two times the speed of sound, and may be the only man with two Soldier's Medals and two Mach-2 cards. Even some of the astronauts were envious of that.

In 1996, Crockett, then a 'cool' seventy-eight years old, was an avid skier and tennis player (two-time senior doubles champion of Virginia). He attended VE-Day ceremonies in Washington as guest of his fellow Arkansan, President Bill Clinton. "In the hangar at Bolling Air Field, a gentlemen walked in with a World War II uniform, a first lieutenant, with his wings and a 15th Air Force patch – the 445th Bomber Group, B-24s. He said, 'You escorted me, and I want to thank you. If it wasn't for you, I probably wouldn't be here.' You get those compliments all the time."

Crockett spent thirty minutes in the Oval Office with President Clinton, whose Secretary of the Treasury, Lloyd Bentsen, had also flown a B-24 alongside the Red Tails. "We never lost a bomber to enemy fighters," Crockett told the President. Clinton sat up in his chair. "Not even one?"

"No sir," Crockett replied, "not even one." The President "was really surprised at that story," Crockett said.

Clinton invited Crockett and his wife, Daisy, to England to represent all American Servicemen at the D-Day anniversary ceremonies. His photo with Clinton and British Prime Minister John Majors appeared on page one of the New York *Times*.

Lou Purnell became a curator at the Smithsonian Air & Space Museum in Washington and helped set up the 1982 'Black Wings' exhibit.

Tom Allen, the early cross-country pioneer, came up from Oklahoma City for the opening.

Another was Chief Anderson. "You know," he told Purnell, "I drove up this time, nine hundred miles, because Gert, my wife, didn't want to fly with me." Purnell shook his head and smiled: "I don't think he'll ever slow down." Anderson succumbed to cancer in 1996.

Purnell tried to reach Hubert Julian to invite him. "I understand he had died," Lou said. "He would have run the whole show!"

Charlie Bussey went to Alaska as consultant on the pipeline there, to Saudi Arabia for the construction of buildings in Riyadh, and to Somalia to report on the U.S. military mission there.

For more than forty years, friends have tried to get the Army to reopen his case for a Medal of Honor. Investigators looked up witnesses to find that many had died, including one man who passed away only days before the interviewers arrived.

Bussey remained philosophical:

> It would be nice to have the Medal of Honor. The only practical advantage would have been a free West Point education for my children, but they're way past college age now. I'm not bitter, but I would have more respect for the American system if there were equity for those who fought and were willing to die for our country. Still I deeply love the U.S. Army, and I am proud to be an American. When I hear our national anthem, I can feel the hair rise on my spine, and goose pimples cover my arms.

Deiz served on the suicide hotline in Columbus for about a year and a half but had to quit because "it gets you down after awhile. When you look at the average Negro pilot, you're looking at a guy who has his sanity. But he fought for it. If we let the things we went through bother us, we could be a bunch of nuts walking around." Deiz died in 1991.

Sheppard served in the Tactical Air Command under, of all people, General Spike Momyer. He didn't show any racial prejudice, Sheppard said, "but he was a miserable man personally, he abused everybody." Sheppard once watched while

Momyer chewed out his second in command, a three-star general, in front of everyone. Shep retired in 1974 as a colonel and survived a heart attack in 1984. He served on the board of the Arlington, Virginia Coalition for the Homeless, played the piano, listened to good music — jazz, classical, and sacred — and was one of the leading living historical resources of the 332nd.

"I wouldn't take a million dollars to do it all over again," he said, "but I wouldn't take a million dollars to have missed it."

The Tuskegee Airmen agree that there have been big changes since they first flew. "When I left," said Lucky Lester, "there were no black generals, just a handful of black colonels. I knew almost every black officer in the military. In the last ten or twenty years progress has been fantastic as compared to the first twenty-seven years. You started to get normal progression, people getting their talents recognized."

Spanky Roberts went on ROTC duty at Tuskegee "and was privileged to have taught, graduated, and commissioned two men who became the first black Air Force major generals — Titus Hall and Rufus Phillips."

Spann Watson went to work for the Federal Aviation Administration.

> They didn't want me under any circumstances; I had to shoot my way in. It was a tremendous battle of double-crosses, but finally, with the help of Bobby Kennedy, they were forced into it. I became the power in civil rights at the FAA, a prime mover for changing the complexion throughout the industry. There were only three or four black air traffic people in the United States then; I'm the man who started the ball rolling and got more in. I knew all the black pilots who were qualified to work in the airline industry, and I did more for civil rights in the F.A.A. than all the civil rights officers since.

C.C. Robinson studied pharmacy and opened a chain of Washington drug stores. He shook his head admiringly:

> When Spann makes up his mind something is right, he goes at it all the way. There's no holding back with Spann. If

he's for you, he'll do anything for you. You always want Spann on your side.

There was a meeting of the heads of the airlines at the F.A.A. building, and Spann complained about not being able to get black hostesses on planes. They said, "We'd hire them if we could find any." So he held classes, taught them how to talk, how to walk, how to do their hair, how to be interviewed, and they hired every one he presented to them, a total of 708 — the first black hostesses. And he got them twenty-five of the first black pilots, all recommended by Spann. He was a crusader.

Of course he made enemies. "But that didn't bother him. Once he made up his mind that he was right, nothing would stop him."

Watson was proud of the fact that "I had the biggest retirement party they'd ever seen in Washington, over 550 people; they came from far and wide.

"The National Aeronautic Association recognizes all records and extraordinary accomplishments and elects big-time aviators like Admiral Byrd and Jimmy Doolittle. In 1990, they elected me as the first black, and I was instrumental in getting Chief Anderson, Ben Davis, and several other blacks elected."

Davis, Sr, retired from the Army in 1948, after fifty years of service. He died in 1977 at the age of ninety-three.

B.O. Davis, Jr. retired as a three-star general and spent several years as an official of the Federal Aviation Authority. He was still referred to by Tuskegee veterans as 'Percy-One,' his radio code name as Group Leader. Despite arthritis, he made daily walks across the bridge from Arlington to Washington and back into his eighties.

Davis:

> The Tuskegee Airmen are one of the major reasons why President Truman was able to sign an executive order ending segregation in the Armed Forces. Major problems still exist, and everything is not perfect — the Armed Forces are an example of improvement, not of perfection.
>
> But for all their warts, they are superior, without any question, to the situation in our civilian society. I can remember when my wife was escorting a young lady from Haiti to a

clothing store in Washington's Georgetown; the lady was surprised to learn that she could not try on clothes in the store.

People talk about the good old days. The good old days are today. We hope for better old days to come.

Babies are not racists. Parents and teachers and others make racists out of them, and they perpetuate these indignities.

I believe victory in the Persian Gulf War can be attributed in some degree to the fact that integrated units fought with a cohesiveness never before attained.

The Tuskegee Airmen made a difference.

Bert Wilson said:

It's hard for young people to understand what the Red Tails had faced. The country was as bad as South Africa. We're not talking a hundred years ago, we're talking fifty years ago. But you can't get mad. When you get mad, you get bitter, and if you get bitter, you lose it all. So you've got to keep your cool. Things have changed for the better, yes, but not as much as I would have liked. You have changed some people's personal views. But you haven't changed them all.

Still, when I see a black airline pilot, I say, "If it hadn't been for our Group, he wouldn't be in that cockpit."

At the Smithsonian, Purnell said:

Sometimes I like to play visitor, slip a camera on my neck, and go downstairs to the exhibit on black aviation and the Red Tails and listen to the remarks of the visitors. You hear such things as, "I can't believe it...," "I never heard of them...," "I didn't know this before...," "It's hard to believe." That's because most of the publicity about us was swept under the rug and after fifty years is just becoming known. The Smithsonian received more newspaper clippings on that exhibit than any other it's put up. At last we're coming out from under the stones and being recognized.

It's good for the morale of the black race, because many are still unaware that there was a black squadron. It's good for history books and for the role image for kids coming up. That's the main thing. I don't care about adults — give the kids something to aspire to.

In the Air Force I think you're subconsciously reaching for higher things, both figuratively and literally. To look back at the accomplishments of the guys who were Tuskegee Airmen, a lot rose to heights — judges, doctors, millionaires, civic leaders — you name it, we've got it, enough to gag a maggot. Lee Archer, one of our highest scorers, was vice-president of General Foods; James T. Wiley was vice-president of Boeing; Jack Rogers was a judge in Chicago; Ace Lawson a city councilman in San Diego; Willie Ashley a PhD with the Environmental Protection Agency; Bill Campbell was a professor in California. Those fellows didn't turn out so bad. All from a little group of guys called the 99th.

I'm not a sentimental person, but by God, just to see the old guys, you get choked up and can't talk. Your memory goes back to little things that happened in combat. When we get together, we laugh about some things, and other things are really touching.

Had it not been for the war, we would never have been able to fly. I think we proved one thing: After the war black fliers became commercial pilots. In Korea and Vietnam the Air Force was integrated. B.O. Davis and Chappie James became generals. We have black astronauts. I think they were all accepted a little more readily than they would have been had we not gone through the Tuskegee experience. It's just another rung on the ladder we were trying to climb. We hope we've done something anyway.

Lee Archer: "One hundred percent to a man, those of us who went through that look back now, and, compared to what is possible today, would say it was all worthwhile."

Will there ever be another outfit like the Red Tails? Roscoe Brown shakes his head.

This effort was unique and will never be repeated. Hopefully there will never be, and there should never be, a time when one group of African Americans has to be so superior.

The real meaning of the Tuskegee Airmen goes beyond what I call the 'combat b.s.' The story on the ground is what it was all about. The stories in the skies are exciting, sure, but they're not unlike those of a lot of white pilots. The thing that makes them important is that we did exactly what the white pilots did and sometimes did it better.

This is the story of some very serious, committed people attacking the most serious social problem of American history.

We fought two wars, one against Fascism, one against segregation, and sometimes you couldn't tell which one you were fighting. It goes back to the ethos of the times. Every black person put up with a lot of crap that they wouldn't think about putting up with today.

The key to the civil rights movement was the Tuskegee Airmen. Our aim was to convince white people that if we could do the job as well as, or better than they, they wouldn't be prejudiced. You and I know that's not really true. The only way people learn not to be prejudiced is if they have a whole range of social experiences. But we neutralized an excuse for excluding us.

It's like baseball. If you're the first black player and you hit .200, nobody remembers you; if you hit .300, everyone remembers you. If we had lost a lot of bombers and screwed up, we'd have been remembered, but not well. But because of our outstanding record of not losing a bomber, of shooting down three jets, of destroying the first enemy naval destroyer, and a lot of other things, we showed that black people could do technical and courageous things and could do them as well as, or better than, white folks. Branch Rickey and Jackie Robinson built on that.

We've made progress. Now when you see a black in a high position in a company, it's a function of what we did. So I feel we made a difference.

Melton:

No question about it: The integration of the Armed Forces was a key, and we were catalysts.

I love this country just as much as you do — this is my turf. Philosophically I guess I've accepted it with its faults. But I don't have any hatred. I'll beat them at their own game. Just plain orneriness has kept me going.

I know this country pretty well, I've been to damn near every corner of it. I have one hell of a faith in the common sense and compassion of the American people. They're a good people. Hell, no one's perfect. I've been around other parts of the world, and there's no place I'd rather live. It's a good country. It has a lot of faults. But that sense of commitment to positive social change seems to be our dedication.

Americans are good people, man, very good people. It will be all right.

Dick Macon became a mathematics professor and was called to Detroit to teach in a black high school – a professor teaching high school.

I've devoted a great deal of time to mentoring young people *pro bono*. I enjoy getting kids jobs, seeing that they get scholarships, and sending them to the Air Force Academy. When I talk to youngsters, I talk about life with no light at the end of the tunnel, letting them know that the tunnel is not as dark as it seems to be. Hope reigns eternal, so don't give up hope and commit suicide but make plans of how you're going to escape and be what you want to be.

Before his death in 1984, Roberts was active in the Tuskegee Airmen.

It's an educational organization which grew out of meeting and doing the war-story bit. Out of this has grown a national organization of twenty-two chapters, now including everyone who is interested in supporting our ideals – people of all ages, all services, all races and backgrounds. We're dedicated to the proposition that there will never be another time when Americans are denied the right to serve their country by virtue of such arbitrary things as race or creed. We believe the best method of accomplishing this is education.

Our scholarships total about $75,000 on a national level and have gone to every racial group – Caucasians, Asians, Blacks, Hispanics. I doubt that fifty percent of the people so assisted have been black. And they've gone predominantly to women, because they have been most qualified and need the help. Our position is, we are against segregation in any form. Obviously there are people who grit their teeth at the thought of assisting people whose fathers or grandfathers have been diametrically opposed to what we stand for, but we think there's a bigger battle to be won. If you want to be a Tuskegee Airman, you can join up.

"Fourteen of us went into our own pockets and contributed money," Ed Gleed said.

Our goal is one million dollars as a memorial to Chappie James. It was his idea to start the fund. There are three criteria:

Scholarship – at least a B average,
Need – at or near the poverty level,
Desire for further education in aero-space fields.

I tell youngsters: You're able to learn and, given the opportunity – and this is important – you can do just about anything anyone else can do. You are not necessarily going to face the same type of barriers out there. But it can be done. You can overcome them. Do one and a half times more than the average white person, that's all right. Push yourselves and do it. This is one of the goals of the Tuskegee Airmen.

Roberts:

Why did it take so long? Or how did we move so fast? It depends on how you look at it.

Americans have always had in their hearts a response that I call 'good-guy violence.' Our heroes have been those who fought our wars, or the Daniel Boones. You couldn't permit blacks to become heroes, because then they would become a part of our political system on an electable basis.

I am amazed at what happened after World War II, when for the first time we were allowed to be heroes. The 92nd Army Division, the Tuskegee Airmen, the Red Ball Express logistics units in Europe, the Japanese-Americans who fought in Italy – look who came out of all that.

Most Americans, I firmly believe, are solid at heart and will do the right thing under most conditions, given a fair chance to do so.

Charles Dryden was chairperson of the 1995 Tuskegee Airmen convention in Atlanta, with astronaut Brigadier General Charles Bolton as a featured speaker. The theme of the convention: "We've made history, now let's make a better world."

The president of the Airmen, Bill Terry, sat on the dais next to Air Force Chief of Staff, General Ronald Fogelman, and the Assistant Secretary of the Air Force, Rodney Coleman, Dryden's 'protege' in ROTC. As Terry recalled it, Coleman rose and read: "By the provision of section so-and-so, the reprimands of the one hundred and one 'mutineers' would be removed from the record." "My name wasn't there. The guys came up and got their papers from the Assistant Secretary, and he still didn't call me. You know what's going through my mind — 'Goddam, they passed me again, the !@#$%&*'s.'"

After they had all gotten their pictures taken, Coleman continued: "Under the provisions of section so-and-so, the conviction of George 'Bill' Terry is also set aside."

"I jumped up," Terry said, "spilling water all over the Chief of Staff, looking for my wife. My speech was short. For the first time in my life, I was speechless. I didn't have a damn thing to say."

19

Epilogue

When the war ended, the 332nd and the 99th had flown 1578 missions and more than 15,000 sorties. They had sent 450 pilots into combat, of whom 66, or more than one out of seven, had given their lives.

Some other totals:

Planes destroyed or damaged in the air	136
On the ground	273
Barges and boats destroyed	40
Locomotives	126
Rolling stock	619
Trucks, cars	87
And the statistic they were most proud of:	
Friendly bombers lost to enemy fighters	0

It is easy to fall into the trap of emphasizing aerial victories, which the pilots themselves regarded as one of the less significant aspects of their job. Their mission was not a game in which both sides kept score. There was much more at stake.

How many bombers and their crews were *saved* because the Red Tails were weaving protectively above them, warding off enemy fighters? The cost of the bombers and the training of their crews alone was incalculable. How many wives, parents, and children welcomed home men who had been spared death thanks to their red-tailed escorts?

And without the brave fighter Groups, black and white, the entire daylight bombing strategy, with its increased accuracy, could not have been carried out. How can one measure the damage wrought against the Axis war industries or how much it may have shortened the war?

Victories

In the air wars over Europe, the Eighth Air Force, based in England and France, scored about seventy-five percent of the victories. The Italy-based Fifteenth Air Force, which included the 99th and 332nd, scored about twenty-five percent.

One important reason was that as the German Air Forces retreated in September 1944 to protect their homeland, the Fifteenth encountered less and less resistance, while the Eighth Air Force, in the North, was heavily engaged.

In the month of December, for instance, the entire Fifteenth Air Force scored only twenty-six victories, while the Eighth downed a thousand planes. Not until March was the 332nd ordered north, where it once more met enemy fighter planes in strength and began building big victory totals again.

"The kills and damages we scored are probably many more than we have records for," Spanky Roberts said:

> If a plane wasn't clearly seen crashing or burning, or the pilot wasn't clearly seen jumping out, we didn't even try to claim it, because we knew we weren't going to get any credit for it.
>
> We were accused of falsifying figures and even pictures. That always seemed interesting to me that we did things to our cameras to make them reveal things that didn't happen. If we were so beastly smart, why did they think we weren't beastly good pilots too? *We* didn't develop the film.

To recap, historian Frank Olynyk made probably the most detailed, painstaking, and authoritative study of every aerial victory credited or claimed in World War II. Using the original squadron records, he found victories that even the official Air Force records do not recognize. His complete study reposes in the National Archives in College Park, Maryland.

Olynyk did credit the three victories claimed for Joseph Elsberry on July 12, 1944, even though they do not appear on the official Air Force list. He also added a probable which had not previously been credited, thus putting Elsberry tantalizingly close to ace status.

However, Olynyk could not confirm the victory which author Charles Francis ascribed to Lee Archer on July 20, 1944, the one which, if confirmed, would make Archer an ace.

Neither could Olynyk confirm two claimed by Charles Bussey on that same date.

Olynyk also failed to find any documentation to support the report of four enemy planes downed over Athens on October 12, 1944.

* * *

The following victories were either claimed by, or officially credited to, the 99th Squadron and the 332nd Group.

(U = Unconfirmed; P = Probable, ½ = shared with another pilot.)

1943

Jul 2	Hall, Charles	99	#1
	Lawson, Walter	99	#1

1944

Jan 27	Allen, Clarence	99	½
	Ashley, Willie	99	#1
	Bailey, Charles	99	#1
	Baugh, Howard	99	½
	Custis, Lemuel	99	#1
	Deiz, Robert	99	#1
	Driver, Elwood	99	P, ½
	Eagelson, Wilson	99	#1
	Lawrence, Erwin	99	½
	Roberts, Leon	99	#1
	Rogers, John	99	P, ½
	Smith, Lewis	99	#1
	Toppins, Edward	99	#1
Jan 28	Deiz, Robert	99	#2
	Hall, Charles	99	#2, #3
	Smith, Lewis	99	#1
Feb 5	Driver, Elwood	99	#1
	Eagleson, Wilson	99	#2
Feb 7	Jackson, Leonard	99	#1
	Mills, Clinton	99	#1
Jun 9	Bussey, Charles	302	U, ½
	Funderberg, Frederick	301	#1
	Green, William	302	U, ½
	Jackson, Melvin	302	#2
	Pruitt, Wendell	302	#1
Jul 12	Elsberry, Joseph	301	U #1, U #2, U #3, P
	Sawyer, Harold	301	#1

Jul	16 Davis, Alfonso	99	U
	Green, William	302	#1
Jul	17 Smith, Luther	302	#1
	Smith, Robert	302	#1
	Wilkins, Lawrence	302	#1
Jul	18 Archer, Lee	302	#1
	Bailey, Charles	99	#2
	Holsclaw, Jack	100	#1, #2
	Lester, Clarence	100	#1, #2, #3
	Palmer, Walter	100	#1
	Romine, Roger	302	#1
	Toppins, Edward	99	#2
	Warner, Hugh	302	#1
Jul	20 Bussey, Charles	302	U, U #2
	Elsberry, Joseph	301	#1
	Johnson, Langdon	100	#1
	McDaniel, Armour	301	#1
	Toppins, Edward	99	#3
Jul	23 Holsclaw, Jack	100	#3
Jul	25 Sawyer, Harold	301	#2
Jul	26 Toppins, Edward	99	#4
	Green, William	302	U #2
	Groves, Weldon	???	½
	Hutchins, Freddie	302	#1
	Jackson, Leonard	99	#3
	Romine, Roger	302	U
	Smith, Luther	302	U
Jul	27 Gleed, Edward	301	#1, #2
	Gorham, Alfred	301	#1, #2
	Govan, Claude	301	#1
	Hall, Richard	99	#1
	Jackson, Leonard	99	#3
	Kirkpatrick, Felix	302	#1
Jul	30 Johnson, Carl	100	#1
Aug	6 Johnson, Carl	100	U, #2

Aug 12	Rhodes, George	99	#1
Aug 23	Hill, William	302	U, ½
	Weathers, Luke	302	U, ½
Aug 24	Briggs, John	100	#1
	McGee, Charles	302	#1
	Thomas, William	302	#1
Oct 4	Gray, George	99	U
	Hayes, Milton	99	U, ½
	Perry, Henry	99	U, ½
	Rhodes, George	99	U#2
	Thomas, Edward	99	U
	Westbrook, Shelby	99	U
Oct 12	Archer, Lee	302	#2, #3, #4
	Brooks, Milton	302	#1
	Green, William	302	#1
	Pruitt, Wendell	302	#2, #3
	Romine, Roger	302	#1
	Smith, Luther	302	#2
Nov 16	Weathers, Luke	302	#1, #2

1945

Mar 24	Brantley, Charles	100	#1
	Brown, Roscoe	100	#1
	Lane, Earl	100	#1
Mar 31	Bell, Raul	100	#1
	Braswell, Thomas	99	#1
	Brown, Roscoe	100	#2
	Campbell, William	99	#1
	Davis, John	99	#1
	Hall, James	100	#1
	Lane, Earl	100	#2
	Lyle, John	99	#1
	Rich, Daniel	99	#1
	White, Hugh	99	#1
	Williams, Robert	100	#1, #2
	Wilson, Bertram	100	#1

Apr 1	Carey, Carl	301	#2
	Edwards, John	301	#2
	Fischer, James	301	#1
	Manning, Walter	301	#1
	Morris, Harold	301	#1
	Stewart, Harry	301	#3
	White, Charles	301	#2
Apr 15	Lanham, Jimmy	301	P
Apr 16	Price, William	301	#1
Apr 26	Jefferson, Thomas	301	U, #2
	Lanham, Jimmy	301	#1
	Simmons, Richard	100	#1

*   *   *

By Name

Jan 27 44	Allen, Clarence	99	½
Jul 18 44	Archer, Lee	302	1
Oct 13 44	Archer, Lee	302	3
Jan 27 44	Ashley, Willie	99	1
Jan 27 44	Bailey, Charles	99	1
Jul 18 44	Bailey, Charles	99	1
Jan 27 44	Baugh, Howard	99	1½
Mar 31 45	Bell, Raul	100	1
Mar 24 45	Brantley, Charles	100	1
Mar 31 45	Braswell, Thomas	99	1
Aug 24 44	Briggs, John	100	1
Oct 12 44	Brooks, Milton	302	1
Mar 24 45	Brown, Roscoe	100	1
Mar 31 45	Brown, Roscoe	100	1
Jun 9 44	Bussey, Charles	302	1
Jul 18 44	Bussey, Charles	302	2U
Jul 26 44	Bussey, Charles	302	U, ½
Mar 31 45	Campbell, William	99	1
Apr 1 45	Carey, Carl	301	2
Jan 27 44	Custis, Lemuel	99	1
Jul 16 44	Davis, Alfonso	99	1
Mar 31 45	Davis, John	99	1
Jan 27 44	Deiz, Robert	99	1
Jan 28 44	Deiz, Robert	99	1

Feb 5 44	Driver, Elwood	99	1
Jan 27 44	Eagelson, Wilson	99	1
Feb 7 44	Eagleson, Wilson	99	1
Apr 1 45	Edwards, John	301	2
Jul 12 44	Elsberry, Joseph	301	3U, P
Jul 20 44	Elsberry, Joseph	301	1
Apr 1 45	Fischer, James	301	1
Jun 9 44	Funderberg, Frederick	301	2
Jul 27 44	Gleed, Edward	301	2
Jul 27 44	Gorham, Alfred	301	2
Jul 27 44	Govan, Claude	301	1
Oct 4 44	Gray, George	99	U
Jul 16 44	Green, William	302	1
Jul 26 44	Green, William	302	U, ½
Oct 13 44	Green, William	302	U, ½
Jul 26 44	Groves, Weldon	302	U, ½
Jul 2 44	Hall, Charles	99	1
Jan 28 44	Hall, Charles	99	2
Mar 31 45	Hall, James	99	1
Jul 27 44	Hall, Richard	99	1
Oct 4 44	Hayes, Milton	99	U, ½
Aug 23 44	Hill, William	302	U, ½
Jul 18 44	Holsclaw, Jack	100	2
Jul 23 44	Holsclaw, Jack	100	1
Jul 26 44	Hutchins, Freddie	302	1
Feb 7 44	Jackson, Leonard	99	1
Jul 26 44	Jackson, Leonard	99	1
Jul 27 44	Jackson, Leonard	99	1
Jun 9 44	Jackson, Melvin	302	1
Apr 26 45	Jefferson, Thomas	301	2
Jul 30 44	Johnson, Carl	100	1
Aug 6 44	Johnson, Carl	100	U
Jul 20 44	Johnson, Langdon	100	1
Jul 27 44	Kirkpatrick, Felix	302	1
Mar 24 45	Lane, Earl	100	1
Mar 31 45	Lane, Earl	100	1
Apr 15 45	Lanham, Jimmy	301	1
Apr 26 45	Lanham, Jimmy	301	P
Jul 2 43	Lawson, Walter	99	P
Jul 18 44	Lester, Clarence	100	3
Mar 31 45	Lyle, John	99	1
Apr 1 45	Manning, Walter	301	1
Jul 20 44	McDaniel, Armour	301	1
Aug 24 44	McGee, Charles	302	1

Feb 7 44	Mills, Clinton	99	1
Apr 1 45	Morris, Harold	301	1
Jul 18 44	Palmer, Walter	100	1
Oct 4 44	Perry, Henry	99	U, ½
Apr 16 45	Price, William	301	1
Jun 9 44	Pruitt, Wendell	302	1
Oct 12 44	Pruitt, Wendell	302	2
Aug 12 44	Rhodes, George	99	1
Oct 4 44	Rhodes, George	99	U, 1
Mar 31 45	Rich, Daniel	99	1
Jan 27 44	Roberts, Leon	99	1
Jul 18 44	Romine, Roger	302	1
Jul 26 44	Romine, Roger	302	U
Oct 12 44	Romine, Roger	302	1
Jul 12 44	Sawyer, Harold	301	1
Jul 25 44	Sawyer, Harold	301	1
Apr 26 45	Simmons, Richard	100	1
Jan 27 44	Smith, Lewis	99	1
Jul 17 44	Smith, Luther	302	1
Oct 12 44	Smith, Luther	302	1
Jul 17 44	Smith, Robert	302	1
Apr 1 45	Stewart, Harry	301	#1, #2, #3
Oct 4 44	Thomas, Edward	99	U
Aug 24 44	Thomas, William	302	1
Jan 27 44	Toppins, Edward	99	1
Jul 18 44	Toppins, Edward	99	1
Jul 20 44	Toppins, Edward	99	1
Jul 26 44	Toppins, Edward	99	1
Jul 18 44	Warner, Hugh	302	1
Jul 23 44	Weathers, Luke	302	U, ½
Nov 6 44	Weathers, Luke	302	#1, #2
Oct 4 44	Westbrook, Shelby	99	1
Apr 1 45	White, Charles	301	#1, #2
Mar 31 45	White, Hugh	99	1
Jul 17 44	Wilkens, Lawrence	302	1
Mar 31 45	Williams, Robert	100	#1, #2
Mar 31 45	Wilson, Bertram	100	1

* * *

Spanky Roberts:

> After the war I found out we were also under-decorated. We thought the Distinguished Flying Cross [the Air Force's highest decoration] was the greatest thing in the world. What we gave the Silver Star for, other units gave the DFC.

The Red Tails earned ninety-five Distinguished Flying Crosses. They also received one Presidential Unit Citation.

Roberts:

> I remember the day in Italy when I stood in parade formation alone in front of my squadron to get the Presidential Unit Citation, surrounded by newspapermen and photographers. The general leaned forward to pin the medal on and in a low voice called me every unprintable name he could imagine: "Baboons can't fly.... Baboons can't fight." He said the gun photos on our planes had been faked. I stood and looked him in the eye and said absolutely nothing. For my money, I proved myself to be a better American than he was.

(above): Colonel B.O. Davis, Jr. receives the Distinguished Flying Cross from his father, General B.O.Davis Sr., during a ceremony in Italy on May 29, 1944.
(below): General Henry H. 'Hap' Arnold, USAAF Commanding General awards Captain George S. Roberts and his unit the Presidential Unit Citation in Italy.

> *There were many whites who were for us and helped us every step of the way. I am thanking all those who helped and forgiving all those who didn't.*
>
> — Spanky Roberts

*   *   *

Per Aspera Ad Astra
(Through Difficulties to the Stars)

ENdNOTES

Chapter 1 - Black Rifles

[1] Bill Pickett is featured on a U.S. thirty-two-cent stamp in the Old West series issued in 1994.

[2] In 1976 the Army reviewed Flipper's court martial and changed his dishonorable discharge to honorable.

Chapter 2 - Black Wings

[1] In 1995, Bessie Coleman was featured on a U.S. airmail stamp.

[2] Powell wrote a book, *Black Wings*, and a play, *Ethiopia Spreads Its Wings*, both intended to popularize flying among black youths. Allen ferried Air Force places in World War II and lived to a ripe old age in Oklahoma City.

Chapter 3 - The Tuskegee Experiment

[1] Ironically, Arnold was very supportive of Jacqueline Cochrane's women who flew military planes on non-combat missions. The women ran into prejudice from male pilots much like that encountered by the black pilots, and Arnold came to their rescue when others tried to scuttle them. However, when Janet Bragg applied, she was turned down. She next applied to be an Army nurse and was told that quota was also filled.

[2] At Pearl Harbor, steward Dorrie Miller was decorated when he manned a machine gun and helped to move a wounded officer.

[3] A retired professor when the author met him more than fifty years later, Campbell was a difficult interview, answering questions slowly, after careful reflection, pausing to express his thoughts precisely. Of course, the author wanted more colorful quotes, but Campbell wouldn't cooperate.

Chapter 4 - The 99th

[1] It may have been the smallest class in the history of the Air Corps.

[2] Walter J.A. Palmer, *Flying With Eagles*, Nova Graphics, 1993.

[3] B. O. Davis, Jr., *An American*, Smithsonian Institute Press, 1991.

Chapter 5 - Combat

[1] After the war Momyer became a four-star general and head of the Tactical Air Command.

[2] Charles E. Francis, *Tuskegee Airmen*, Boston: Branden Publishing Co., 1988. p. 40.

Chapter 6 - Triumph at Anzio

[1] A vertical turn in which the pilot rolls over and then dives so he is going back the way he had come.

[2] A victory roll is a slow roll down near the ground (later outlawed by the Air Force for safety reasons).

[3] Eagleson must have had trouble with his guns. Later, after the 99th joined the 332nd, Harry Sheppard said, Eagleson joined Sheppard's plane, easing in from the left. "I thought I saw a lot of flames coming from his wings," Sheppard said, so back on the ground he asked, "Did you fire your guns?"

"Yes," Swampy said. "Ever since I ended up over Anzio beach and my guns jammed, I decided I'd never let that happen again. That's why I always fire my guns."

"On joining up?" Sheppard exclaimed.

Chapter 9 - 15th Air Force

[1] Negative Gs is the feeling of weightlessness when a roller coaster goes over the top; centrifugal force is the feeling of being pushed against the side of the car when it roars around a bend.

[2] *Tuskegee Airmen*, p. 92.

[3] Mary Taylor Mottley, ed., *Invisible Soldier*, Wayne State Univ. Press, p. 162.

Chapter 10 - Walterboro

[1] An overseas site would have permitted censorship of outgoing mail to prevent criticism from reaching the black press.

[2] *Invisible Soldier*, p. 200.

[3] *Ibid.*

Chapter 11 - The Red Tails

[1] *Invisible Soldier*, p. 220-1.

Chapter 12 - Air Wars

[1] *Invisible Soldier*, pp. 219-20.

[2] Robert A. Rose, *Lonely Eagles*. Los Angeles: Tuskegee Airmen, Inc., pp. 70-71.

[3] *The Tuskegee Airmen*, pp. 107-108.

[4] Frank Olynky, personal conversation with author, October 19, 1996. confirms three disputed kills by Elsberry on July 12, which the Air Force does not; he adds a probable for Elsberry on that date which Francis did not have. Olynky cannot confirm Bussey's claim of two on July 20, and has no record that Archer got the disputed second one that would have made him an ace.

[5] *Invisible Soldier*, p. 234.

Chapter 13 - Ground Wars

[1] *Tuskegee Airmen*, pp. 146-47.

[2] Olynky, personal conversation with author, October 19, 1996. Olynky agrees with Bill Campbell that the 99th did not claim any victories in the strafing raid over Athens on October 4.

Chapter 14 - Christmas

[1] *Tuskegee Airmen*, pp. 150-51. The bomber captain turned out to be the cousin of a former Mississippi governor.

[2] Almond's controversial career would continue into the Korean War, where he was praised for his brilliant planning of the Inchon landing but blamed for much of the Army's troubles during the headlong retreat from the Yalu.

[3] In January 1997, Fox and six other African Americans were retroactively awarded Congressional Medals of Honor for their heroism in World War II.

[4] *Invisible Soldier*, p. 259.

[5] Eric Hammel, *Aces Against Germany*. Pacifica, CA: Pacifica Press, 1993, pp. 256-67.

[6] *Invisible Soldier*, p. 234.

7 *Ibid.*

8 Melvin W. McGuire and Robert Hadley, *Bloody Skies: A 15th AAF B-17 Combat Crew, How They Lived and Died.* Las Cruces, NM: Yucca Tree Press, 1993, pp. 298-302.

Chapter 15 - Victory in Europe

1 Adolf Galland, *The First and the Last.* New York: Henry Holt & Co., 1954.

Chapter 16 - Homecoming

1 Ms. Douglas would lose a bruuising Senate campaign to Richard Nixon amid charges that she had Communist sympathies.

SOURCES

Bussey, Charles M., *Firefight at Yechon*, Washington, D.C.: Brasseys (US), Inc., 1991.

Davis, Jr., Benjamin O., *Benjamin O. Davis, Jr., American*, Washington, D.C.: Smithsonian Institution Press, 1991.

Davis, Burke, *Black Heroes of the American Revolution*, San Diego: Harcourt Brace & Company, 1976.

Carisella, P.J., and James W. Ryan, *Black Swallow of Death*, Boston: Marlborough House, 1972.

Francis, Charles E., *The Tuskegee Airmen*, Boston: Branden Publishing Co., 1988.

Freydberg, Elizabeth, *Bessie Coleman*, New York: Garland Publishers, 1993.

Greene, Robert Ewell, *Black Defenders of America*, Chicago: Johnson Publishing Co., 1974.

Gropman, Alan, *The Air Force Integrates*, Washington, D.C.: Office of Air Force History, 1985.

Hammell, Eric, *Aces Against Germany*, Novato, CA: Presidio Publishers, 1993.

Hardesty, Von, and Dominick Pisano, *Black Wings*, Washington, D.C.: Smithsonian Institution Press, 1983.

Leckie, William H., *The Buffalo Soldiers*, Norman, OK: Univ. of Oklahoma Press, 1967.

Lee, Ulysses, *The Employment of Negro Troops*, Washington, D.C.: U.S. Army Center of Military History, 1994.

McGuire, Melvin W., and Robert Hadley, *Bloody Skies: A B-17 Bomb Crew, How They Lived and Died*, Las Cruces, NM: Yucca Tree Press, 1993.

Motley, Mary Penick, *Invisible Soldier*, Detroit: Wayne State Univ. Press, 1975.

Palmer, Walter J.A., *Flying with Eagles*, Indianapolis, IN, Nova Graphics, Inc., 1993.

Phelps, J. Alfred, *Chappie*, Novato, CA: Presidio Press, 1992.

Pyle, Ernie, *Brave Men*, New York: Holt & Co., 1944.

Rich, Doris, *Queen Bessie*, Washington, D.C.: Smithsonian Institute Press, 1993.

Rose, Dr. Robert, *Lonely Eagles*, Los Angeles, CA: Tuskegee Airmen, Inc., Los Angeles Chapter, 1976.

Sandler, Stanley, *Segregated Skies*, Washington, D.C.: Smithsonian Institution Press, 1991.

Spencer, Chauncey E., *Who Is Chauncey Spencer?*, Detroit: Broadside Press, 1975.

Index